THE PERFORMANCE CEO

An Extreme Cognitive Protocol
for Entrepreneurial Success

MICHAEL KOCH

Copyright © 2023 Michael Koch.

All Rights Reserved. This book contains material protected under International and Federal Copyright Laws and Treaties. Any unauthorized reprint or use of this material is prohibited. No part of this book may be reproduced or transmitted in any form or by any means, electronic or mechanical, including photocopying, recording, or by any information storage and retrieval system without express written permission from the author/publisher.

This book contains advice and information relating to health care. It should be used to supplement rather than replace the advice of your doctor or another trained health professional. If you know or suspect you have a health problem, it is recommended that you seek your physician's advice before embarking on any medical program or treatment. All efforts have been made to assure the accuracy of the information contained in this book as of the date of publication. This publisher and the author disclaim liability for any medical outcomes that may occur as a result of applying the methods suggested in this book.

Hardcover: 979-8-218-27172-5
Paperback: 978-1-960346-08-7
Ebook: 978-1-960346-12-4

Published by Performance Press

Dedication

For Mom and Dad.
I am who I am because of you.
Your love, belief, and unwavering support
allowed me to always dream big.

Contents

Foreword..vii

Introduction..1

The Ten Principles....................................13

A Day in the Life.....................................37

Part I: Fasting/Nutrition.............................45

Part II: Strength....................................77

Part III: Recovery..................................107

15-Day Jumpstart....................................133

30-Day Extreme Cognitive Protocol...................181

Final Thoughts......................................275

Bibliography and References.........................281

Endnotes..287

Foreword

By
Kevin Newell
Former Global Chief Brand Officer, McDonald's

As a leader, executive, and track Hall of Fame athlete, I had the opportunity to be part of some truly remarkable teams. I understand the essential dynamics of a winning team—but more importantly, the rare qualities of the people who lead these high-achieving teams. These leaders possess an uncommon blend of drive, vision, laser focus, determination, inspiration, high standards, an intense desire to do the hard work, and must also possess an unparalleled ability to galvanize the team toward a common goal—to win.

In the early 2010s, I became the Global Chief Brand Officer of a little-known restaurant company called McDonald's. I jest, of course, because everyone knows Mcdonald's. As one of the most recognizable and valuable brands in the world, ever, it's no surprise that everyone has their own personal McDonald's story. When I assumed the role, McDonald's was riding high on the waves of success but faced several headwinds and challenges. At the forefront was an evolving customer base with very different ideas on what leading companies ought to do in this new digital world. That's the thing about winning teams; it's not just about reaching a certain destination, but about ongoing leadership that prioritizes evolution, adaptation, and continually seizing new opportunities that arise.

Our customers were evolving at warp speed, expecting leading companies like McDonald's to rise to the challenge in ways we hadn't considered. More than just convenience and value, they wanted us to move from traditional means of communication to the new burgeoning world of digital. This would completely modernize the way we connected with our consumers. The need to embrace digital offerings was clear, but actually making this shift was a whole different ball game. This was a top priority for me and our CEO, Don Thompson.

Amidst this digital headwind, I was made aware of and encouraged to meet with a young tech CEO in 2013, who was doing some phenomenal work in the digital space with other big brands like P&G, Visa, and FedEx.

We set up a meeting and this guy walks into my office. Not what I expected. My idea of a "tech guy" had been shaped in large part by Hollywood with films like *The Social Network* and of course, my own IT people. My stereotypical view of techies was that they were supposed to be these thick-rimmed, eyeglass-wearing, super-intelligent nerds. That was not who walked into my office. Everything about him was different. No thick-rimmed glasses. No nerdy demeanor. In fact, my initial impression was that he could have been a former professional athlete, but as soon as he started to speak, it was clear—he unequivocally fit the super intelligent portion of my "tech stereotype."

He demonstrated deep technical knowledge, unflappable confidence, and a blend of leadership, thoughtfulness, and ingenuity that struck me immediately. I sensed a visionary: someone who thought big, dreamed bigger, and possessed an insatiable appetite for innovation.

Within minutes of entering the boardroom, this CEO had passed me an airplane napkin from his flight into Chicago. On it were five handwritten points outlining the exact steps McDonald's needed to drive our digital evolution and capabilities. With captivating conviction, he understood the mission to craft an unparalleled digital customer experience that spoke to our core brand values—quality, innovation, and connection. I was sold.

And so, with an airplane napkin as our compass, we embarked on a journey that would reshape the digital roadmap of McDonald's. Michael Koch's audacious vision and unyielding determination set the stage for a series of transformative projects that would revolutionize the way we interacted with our customers and the world.

Michael proved to be an incredibly big thinker, an innovator, and a tireless worker. He and his company developed nine global tech platforms for us. He built an artificial intelligence/machine learning system back in 2013, well before people understood that artificial intelligence was not The Terminator. He built for McDonald's the first augmented reality execution in the United States, best known as "Dancing Ronald." He is the innovator who, in 2014, envisioned and created a digital world in which customers could build their own McDonald's and were interconnected. In addition, he built a local tech ecosystem for the 14,500 McDonald's US restaurants: a hiring platform, mobile apps, and on top of this, our entire Global Creative Review Center. The speed of innovation and output was astounding, all whilst traveling between Europe and the U.S. every two weeks. He had a real love for our brand values and a passion for bringing world-class technology to our business. He had a big vision, he was committed, and he was disciplined; all things that I had grown to appreciate and value whilst being on winning teams.

We often wondered how he was able to accomplish so much in a compressed time frame. *How* did he do it? He's everywhere, always on and always ready to deliver. All this, while spending half his time in Europe, and half in the US, working around the clock and delivering phenomenal tech-driven business solutions. What's his secret sauce?

After getting to know Michael personally and working alongside him, I began to understand how he could run at that extended speed, continue to be innovative, lead his company of 150 developers, travel, and still attend all our key franchisee meetings. It was due to his extreme daily protocol, which made sure he had the energy, output, and cognitive wherewithal to drive technical innovation at McDonald's.

Extreme daily protocol. What exactly is that? Here's a hint. Seven years ago, I learned that Michael would fast 23 hours a day, eat only one very specific nutrient-designed meal, wake up at 4:00 am to work out, and then meet with his European development team. Did I mention the 39-degree ice baths? But that's not all—it goes much deeper. But you'll have to read the book to learn the rest!

After I retired from McDonald's, I learned that Michael, like many serial entrepreneurs, exited his tech company. But I kept tabs on this renegade tech innovator. I got a good laugh when I heard he had moved to Thailand to live in a Muay Thai camp and fight professionally. Seriously, who does that? Who does that after amassing tech millions? Michael does. He lived a spartan lifestyle—no-frills, bare-bones, fighting professionally in what is arguably, the most violent martial arts form. And why? He needed it to stay humble and hungry to innovate. He's driven by a hunger for innovation, an unquenchable thirst for staying grounded, thinking big, and honoring a higher purpose.

One thing I've always admired about Michael is his private demeanor. You won't see him flaunting luxuries on a super yacht in the Mediterranean. That's because his passion lies behind the scenes, working for his clients and surging towards the next tech breakthrough. His philosophy is simple: being famous and being great are two very distinct and different ideologies. Keep the fanfare, he just wants to be innovative and do great things. It's evident in his actions and the meticulous life he lives: to stay sharp and to win for his clients and team is the top priority.

I applaud the reader for picking up this book and taking on this protocol. It's not for the faint of heart, but if you're passionate, all-in, and want to be optimized for entrepreneurial success, you've come to the right place. Michael will deliver like he always does and get you across the finish line. Good luck, and enjoy the ride.

Introduction

The Performance CEO

You have picked up this book for a reason.

As entrepreneurs and high achievers, we like to think we utilize all available resources at our disposal to attain a competitive advantage in creating our success. This chosen path of entrepreneurship is not destined for everyone. We are a rare breed. Ours is a demanding, performance-based profession that requires peak mental acuity, demanding physical output, and elite cognitive performance to attain our herculean dreams.

But let me ask you a few questions.

What if you could do more biologically to ensure your brain always performs at maximum capacity for all your entrepreneurial endeavors?

What if you could turn your brain into a supercomputer, one that works smarter, faster, longer, and harder than those of your competitors?

What if within 45 days you could become the smartest, strongest, leanest, most focused, and most driven person you know?

A decade ago, I asked myself those same questions. And I found the answers. That's why you're here with me now.

This book, *The Performance CEO*, is the key to unlocking that cognitive potential. In the pages ahead you will uncover an extreme Protocol for cognitive function, entrepreneurial output, and a framework to upgrade your brain and body through a demanding, science-based daily Protocol. You will maximize performance—gaining every biological competitive advantage, and becoming cognitively and physically the most optimized human, leader, and entrepreneur you can be.

Using the data, neuroscience, cutting-edge research, and proven biohacking techniques that I've aggregated from world-renowned experts—and which I have implemented personally, now, for over a decade—I have fused a wide array of key modalities together for the first time, creating an entrepreneurial Protocol that will accelerate your capability to outthink and outwork everyone.

From this moment forward, you will live in a world of daily high performance. You will do the things others will not and will always be primed to seize every opportunity that arises each day building your business. With this state-of-the-art Protocol, you will feel like the lights in your brain have been turned on, accelerating key functions like neurogenesis, BDNF (Brain-Derived Neurotrophic Factor), and neuronal regeneration, to optimize your cognitive capabilities while becoming the strongest and most powerful human you can be.

You already have all the biological tools you need. Your weapons are sitting in your arsenal, waiting to be used. Now you need to learn how and when to deploy them.

What we will do is intricately fuse the tools and behaviors: fasting, nutrition, autophagy, strength training, deep work windows, cognitive recovery, optimized sleep, and exact biological timing. We will do this throughout your day, according to a carefully planned Protocol, so that you can execute all entrepreneurial endeavors when you are best biologically primed to do them. We will weaponize your business pace, output, drive, and spark your brain into the optimal neuronal state it needs to be in, if you're to be at your very best and accomplish what might otherwise seem impossible.

The brain is the most valuable arrow in an entrepreneur's quiver, and it needs to always be in an optimal state, so we can take on the cognitive demands our roles require of us. As leaders we never know when one of those demands will present itself. We must always be ready, and luckily, intelligence is not fixed. The brain is an organ that can be prepared, improved, and built upon. It can become sharper, smarter, and trained to achieve better recall and operate at a speed to solve the most complex issues. The symbiotic relationship between biology, neuroscience, nutrition, fasting, sleep, cold, physical activity, and the optimal timing of each, is hardwired into the brain's circuitry.

The Performance CEO Protocol will harness these imbedded capabilities. After following the Protocol precisely for 45 days, you will be completely optimized to continue living day in, day out a life of optimization. Once you experience the clarity and energy, you will never go back.

On the way to cognitive acceleration, we will leverage my own personal journey through trial and error as I went on my quest to upgrade my brain and business output, becoming a top tech entrepreneur.

The goal of the Performance CEO is to function better at everything we do as human beings. I have no doubt that with science, dedication, determination, and grit, you can reach heights you always dreamed of. You've picked up this book, and that is a great first step—but what comes next is not something everyone can manage.

You will have to go to levels you never thought possible. To get something you never had, you must do things you have never done.

A Word of Warning

Let me be clear. This book is not for everyone. Not even close.

It's not the right book for 99 percent of the people out there who have entrepreneurial aspirations, or even many of those who are currently successful. Plenty of those who operate at high levels simply don't have what it takes to live a life of true optimization and innovation. And that is okay. This book is simply not for those people.

But those who don't evolve will be left behind as a new breed of optimized CEOs emerge.

It takes a different type of person to walk this path. It takes drive and mental toughness the likes of which many people simply lack. Not everyone is cut out to join us. Welcome to rarified air.

I meet people every day who say they want to succeed, to achieve more than they ever have and to function at a maximal level. But when it comes time to adopt the lifestyle that will enable them to do that, they make excuses or are just not willing to commit to the arduous work and live the disciplined life that will get them there. This is why I value people of action and commitment.

And so, to reiterate, I am not writing this book for the faint of heart, or for people who seek a better work-life balance. This is not a wellness book, nor a fitness transformation book. This book outlines an Extreme Cognitive Protocol for entrepreneurial success in which the end result will have your brain acting as a supercomputer, while attaining elite physical benefits as well. But the most important aspects will be your brain's performance, drive, energy, and output because of your daily focus on maximizing cognitive performance.

I am writing this book solely for obsessed entrepreneurs. I'm writing this for those who are tenacious, who possess an all-encompassing passion, and who are infused with just the right amount of crazy. Who realize by focusing on the optimization of their brain, the body will always follow becoming the strongest, leanest, most productive humans they can be.

I'm talking about those who love the grind, who need to operate at the most extreme levels of optimized cognitive and physical performance to fulfill their visions. I'm talking about those who run startups, and established leaders who want to push themselves and go beyond where they've been. For people who want to lead the future.

This is not a plan where I wave my entrepreneurial wand and make hard things magically easier. Instead, we will embrace the grind that so many out there are shying away from. We will roll up our sleeves, push our bodies daily to extreme levels, and spark our brains to attain their true genetic and cognitive capabilities. Focus on the brain and the body will respond.

It's time to be the founder and entrepreneur who wins in the trenches, who has the ability to outwork everyone, and who always leads their company from the front. This Protocol isn't something you should try out; you don't *dabble* in something like this—this is something you *must incorporate* into your daily life, if you want to take your performance to an elite entrepreneurial level in this new, fast-paced world of entrepreneurship that's led by optimized builders like me.

Ultra-successful people make the conscious decision to use every minute available in a day to attain their dreams and support a high-achieving lifestyle. Our life's purpose is greater than any short-term pleasure, gratification, party, night out, or unhealthy meal. The habits created in this Protocol will allow us to follow the path to greatness through discipline.

My Protocol may seem extreme, initially—and let's face it, it *is* extreme—but so are the legendary habits of Kobe Bryant, Michael Jordan, Tom Brady, and others who possess an unrivaled dedication, mentality, and focus to do what it takes to win.

As in my life, I don't just talk the talk. I live this Protocol every day, and I have done it for over a decade, following this exact Protocol for the past five years. That was back before anyone understood or knew biohacking, or thought it was a cool trend to post ice bath vids on Instagram.

I don't live this Protocol every day because it's a popular trend, or for bragging rights. I'm also not doing it to show off how "optimized" I am. I do it because I *need* to be my very best. I have to ensure that I am always leading innovation for clients, partners, employees, and most importantly so that I can create cutting-edge technological AI solutions that change history.

With this singular focus, I will show you how to push the limits of modern science to drive unprecedented results. So go ahead and tweet @ your competitors right now because there is about to be a seismic shift once we get you fully optimized.

A Bit of My Background

In my career as a tech entrepreneur, I have been honored to grace the cover of *Forbes*, receive numerous tech industry awards, and founded, built, and exited four tech companies. My most important accomplishment, however, has been my ability to clear the way for others to be wildly successful, dream big, and create life-changing opportunities, all while propelling the world's leading brands and companies to unprecedented technological innovation.

As a young tech mogul, I took the bold entrepreneurial leap and through pure tenacity was blessed to exit my first company at 26. I then founded, grew, and exited my second tech company before I was 30 years old.

Never becoming comfortable, still having a passion for innovation, I built my other two tech companies during my early 30s and exited both before my late 30s.

My companies and technologies were built to solve complex problems, with real impact. We focused on conceptualizing global solutions that drove tangible business results, not on building well-known household brands, fame, or using PR and marketing to grow company awareness for ego. Client success was the only success metric I focused on. That created our value.

I am self-made, I never took a single dollar of VC funding. I pushed in all my chips, risked everything I had into what I was doing, and I have earned everything I have ever accomplished through intrinsic competitiveness, tenacity, resilience, vision, and passion to innovate.

Here is a simple truth. When you are self-made, you need to work harder. Do more. Be more. Be ferocious. Do the lonely, quiet, hard work you need to compete, be bold, and be fearless. And you need to perform when the pivotal moments arise because you have more to lose.

I had an unwavering passion and a calling to lead the future of ethical artificial intelligence, which I have done through building real-world AI solutions for the world's largest companies.

Currently, as I write this book, I am Co-founder and CEO of my fifth technology company, HubKonnect, the leading artificial intelligence platform for data-driven local store marketing in the world. I am building another juggernaut of an AI company, and through my Performance Protocol I am operating daily at an unrivaled cognitive level, because I have quietly upgraded my brain and body. My days are structured specifically for performance and brain function to be at its peak. I know I need to be at my best to drive innovation and conceptualize the future of tech, artificial intelligence, and what's beyond in the future iterations of the Web.

I love the pressure to perform when the stakes are high. That is why I do the hard, lonely, early daily work to be at my best always. With a laser-like focus, discipline, and work ethic, I built a reputation as someone top executives go to when they need digital innovation, and the ability to execute the most critical digital initiatives at the highest technical level. I thrive in solving business issues with revolutionary technology, and I make sure I am always at my cognitive best to give my clients everything I have.

During these years, I have had the sincere honor of working with some of the top brands in the world, like P&G, Nike, Visa, McDonald's, Meta, IBM, Google, and their brilliant leadership teams, to build the technological future.

With every success, every win, I am hardwired to never want to feel a sense of comfort or complacency. Comfort is the enemy of innovation. I am built to look for a challenge, to do what others deem impossible. I push myself to do more, stay humble, and set another goal, to see if I have the talent, vision, leadership, and drive to build another impactful company to create opportunities for others.

As I look back over my early career, life was awesome. I was kicking ass. Living across Europe, I had built a reputation of never being outworked. I was known as one of the hardest-working founders in the tech space.

I was profoundly successful—but still I had that voice in my head telling me, "Work harder, stay humble, do more, there is a bigger calling." So I did.

I was creating real impact—but I didn't listen to my body. I barely slept—but damn, I was building revolutionary companies and I just conceded this was the price of success. I was happy, tired, and fulfilled. I was changing people's lives, making my parents proud, jet-setting around the world, following my passion, and scaling my companies to thousands of employees.

I know my life was extreme, but I was built for this, fulfilling my dreams, and flourishing in the global grind. I thrive pushing through discomfort and creating what others can't or don't work hard enough to do. I just kept going.

The Epiphany

On one day I will never forget, after flying back twelve hours from Europe to the United States for a meeting, I was just physically and cognitively drained. I was jetlagged and pulling myself along to the next task, the next meeting. Let's be clear, I still crushed every challenge, and met every goal—but I was running myself down in the process and had that same voice telling me I needed to do more to continue creating opportunities for others. Think bigger.

I dragged myself into a meeting with my top client at that time. And as I sat at the boardroom table, across from the CEO and CMO, they awarded me a huge chunk of new global business. I remember thinking "how in the hell am I going to be able to deliver this? I am exhausted" and right there I realized that to lead this initiative, I needed to find a way to take my energy and output to a new level, fully optimize my cognitive function and accelerate output to scale to meet this mission. I always deliver no matter what it takes. That was my "aha moment."

I did not want to do less or pull back—I needed to do more! I knew there must be a biological and scientific way to enable myself to always have the energy to crush anything I needed to do.

What if I could go deep into the science of human performance, to create habits, workouts, modalities, and work windows that would allow me to have unrivaled energy and brain function to optimize my days as a CEO?

Could I raise my cognitive function, recall, reasoning, judgment, and problem-solving above any of my technology CEO contemporaries? Could I unleash my brain's full potential?

As a builder of tech, it hit me. Right there in that meeting, I realized I needed a way to upgrade myself like a technology platform and go find the secrets of brain performance that only top neuroscientists knew.

I must seek out and uncover new and modern advancements in performance science—to learn all the new findings on nutrition, athletic training, and fasting, so I could specifically apply them to my life, solely for the purpose of increasing entrepreneurial impact. I knew I was on to something. By the time that meeting was over, it had become imperative that I create a business performance Protocol strictly for entrepreneurs.

So, just like anything I do in life, I went all-in.

Down The Rabbit Hole

With all my artificial intelligence applications, before I get started, I gather all data possible, understand the user, and then analyze product market fit. And so, after my epiphany I went about discovering how to become the Performance CEO in much the same way.

I sought out and consumed volumes of any medical research I could get my hands on—and it became a strategic imperative, to meet with the smartest people in the world, so I could aggregate all their best practices and find a way to elevate my entrepreneurial performance. I was determined to learn how to structure my day, actions, and habits, to increase my performance to unseen output into one Protocol.

I wanted to still work just as hard (or harder), just as long (or longer)—but with a new focus on my biology, to make sure my body could keep up this tenacious speed of business and go to levels I never before thought possible.

I set off on a whirlwind journey around the world, on a quest to find a way to completely optimize my brain. I immersed myself in biology and neuroscience. I met with top doctors, trainers, neuroscientists, biohackers, Navy SEALs, monks, athletes, and healers. I became a voracious reader, going through stacks of medical books, volumes of scientific studies, and lectures from MIT, Stanford, Johns Hopkins, and Harvard. I absorbed decades of research at a fanatical pace. I like to joke that, having studied as hard as I have, and taken in all this information, I could probably ace the MCAT.

I began testing on myself techniques aggregated across all disciplines. I merged different modalities leveraging my personal data, blood work, DEXA scans, and biomarkers to determine what works uniquely for entrepreneurs, and to begin to create the Performance CEO Protocol, specifically to follow it day in and day out, and to be my absolute best. I built and trained the model just like machine learning and followed the performance data.

Through trial and error, I progressively introduced new components, science, workouts, diets, fasting, and spiritual concepts. I eliminated all elements of my life that drained my energy physically, personally, and emotionally. I created my own individual ecosystem, rigorous Protocol, key recovery modalities, and spartan living environment for simplicity and optimal cognitive performance.

Through my experimentation, I found results that I'll share with you throughout this book. I did it using long fasting windows, specific compound strength training, exact nutrient consumption ratios for cognitive nutrition, macro- and micronutrients, optimized deep work windows, advanced brain recovery techniques, and mastering sleep, to ensure I wake up early every morning at 4:00 am completely energized. I found that these techniques could be fused together, with the right timing, to create the daily entrepreneurial Protocol for the CEO human machine.

I experimented even further, investing in modern technologies, like daily red light therapy, brain photobiomodulation (PBM), and HBOT (hyperbaric oxygen therapy) for cellular regeneration. I tried more familiar, tried-and-true practices like ice baths, sauna, extended fasting, heavy lifting, hydration, sprinting, nature, and morning sunlight. I was going to build myself the most comprehensive performance Protocol for entrepreneurs the world has ever seen.

I captured and applied data, and saw all the benefits for my health, such as impeccable bloodwork, strength increases, single digit body fat, glowing skin, and unrivaled energy levels. I combated aging, both inside and out, and became the strongest and leanest I have ever been. But that was just a byproduct of my healthy brain. My mind felt like a supercomputer.

In short, I built myself into a new breed of optimized CEO, so I could be my best for others, setting an example of passion with an extreme focus, and determining the most effective Protocol to always run at an unrivaled business speed and intensity. And it worked.

This is where *The Performance CEO*, the book you're reading now, was born. I quickly realized that neuroscience is too important to be left to neuroscientists (no offense). I knew I had to share my competitive advantage I have found over the past five years with likeminded entrepreneurs who understand the level of work and sacrifice it takes to attain your dreams. There is enough success out here where everyone can win. This Protocol will get you there.

Your Time Is Now

I wrote this book like an executive summary: actionable, direct, and in a digestible format. I'll share the science behind the way I live, and I won't overwhelm you with medical school jargon. I'll be straight to the point, with clear plans, schedules, and formulas to optimize your cognitive capabilities.

I am not writing this book to show off my knowledge or create a volume of overcomplicated, over-scienced explanations. I want to be a facilitator and aggregator of digestible information, demystifying biohacking, and creating a clear, direct Protocol to get this information into the hands of as many driven and likeminded entrepreneurs as possible. This book will focus on *what* you need to do, and not so much on *why*. All you need to do is follow it.

As entrepreneurs, we want a plan, and we will execute the plan once we have it. In my opinion, brilliance lies in simplicity, and so I want to keep things simple.

I am not writing this book so I can be a content creator or a leading biohacking personality. I do not have time to take that on. I am in the day-to-day fire, just like you, building my company every day. My days are consumed as a top tech CEO. I am busy building the future of ethical artificial intelligence and creating life-changing opportunities for others.

But my mission with this book is clear: to put this Protocol into the hands of the new breed of optimized CEOs and future changemakers so they have the tools to be at their best and build their dreams like I have done. The rest is up to you.

So, if you are built differently, and have a laser-focused passion and obsession with reaching your goals, you have come to the right place. The Performance CEO Protocol will get your brain in peak condition, provide unrivaled energy and output. In parallel, your body will become the leanest and strongest it has ever been, as you perform your daily tasks at the highest level. We will weaponize your entrepreneurial pace.

This newly sparked brain function will provide you with the ability to outwork and outthink everyone. We will make your brain reach its fullest potential, creating boundless mental energy and power to attain your dreams.

This book will not hand you a participation trophy for trying. This road is not easy, and only a few will take it, and fewer will arrive at the destination. To reach this level of optimization, you must have an unrivaled passion for doing the impossible and a fire inside you that is indomitable.

Are you getting fired up? I know I am. Do you realize the power you are about to unlock?

Let us ignite your dopamine, spark your competitive intensity, and crush this together.

Your time is now.

The Ten Principles

Our brains control everything we do: what we say, how we say it, and how we move, as well as our toughness, pain threshold, and ambition. Throughout my quest for cognitive optimization, I have developed ten powerful principles and used them as the core building blocks to fuel my entrepreneurial success and weaponized work pace. These key principles build upon each other and weave in and out of the three major pillars of the Performance CEO Protocol that I will expound upon later in the book: **Fasting/Nutrition**, **Strength**, and **Recovery**. This Protocol will get you as close to superhuman as possible.

The Performance CEO Protocol is a science-based plan to optimize brain function while becoming the strongest, leanest, most energetic leader you know. When looked at individually, each of these principles is impactful on its own, geared for optimizing the performance of our brains. When fused into one Protocol, with optimal biological timing, they can help you conquer your highest business goals, no matter what they may be. By implementing all of these principles on a daily basis, I have seen proven results time and time again, success after success, also providing the strength to get back up when I get knocked down. Build the brain, and the body will always follow.

I wrote this book for two types of people: the entrepreneurs who always need to know *why*, and the people who just want to know *how*. Both have come to the right place. I will give a deeper explanation of the science in the three pillars, while the action-oriented entrepreneurs—who want to go and crush it right away and only need to know how—can go straight to a concise cognitive action plan, and begin the 15-day jumpstart adaptation period.

I, for one, share in both of those tendencies. I am always ready to take action—but I am also always curious as to how everything works. And so, as I walk you through the Performance CEO Protocol, and show you what it's done for me and what it might do for you, I'll give you all the knowledge I've acquired along the way. You choose your path forward.

The ten principles are the result of more than a decade of working and personal experimentation. You have everything you need, biologically, to be buzzing with the same electricity, cognitive focus, passion, and motivation that I do daily. The development and incorporation into your life of the Performance CEO Protocol principles can make you the best executive and most powerful human you have ever been. Let's build.

Principle 1. Fasting as a Weapon: 23-48-72

Elongated Fasting is the most powerful component of the Protocol for both physical and cognitive performance. It provides many benefits an entrepreneur needs, like improved brain neuronal autophagy, decreased inflammation, increased fat loss, increased natural HGH (human growth hormone), optimal biological environment for muscle growth, lower insulin, lower cortisol, and even raised energy levels. By simply not doing anything—let me say this again, by NOT DOING ANYTHING—we can begin to heal our bodies, get smarter, leaner, stronger, and quickly attain the optimal body composition that is unique to each one of us. Fasting is a timeless technique, used throughout history, which will unequivocally accelerate your path to becoming the best human you can be.

What we do:

Within this Protocol, fasting is an essential foundation, during which 23 hours a day we are not eating. For optimization, we do OMAD (one meal a day), where we consume all the key nutrients in one meal that our brain and body need to thrive. This provides our body with the right environment to spark the biological tools needed within us to operate at the highest cognitive level, while evoking the optimal fuel-burning system with improved reasoning skills.

To the female entrepreneurs reading this book: your fasting Protocol will be a bit different (more on that in the Three Pillars), due to the beauty and complexity of the female hormonal process and cycle. But rest assured, you will still maximize all of the benefits of fasting.

Why we do it:

Fasting has been shown to increase the production of brain-derived neurotrophic factor (BDNF), which is the protein that plays an important role in promoting the growth and survival of brain cells. Fasting can lower oxidative stress and cognitive inflammation; trigger neurogenesis, autophagy; and increase neuroplasticity, or the brain's ability to change. When fasting, your cells go into survival mode, eliminating unhealthy mitochondria and replacing them with new ones. With this increased mitochondrion production, your brain will be rejuvenated and more laser-focused than ever before in learning, memory, executive function, and overall brain health. Fasting also keeps insulin levels from spiking, and increases levels of natural human growth hormone, which stimulates cell growth and regeneration, along with the release of the neurotransmitter norepinephrine, which helps with your mood.

This is one of the most powerful components of the Protocol. All of these benefits are brought on by doing *nothing*. You don't need to be a successful tech entrepreneur and spend millions of dollars. It's FREE.

The only cost is mental discipline. So, embrace the power that comes with the act of doing nothing. We will determine when fasting is best for your schedule, to optimize all of its tremendous benefits, with the ultimate goal of crushing your business day.

How we do it:

We follow an exact fasting formula of 23-48-72 which is defined as: 23 hours a day, with a 48-hour fast once a week, and a 72-hour fast once a month, to gain all the cognitive repair, increased autophagy, improved brain function, reduced inflammation, and increased resilience to stress. Over the course of the first 15 days of the adaptation jumpstart, you will shrink your eating window from four hours a day to one meal a day (OMAD).

This may seem initially daunting, but I have been following this exact Protocol for five years. When I look at the frequency with which others eat, I just can't imagine consuming food that often and at those volumes. But this is also why I measure at single-digit body fat and naturally retain my muscle mass.

Fasting will ensure utilizing a clean, fuel-burning system that propels you energetically and improves brain function. Any Performance CEO who makes fasting a pivotal component of their day will see tremendous results, maximizing their physical output and cognitive abilities. So, to keep it simple, remember: 23 hours a day, 48 hours a week, 72 hours every month. You are one step closer to being the Performance CEO. Always remember **23-48-72**.

Principle 2. Feed Your Brain

We accelerate cognitive function through our one meal a day (OMAD) of a specific cognitive diet. So with the fusion of extended fasting and OMAD, we create an optimal biological environment—you have the nutrients your body needs to perform, while giving you the fuel to execute all your entrepreneurial endeavors. Not eating is just as important as eating—and when we eat, we consume ONLY specific foods and nutrients, consuming the core key foods every day to ensure our brains and bodies are given what they need when we need to seize those moments.

Let me be clear: we eat the same things every day. Food is for fuel, not enjoyment or reward. Understanding that, changing the mindset society has put on food, and practicing it, will enable us to get all of the nutrients we need, while creating extra time in the day that would have otherwise been devoted to "when do I eat?" and "what do I eat?"

Food is fuel. We fill up our entrepreneurial fuel tank, and then we get back to thinking big, dreaming big, and tackling any strategic initiative that gets placed in front of us.

What we do:

Consume and eat the same cognitive foods on a daily basis. This may seem boring, but because we eat the most organic, bioavailable foods on Earth, the things we consume are always delicious and nutritional. These foods contain the exact nutrients our bodies and brain need to drive cognitive performance, and to prime our bodies for any entrepreneurial task.

By changing our food, following the Performance Protocol, we evoke our optimal fuel-burning system to utilizing ketones, a type of chemical your liver produces when it breaks down fats, and your brain's preferable energy source. In a fasted state, you will have access to the cleanest, most efficient, and steadiest energy source your body and brain have ever enjoyed: clarity with a hunter's mindset.

When we consume the exact nutrients at the right time, we create the cleanest fuel-burning system in the human body and ignite neurogenesis for our brains. We were created to run lean, not eat frequently, and cherish key nutrients that work well with our biological makeup.

I bet you never thought you would use your biology as a competitive advantage in business. Let's use every tool at our disposal to win.

Why we do it:

For proper nutrients to support cognitive optimization, we must provide our brains and bodies with foods that contain exactly the right nutrients. No more, no less. We eat more fat than usual, but only the right kinds, not only to provide the macro- and micronutrients our bodies thrive on in a highly stressful and competitive environment.

It's also key to intertwine our diet and fasting, for the symbiotic relationship between nutrients and giving the body its time to heal. This sparks cognitive performance, evokes neurogenesis, and starts BDNF (brain-derived neurotrophic factor)—all of the elements an entrepreneur needs to function at their highest cognitive level.

By eating the same things every day, we limit decision fatigue, and we look at food only as fuel to accelerate our goals. It is freeing, to not have to chase the next meal, and to eat identical food choices daily.

This way, we can eat and then get back to building our companies and our dreams.

How we do it:

We consume only these specific foods daily, at our one meal a day:

(1) grass-fed beef or wild-caught salmon (salmon only one day a week)
(2) two oz. organ meat
(3) organic bone broth
(4) organic avocado
(5) organic raspberries
(6) organic nuts (pecans/almonds)
(7) free range eggs
(8) organic raw cheese

We simplify our diet, and take in only clean organic nutrition, with the fats, protein, fiber, vitamins, minerals, and antioxidants your brain and body need to run at their best. We only eat in the one-hour window (hence the twenty-three-hour fast), and then we fast the rest of the day, letting our bodies properly digest, deploy, and utilize these bioavailable foods.

When these foods are combined, it's like consuming the world's most potent and most natural cognitive multivitamin. Grass-fed beef and liver are excellent sources of iron, zinc, riboflavin, niacin, vitamin A, vitamin D, vitamin K, vitamin B12, copper, folate, and B6. Avocado and berries are great sources of fiber, vitamin C, potassium, magnesium, vitamin E, and antioxidants. Avocados are also an optimal source of healthy fats, particularly monosaturated and polyunsaturated fats. Eggs and raw cheese provide B12, vitamin D, calcium, choline, selenium, zinc, vitamin K2, and other important nutrients. The raw cheese contains enzymes and good bacteria, which are good for digestion and gut health. Bone broth has vitamins A and B, and minerals like zinc, iron, calcium, and selenium.

Since your brain is composed of 60 percent fat, this diet increases your cerebral circulation, grows new neurons, and reduces inflammation, giving you what your brain needs to form neuronal membranes and for cells to function correctly.

Cholesterol is an essential nutrient of the brain and plays an essential role in brain function. A byproduct of this diet? Your body also has all the necessary foods that promote muscle growth and strength. You'll consume .8 grams of grass-finished, raw, organic protein per pound of body, which creates the perfect environment to get you to your optimal body composition, so you'll build muscle and have energy for days.

I have such conviction for power of nutrient-dense, certified organic grass-fed and grass-finished beef, free range eggs, organic berries that I purchased a 30-acre farm in North Carolina where I will produce only the highest-quality food for my personal consumption. I want to know the quality of everything I ingest, from organic produce to pasture-raised eggs, to grass-finished beef and organs, to ensure I am always at my best to lead my company. As Performance CEOs, we need to know everything that we ingest and know the quality of the food. This is where you should invest in yourself and ensure the quality of organic food you consume.

Principle 3. Win the Morning, Win the Day

Greatness happens in the solitude of the morning. The darkness and silence of the early hours creates the space for mental clarity, and when we are best biologically equipped to make the most important decision of the day. So, wake up early naturally, and maximize the time and space of the early morning.

The science speaks for itself. When you first awaken, your brain operates at a much higher electrical frequency, through which it is capable of deep and profound learning. Your brain is moving into the Alpha stage, when you are fully aware and focused, with a calm mind. You are relaxed and thinking. When you wake up, your subconscious mind soaks in what you do or listen to in the first 20 minutes. Therefore, some people meditate, read the Bible, or just sit with themselves and think big about the most pressing strategic issues in silence, without checking their phones, to consciously choose the tone of their day. Regularly expressing gratitude changes the molecular structure of the brain. Let your mind take you where it wants to go. Some of my best ideas and biggest issues were created and solved in this early morning quiet.

The output you get from these early mornings is worth setting up a routine, where you work before the sun rises and set up a nightly sleep schedule, to go to bed early and get the proper sleep while maximizing the early morning. Using those quiet, dark hours of the day is a real strategic advantage. As entrepreneurs we must normalize using all our biological tools to be at our best to build our dreams.

What we do:

Great leaders need to use every minute of every day to their advantage. Take advantage of the early morning hours, when competitors (on your side of the world, for a Global CEO) are sleeping. We will adapt our sleep schedules and NATURALLY wake up every morning from 3:45 to 4:00 am, creating the time and space for us to think and just be brilliant. These early hours are when your brain is most receptive to processing information and making strategic decisions.

Let me be very clear: this is not a Protocol to sleep less and to "out optimize" other people. Getting our proper seven-plus hours of optimized sleep with two hours of REM and two hours of deep sleep is key (I will go into this more later). This is just building a schedule to where you get your sleep *and* maximize winning the early morning. There is no sleep-is-for-losers dogma in this book.

We want to leverage this as one of our initial strategic deep work windows. In the darkness of the morning, there is peace and tranquility, allowing us to think through our most complex business problems. We also perform early morning fasted strength workouts, where we are primed with increases in HGH and testosterone and have the tools to crush our strength workouts while we think about our businesses. Exercising in the early morning improves focus and the brain's ability to ideate, create, and learn. After winning the morning, we have the rest of the day to go and execute our thoughts and ideas.

Why we do it:

When we first wake up, our brainwave chemistry is around 10.5 waves per second. At this speed, between the Alpha and Theta stages, the mind is capable of profound learning through calm focus and effortless thoughts. Capitalizing this state of mind can help you get ahead in the day and conquer the daunting tasks every entrepreneur faces, whereas sleeping in only puts you behind, because you're missing a window in which your brain is biologically triggered to give you the optimal decision-making process to handle anything that's thrown your way. We must use all the biological tools at our disposal if we want to win.

My early mornings began not trying to be the "most optimized human" on Earth. It was because I was a young, global CEO who had teams in Europe, Asia, and in the US. If I got up at a normal time, my tech team in Eastern Europe (which was +7 hours ahead), would be almost through their day. But through this process I saw the power of my thinking, my quiet time. In the early darkness of the morning, I created a space where I could spend time with my thoughts, solving complex problems, creating the time and space for me to think big, and really have my time where people were not pulling me in many directions. I have been doing this for over ten years. I have never looked back.

How we do it:

With a 4:00 am start, you've already begun to structure your day to embrace the solitary morning. To best utilize this time, focus on planning and making all your critical decisions in the early morning. By waking up fasted, you're giving your body and brain the best chance to think like a supercomputer—especially when you introduce black coffee! Caffeine will optimize your cognitive abilities with recall, memory, and quality decision-making—way more than your mind would in just a fasted state. We then go and crush our fasted early morning strength workout, optimizing our body's functions and the ability to think big, create, and learn. I would just like to point out that getting up early is also free. Don't let the biohacking world tell you optimization requires a $2 million spend on yourself each year.

Principle 4. Lift Heavy Shit, Sprint, Get Smarter

Building strength is essential for long-term success. This Protocol is geared toward putting myself in the best optimal cognitive state to handle my business tasks and be a visionary for my clients. To do that, I learned I must get into world-class physical shape, so lifting heavy things is an integral part of the Performance Protocol for a simple reason: exercise maximizes blood flow to the brain. But there are also tremendous physical benefits to following this cognitive strength Protocol and lifting heavy things. By focusing on strength training (for the brain)—and those actions that evoke the right responses to provide the brain with blood flow, cognitive focus, increased BDNF, and improved brain plasticity—we can reduce stress while triggering the right hormones that are induced through lifting heavy weights and sprinting. It activates areas that dictate mood and cognitive function. So, even though this is a cognitive Protocol, through following my specific strength training program in an exact order, you will be the strongest, leanest, fastest human you can be through crushing fasted workouts, where we lift heavy things and push our bodies to the limits, always getting stronger and ensuring we're physically primed to lean into work at the pace and tempo every successful entrepreneur needs. Strength is an essential component of this. Strength is the main focus. And you might get a compliment every now and then about being in elite shape.

What we do:

Thrust your foot down on the gas pedal—fasted—in the early morning through the Protocol's low rep strength training, followed by the Cognitive Walk/Sprint interval training (HIIT) sprints to spark neurogenesis. Follow a foundational strength Protocol, to leverage each power system in the body and maximize the rep range, to get stronger, leaner, and more powerful. Lifting heavy doesn't mean getting bigger or bulkier. Through this workout Protocol, which we will get into later, your body will naturally find your optimal body composition strength and fitness for you and your body. For example, heavy deadlifts in particular (the top full-body exercise for building strength) creates blood flow to the brain, which creates a better decision-making environment for you to accomplish and take on anything you need—becoming a badass naturally follows suit.

Why we do it:

As you build more strength physically in the gym, you'll feel more powerful in the boardroom. Lifting heavy not only brings you great cognitive, aesthetic, and health benefits, it will also help you gain confidence to take on every challenge head-on.

Know that you have the physical and mental strength to pull through. By focusing on critical lifts, key body parts, and recovery time, you can create the best environment to help you achieve peak performance—mentally and physically. Sprinting is a proven way to drive cognitive function while the physical byproduct is to become lean, powerful, and shredded, activating your Type-2, fast-twitch muscle fibers for speed and power.

By focusing on Strength and HIIT, you can train your body to spark neurogenesis and drive blood flow for brain performance. And since you're lifting heavy, sprinting is the perfect complement to your body's muscle-building process. By following the workout Protocol I will outline later, you can optimize your time working out to get the results to look and feel your best. Your body is your resume. It shows how well you take care of yourself. It shows me how much you respect yourself.

How we do it:

To build cognitive strength, I will introduce exercises to you in a scientific manner that can help supercharge your brain and body through muscle growth, power, and endurance.

- Strength: 5 sets x 5 reps (3-min rest)
- Accessory: 4 sets x 6-8 reps (2-min rest)
- Volume: 4 sets x 10 reps of 4 exercises (30-sec rest)
- Burnout: 2 exercises x 50 reps each

- GPP: 3 rounds - 30 secs on, 30 secs off: Farmer's Walk, Sled Pulls, Box Jumps
- Cognitive Walk/Sprint: 30 minutes (HIIT Sprint) 2:30 walk, 30-sec Sprint, 10 Rounds

Strength Training Automation. Every exercise, rep range, sprint, and movement in the Performance CEO Training Protocol is automated with the proper timing in a boxing app. By not having to worry about timing, rest, sets, when to do the next exercise, we are able to think about business during the entire workout. It is a physical ideation session we automate for physical activity. Lift heavy. Think Big.

Principle 5. Thrive in Deep Work Windows

A deep work window is a blocked space in which you have no distractions for a set period of time, when you can focus on and execute your mission. "Deep work window" refers to twenty minutes of uninterrupted performance during which we exclusively focus on high-concentration, cognitively demanding tasks without distractions or interruptions. These deep work window sprints yield results.

Your critical analyses, key meetings, and ideation sessions should be completed in your deep work windows throughout the day, specified with the exact biological timing of the day you are most primed to perform these tasks. Early morning ideation starts the day moving into midmorning output, and that is when you're cognitively at your best for client interactions. Your output is unrivaled in afternoon production windows, and then you have the night for planning to be more tactical, organizing your day, and maximizing your strategic windows, because that is when you are most logical. Our bodies naturally know the best time of day to experience their peak performance, create new ideas, and learn new abilities.

Fortunately, the human mind and body run in a predictable pattern that fluctuates throughout the day. Although it may change from person to person, most of us are peaking in the late morning or around noon in mental acuity. Therefore, if you need to complete any tasks, the boosted speed and accuracy are both heightened in the morning.

Eliminate the sedentary lifestyle. Most people sit when they work and, in our windows, we stay active as inactivity is killing our brains, physically shriveling them. Hack the work environment for optimal performance, to allow yourself to engage in low-level physical activity all day long. We perform kettle bell for swings, use a standing desk, and partake in an afternoon nature walk. We will change your work environment to be optimized for full cognitive performance, across all of your optimized work windows. It's a biological imperative that we move.

What we do:

Perform tasks when we are biologically primed to do them. We time and perform tasks that spark the brain to do the optimal work our biology was created to do within our 24-hour cycle. Build your daily schedule around your biology, to execute your tasks expertly. We do strategic exercises after the point when BDNF is highest, when we are the most energetic, motivated, and inspired, to perform the designed tasks in the optimized work window.

Why we do it:

We engage in these 20-minute deep work windows so that we can create a zone in which we are not distracted, when we can focus with the time and space to maximize every hour of the day. A focused deep work window will create a level of output and a level of productivity that would be very hard to achieve if you didn't plan them. During a deep work window, we intentionally set aside distractions like social media, email, and other non-essential tasks to immerse ourselves fully in a specific task or project. The goal is to achieve a state of flow, where deep focus and concentration leads to increased productivity and higher-quality work. In short, crush the day.

A scientific study of brain circuits confirmed that our creative activity is highest during and immediately after sleep (Morning Ideation), while the analytical parts of the brain (the editing, researching, and proofreading parts) become more active as the day progresses[1]. You can start to see why I have built out my day as such. As we progressively go about our day, our mood tends to become warmer, with good feelings typically peaking around noon, meaning you should most likely book important calls or meetings when your mood is most elevated.

How we do it:

We have five optimized windows throughout the day. We crush the deep work window with 20-minute deep work productivity sprints, and then we do a physical activity (ten kettle bell swings) right before the next deep work window sprint, to spark the brain. We also take the time to get out in nature in the afternoon to clear our heads, and to finish every day cognitively strong.

1. Early Morning Strategic Ideation Session: fasting and coffee. Think Big.
2. Morning Cognitive Production: Post-workout Deep Work Window.
3. Midafternoon Deep Work Window Post-nap, BDNF-sparking office movements.
4. Nature Walk: 30-min to 1-hour walk outdoors.
5. End of the Day Tactical Deep Work Window.

All of these windows are greenlighted to maximize each minute of the window based on when you are best biologically primed to work. This also has no cost. Do you see a theme forming with my demystifying biohacking for entrepreneurial performance?

Principle 6. The Power of the Morning Sun, Nature & Afternoon Stroll

Each day, find time after your workout to get 20 to 25 minutes of morning sunshine. It offers so many vital components for the optimal functioning of the body. Research indicates that an hour of natural light in the morning will help you sleep better[2]. Sunshine regulates your circadian rhythm by telling your body when to increase and decrease your melatonin levels. So, the more daylight exposure you can get, the better your body will produce melatonin when it's time to sleep at night. Sunlight also reduces stress, and melatonin lowers stress reactivity.

We also go out in nature daily for an afternoon hike or nature walk. Research shows that a walk can increase cerebral blood flow, creativity, and overall executive function[3]. If you need to clear your head or prepare for a big afternoon meeting, do your brain a favor and go for a walk in nature. A hike in the woods—taking the time and space in nature—does wonders for the brain, so you can finish your day strong and cognitively energized. The more I am in tech, the more I am pulled to nature.

What we do:

Post-workout, daily, we go outside and get that morning sun for 20 to 25 minutes. We absorb all the benefits that the sun has for us to optimize our internal bodies and circadian rhythm. The morning sunshine zone between 7:00 am and 10:00 am is ideal. This can be during your Cognitive Walk/Sprint or in a separate session.

Getting out in sunlight charges you and optimizes sleep down the road; it has a deep relationship within our performance. The sun plays a huge role in keeping our body functions on the right clock and the right timing to perform at our best. Every afternoon, we also get out in nature for a 30-minute to hourlong walk or hike. I love to go to my 28 acres in the North Carolina mountains and do my afternoon stroll on my land. Or I go to the farm and walk along my creek. I hear the babbling trout stream while thinking about technology and AI architecture, taking in all nature. The fresh air, blue skies, and space put me in a cognitive state for big thinking and innovation. If I am in the city, I will still make sure to get outside for my walk.

Why we do it:

We need our bodies to produce essential vitamin D when exposed to sunlight. Vitamin D helps maintain calcium, and prevents brittle, thin, or misshapen bones. For men, 15 minutes of sun boosts a man's testosterone level by up to 69 percent.

The morning sun also helps us with our sleep. By exposing ourselves to the sun, it is a free way to optimize our sleep, and mood, and spike the right hormones.

Being out in nature for a hike or walk improves working memory, cognitive flexibility, and the other brain functions a CEO needs. It also provides the environment to think big and clear your head. Chase real dopamine: sun, ice, sauna, weights, runs, walks, hard work. Do the real work. Don't settle for fake dopamine. Take care of your brain and give it the time and space it needs to think big.

How we do it:

Every day we go outside and get 20 to 25 minutes of morning sun and go for the cognitive 3:00 pm walk. It's free and its simple, but so powerful. Get the power of nature to spark the internal biological triggers that you need to optimize your entire day and put you on the right trajectory, not only in your current, active state, but also prepare you for an amazing night's sleep. Daytime exposure to sun creates a relationship with a great night's sleep, making sure you're getting your deep and REM sleep because your circadian rhythm is in sync with the rising and setting of the sun.

Every afternoon we go for our walk in nature, which helps restore emotional and cognitive resources that are depleted throughout the demanding life of an entrepreneur. Yup, you guessed it. The sun and walking outside are free as well. Interesting theme, coming from a four-time-exited tech CEO. I hope I am not destroying a $25 billion biohacking industry and crushing the optimization dreams of these biohacking "gurus" who are selling you things you don't need and telling you things that won't help you optimize yourself as an entrepreneur. My talent as an entrepreneur is eliminating redundances and simplifying execution. Looks like I am doing it again.

Principle 7. Recover Like a Boss

Recovery is cognitive as well as physical. We engage in recovery modalities that reduce inflammation, as inflammation is detrimental to the brain and cognitive function. If there is one area in which I do invest in myself, it is recovery. I am a believer in having the most scientifically effective recovery modalities that I then fuse with traditional and ancient recovery techniques to attain unrivaled cognitive optimization. Focusing on lowering our inflammation enables increased brain performance. We create the optimal environment to avoid sensory overload while we recover our bodies, to put our brains in the best biological state to perform in our biologically primed work windows. We will ensure the mind and body are able to not only meet—but exceed—what needs to be done daily.

For example, I believe this is the area where investment in yourself makes sense. We should normalize an HBOT (Hyperbaric Oxygen Therapy) chamber in every CEO's bedroom. Sounds funny, but I am not kidding. An HBOT chamber triggers the body's ability to heal itself as it increases energy at the cellular level. It improves cerebral blood flow, promotes new blood vessel formation, mobilizes stem cells, reduces inflammation, and increases oxygen to build and repair damaged cells. This is just one of the modern tools I use, just like a professional athlete, to make sure I am at my best to perform at an optimal level and handle the stress we put on our bodies as a hard charging entrepreneur.

The body and brain need time to recover and grow after an entrepreneur's high-impact days. And I am not simply geeking out on recovery. This is what science has created, to gain that competitive advantage. You need to focus on the recovery stages of your physical, mental, and central nervous system. Why would you not utilize the tools the best athletes in the world use for their recovery? Why is it normal for them to do it, but not for a CEO or startup entrepreneur? The Performance CEO will change that.

As you make your way through this book, you'll discover a comprehensive list of tactics you can use to enhance the physical and mental healing processes, so you're able to bounce back as soon as possible from a workout, business trip, or stressful day. There are multiple ways to get the benefits of recovery, depending on your budget and levels of success, but remember: you are always your best investment.

What we do:

Throughout our days, we structure and schedule time to utilize the proper recovery modalities that continue to fill and heal our bodies and our brains, putting us at the best cognitive state to continue working harder and faster. By scheduling these recovery modalities into every one of our days, we ensure that our bodies can continue to operate and run at the speeds needed to be an entrepreneur and build our empires.

Why we do it:

As the Performance CEO, finding success means recovering your mind and body from daily stressors. By focusing on the recovery stages of your muscles and your central nervous system—which are (unfortunately) often neglected by hard-charging achievers—you can optimize recovery and maximize your "time off" to move onto your next meeting, crush through precise biological mechanisms, and do it all over again every day.

When done correctly, recovery can be one of the most comprehensive and most important Protocols. For your brain and body to be at their strongest, they need to be at their most rested. Being prepared for battle when walking into that shareholder meeting can give you the confidence to tackle any obstacle you will face in your professional career.

How we do it:

The following may seem like an extensive list, but if you want to achieve your best, you need to consider using the various tools that help bring out your best biologically.

In my daily Protocol, I use tools like:

- ice baths
- red light therapy

- compression
- vibration therapy
- electrical muscle stimulation (EMS)
- infrared sauna
- hyperbaric oxygen therapy (HBOT)
- deep tissue massage
- brain photobiomodulation
- breathwork: Navy SEAL Box Breathing
- fasting

I do all of this to help me physically, mentally, and spiritually recover. I will go over how you can implement these tools, no matter your budget, later in this book. Based on your financial standing, there are different levels for what you can do for free up to full investment in yourself, from "bootstrapped recovery" all the way to "billion-dollar exit recovery." Just always remember you are your best investment.

Principle 8. Evoking Natural Hormonal Balance for Brain Function

Several key hormones and functions play a pivotal role in driving cognitive function and performance. We have all the tools to naturally support and enhance these critical functions. Natural HGH is produced by the pituitary gland located at the base of the brain. It plays a crucial role in muscle growth and cellular repair. Cortisol regulation is crucial for managing stress and maintaining mental clarity under pressure. Dopamine, often referred to as the "reward" neurotransmitter, fuels motivation and creative thinking, essential traits for successful entrepreneurship. Serotonin, known for its impact on mood, also contributes to confidence and effective decision-making. Testosterone plays a role in cognitive function, mood, and energy levels in both men and women. Optimal thyroid hormone levels are vital for sustained energy and focus. Additionally, balanced levels of brain-derived neurotrophic factor (BDNF) facilitate learning, memory, and adaptability—all fundamental for entrepreneurial growth.

What we do:

We focus on key Protocol activities daily, such as our elongated fasting, walk/sprint, strength training, HIIT (High Intensity Interval Training), ice baths, sauna, sleep, and proper physical and cognitive recovery though our recovery modalities, to optimize key cognitive hormones.

Why we do it:

Your performance depends on the quality and capability of your brain health. When working the hours an entrepreneur does, we need to be able to have the brain continuously heal itself from the inside, because of all the stress we put on our bodies and brains. Internally, we have all the biological tools needed to heal and repair ourselves, and to ignite the essential processes needed to ensure we can run with the workload and the pace needed to be successful in business.

This Protocol is not about slowing down; it's about accelerating, while ensuring we utilize the right modalities to evoke the proper natural hormones for our brain and, at the same time, provide the biological environment for our bodies to heal all the way down to the cellular level. A vibrant brain with a high rate of balanced hormones and BDNF is the goal. All can be attained following the Performance Protocol.

How we do it:

To enhance key cognitive hormones and functions, the Protocol uses a multifaceted approach. We boost dopamine through goal achievement, kicking ass, training hard, and consumption of dopamine-rich foods like eggs, nuts, and raw dairy. Elevate serotonin levels by spending time in sunlight, practicing mindfulness, training, hydration, and fostering positive social interactions. The Protocol supports thyroid function through managing stress with recovery and prioritizing optimized sleep. We foster brain-derived neurotrophic factor (BDNF) through our cognitive walk/sprint, mentally stimulating activities, optimizing our sleep, consuming brain-healthy nutrients during our OMAD, and implementing 23-48-72 Fasting Protocol.

So, in essence, we simply focus on the daily Protocols that are built on activities, specific training, workouts, diet, and fasting, which spark the brain and put us in the best cognitive state to perform. I want to reiterate that I am a millionaire tech CEO telling you that you don't need to spend ANYTHING to optimize your brain.

Principle 9. Optimized Sleep—the Non-Negotiable

If you are not prepared to make optimized sleep a priority, put this book down. You should not try to follow this Protocol, as it will be for naught. You need to rebuild your sleep balance.

To be the best you, you must be rigorous with your sleep routine. Use the available modern tools to maximize and NREM Stage 3 (Deep Sleep) and REM sleep. If you are not prepared to build sleep into your work schedule, don't even bother trying this Protocol, because you won't be able to do it. Sleep is your superpower, to regenerate your brain and your body, to be able to attack the next day. We master the science of sleep and make it pure, deep, uninterrupted, and extremely efficient.

In the Performance CEO Protocol, you will learn science-backed tricks to help you get the deepest sleep with REM sleep. As the Performance CEO, you should begin to see sleep as one of the most important tools for fueling your greatness.

You'll learn the secrets of leveraging technology, like a temperature-controlled sleep pad, keeping your room at 65 degrees to induce better sleep and a slower resting heartrate, and planning out when you have your last meal or partaking in your last activity.

Every decision contributes to the perfect nighttime routine, to optimize your sleep.

What we do:

Work hard and sleep even harder. As the Performance CEO, prioritize an optimized night's sleep to help recharge your performance levels for the next morning. We focus on optimizing our sleep to hit two hours of REM and two hours of NREM Stage 3 Deep Sleep every night.

Why we do it:

Although you may have been pulling all-nighters to create the perfect presentation for your next meeting, staying awake rather than sleeping is likely to hinder more than help you.

This principle is one of my most interesting and unexpected discoveries. I spent most of my career running away from sleep. People have even heard me say, "Sleep is for losers."

However, now I know that sleep quantity and quality are crucial to my success and critical for optimum cognitive function and focus. A bad night's sleep can completely mess up your body, blood sugar, cravings, energy, recovery, and hydration levels. It can undo all the work you've just put in at the office, gym, and kitchen.

How we do it:

Set up your bedroom as the ultimate Recovery Center, with proper room temperature. I take an ice bath at night, to lower my core body temperature. Invest in a great bed, wear blue-light blocking glasses, use a product to chill your bed mattress, hang blackout curtains, and leave your phone out of the bedroom. I implement all the tricks daily that I've learned while researching sleep. Every decision contributes to the perfect nighttime routine to optimize your sleep. Sleep to win.

Principle 10. Live a Spartan Lifestyle

Throughout my career and success, there have been distant stages in my life where I've had multiple homes all over the world, and a lot of unnecessary things, like thirty pairs of jeans, seven luxury watches, and my Bentley. I loved having these things initially, but I quickly learned that they were just unnecessary *things*. Just stuff. I realized that simplicity creates the environment for genius.

The Protocol I developed is meant to create the optimal minimalistic environment around me to focus solely on being at my best for innovation. The simpler the environment, the less clutter in the environment, the more the brain's ability to think clearly and think big is enhanced. So, it's imperative that we whittle down our belongings and focus only on the things we need to pursue our dreams—and live in a very clean, simplistic environment, without clutter and excess luxury. Be non-materialistic. Absence of clutter creates a clear mind to drive your dreams and businesses forward. Living in a spartan environment gives you everything you need and nothing you don't to build your dreams. Resist comfort. Comfort is where innovation goes to die.

What we do:

Comfort is a drug. Once you become addicted, you forget about your dreams and goals. By reducing your surroundings to the bare minimum, you can create an environment that will help you reach and sustain success. A spartan lifestyle or existence is very simple and strict. Instead of indulging in the creature comforts and pleasures that money can buy, invest in your mental and physical health by getting the tools your brain and body need to perform their best. We focus on following our passions, not accumulating stuff.

Why we do it:

After working so hard, it can be easy to entertain the ideas and stereotypes of what objects signify success. In my career, I had indulged in fancy cars and a big house full of "stuff." But all of that was ultimately just a distraction on my journey toward higher success and the goal of brain optimization. By living a life of simplicity, we can rid our day-to-day lives of distractions that don't contribute to biohacking or optimizing our entrepreneurial performance. Remember, biohacking is not only for your biology, but also about creating the environment around you. Marvin Hagler, the famous boxer, said it best: "It's tough to get out of bed to do roadwork at 5 am when you're sleeping in silk pajamas." Stay lean, stay hungry, stay simple.

How we do it:

I want to reshape what it looks like to be a high-performing and successful CEO, and what success looks like. Through this Protocol, in our sole quest to become the most optimized human mentally and physically, it's my goal to normalize a standing desk, whiteboards in the living room, kettle bell swings in the office, and complete simplicity in your surroundings. Living a spartan life can help you isolate the absolute necessities your brain and body need to outperform everyone, and eliminate all the rest as a distraction on your journey to greatness. Having a strict diet isn't just about the food you eat. It's also what you consume outside of food. It's what you feed your brain informationally, and that's just as important as the nutrition you supply it with. This is why with a minimalistic lifestyle we control the environment to ensure we are at our best.

Don't let social media fool you. The new wealthy are not driving Bugattis, but are low-key and self-sufficient. They are not materialistic; they are living off the land, farming cattle, growing organic food, increasing physical strength, getting more sun, walking in the woods, off the grid, focused on innovation, and concerned with something higher than modern materialism. This is the life of the true Performance CEO.

Now let's take a look at how these Ten Principles fall into my typical day. Like I told you in the introduction, I am really about this life and live my perfect day, every day, to live a life of innovation and impact.

Then we will go deeper into the three major Performance CEO pillars of Fasting/Nutrition, Strength, and Recovery, and *why* they are intricately incorporated into the next steps of the Performance CEO Protocol adaptation period 15-day jumpstart. It's a window into the exact Performance Protocol you will be following—just like I do every day—in the next 45 days.

A Day in the Life

I want to take some time to transparently show how I have optimized every workday, so I am at my best for my clients, employees, family, and live a life of innovation as I lead the future of artificial intelligence. This is truly my perfect day, a day I am uniquely able to create as an entrepreneur. I walk this path day in and day out, not to show how "optimized" I am but to solely reach my full capability and evoke my brain's greatest potential for creating new neurons and brain cells to perform when I need to. The brain influences far more than just your mental acuity, and that is why I put so much importance in my daily cognitive Protocol.

I am really about this life. I am a builder, a man of action, and have the honor as a leader and entrepreneur to live my perfect day, building people and technology, every day. The reason I live this extreme life, is not about me. It's about being my best for others.

Every morning, I jump out of bed ready to face the world. I wake up each day obsolete and every day I need to learn, grow, and earn my success. What I knew yesterday could be incorrect today because technology moves so fast. And every evening, I ask myself a simple bottom-line question: did I do everything I could to prepare myself to seize moments when they arise in my business, did I actualize all my God-given talents?

I am built to do the hard, lonely things to stay humble and hungry.

I am aware that the Performance CEO's daily schedule is intense, but so is being an entrepreneur and building a company from nothing. Performance CEOs have a different calling—a requirement to be great.

We are all given the same hours. Let's be meticulous about how we use them.

My Daily Schedule

It's important for you to see what this Performance Protocol looks like daily, so you can envision my day-to-day life and ask yourself honestly if you have the passion, desire, and discipline to live it. Once again, I get it. Living this spartan life of innovation is not for everyone, but the real ones know. Here we go.

4 AM: Wake up naturally anywhere from 3:30 to 4:00 am daily. I never set an alarm clock. Waking up naturally shows that your body is getting the sleep it needs. Upon awakening, I get right out of bed and never linger. I always wake up with purpose and count my blessings for another day to pursue my calling, build my dreams and change lives.

- Test Ketones: Goal 1-1.5 mmol +
- Measure Body Composition (weight)
- Drink my Super Water - 24 oz. Water with 1/2 tsp. Vitamin C, Minerals, and 1/4 tsp. Salt
- Drink Organic Black Coffee. As I sip on my coffee, I enjoy the silence of the morning.
- Red Light Therapy, Full Body: Ten mins – while doing therapy, I pray, read a verse of Proverbs, and embrace the silence of the morning to go where my mind takes me. Red light mimics the natural sunrise.
- Cold Plunge: I pride myself on being mentally strong - 3 min at 39 degrees (while in the tub, practice Navy SEAL Box Breathing). Performing this task at 4:00 am, I set the tone for embracing the hard, uncomfortable tasks all day long. I am too strong, mentally, to waver. I am indomitable.

4:20 AM: Next is my Morning Ideation Session: First Strategic Deep Work Window. Think big and be brilliant. I sit in the dark, silent solitude of morning. This is my time in the quiet of the early day to create and solve my most pressing issues. This time varies each day based on how early I wake up and where my brain takes me, whatever strategic task that might be.

- Second Organic Black Coffee (Max 400mg in total)
- Add - 1 mL of Lion's Mane and L-Theanine to create my cognitive coffee
  At this point, I am 16 hours fasted (black coffee and water do not count). For my brain, BDNF is in full effect with learning and memory, making neurons more resistant to stress. With neurogenesis sparked, this is the time and space to be brilliant. I continue to embrace the quiet and stillness of early morning. Think big. Create. Solve. All of my big decisions and ideas come in the quiet of the morning.

4:50 AM: Morning Strength Workout. Time for this 4:00 am CEO to do his thing. Depending on where I am, I will go to the gym or use my home strength performance center. Using a timing app, I have programmed the times for each set, rest, and exercise, so I can work out on autopilot and think about business, not sets. I preset into my phone, so this becomes another ideation session while I hit the weights and think big. I have two whiteboards in my home gym for brainstorming, notes, and problem-solving or I use the notes section on my phone. I am always thinking about innovation and business as I dominate my strength workout. My best ideas come while I am lifting heavy things. Heck, I have written over half of this book during my Strength Session, as my brain and creativity are optimal as I crush weights.

Strength Training Protocol:
- Warmup: 20-20-10
- Strength: 5 sets x 5 reps (3-min rest)
- Accessory: 4 sets x 6-8 reps (2-min rest)
- Volume: 4 sets x 10 reps of 4 exercises (30-sec rest)
- Burnout: 2 exercises x 50 reps each
- GPP: 3 rounds - 30 sec on, 30 sec off

- Cognitive Walk/Sprint: 30 Minutes (HIIT Sprint) 2:30 walk, 30-Sec Sprint, 10 Rounds (I always catch the sunrise during this time. It helps in so many ways, especially with my circadian rhythm and morning sunlight.)

At 16-18 hours fasted, during the workout my natural HGH starts to peak, to be able to build muscle and maximize benefits. My mental clarity is unrivaled. I feel unstoppable. I have been thinking about my business now for three-plus hours, as I power through the early morning, before my competition has even hit snooze.

7 AM: Post-Workout Recovery Modality Routine.
- Post-Workout Infrared Sauna: 25 min (when accessible)
- Natural AM Sunlight Outside (raises Vit D & natural testosterone): 20 min
- Consume 3g of Creatine Post workout
- Finish Off my first 85 oz. of Water

8 AM - 12 PM: Uninterrupted 20-minute deep work window sprints. In 20-minute increments, this is the best time cognitively to get the most important work done. These are the eight most important meetings of my day. This is when I am at my best. Set up your Office Control Center to have all the tools you need at your disposal and do only the most mission critical tasks and client video meetings. I work from my standing desk. Even with all the vigorous training in the Performance CEO Protocol, you must keep moving; it will never be enough to offset nine hours executives spend sitting each day.

- At this point 20+ hours fasted during this time
My Office Activity Rules: to keep my brain sparked, for the last ten minutes of every work sprint, I do ten kettle bell Swings in my office, at the end of my deep work windows. I also make sure to look outside, into the distance, so my eyes are healthy considering all of my screen time.

12 PM: OMAD Time for Brain Fuel. I eat the same thing daily for my brain and optimal neuro healthy nutrition that supports neurogenesis and optimizes brain function. I am 23 hours fasted when I consume my first sip of bone broth to break my fast.

- Break my fast with Organic Bone Broth [2 Cups]
- Protein Formula Calculation: 0.8g protein x BW (grass-finished beef or wild-caught salmon). We weigh *after* cooking as cooking process loses 25% of protein weight.
- Grass-Finished Liver or Organ Meat [x2 oz] or a liver/organ supplement
- Pasture-Raised Eggs [x4 men; x2 women]
- Organic Pecans [20 halves or 1/4 cup]
- Organic Raspberries [x40]
- Organic Avocado [x1 large]
- Grass-Fed Raw Cheese (50g, or consume enough to hit your Total Protein Formula Goal)

12:30 PM: Afternoon Recharge HBOT/or Compression Boots. One-hour midday recovery.
*I learned this from NASA Astronauts and how they prepare to reset for the afternoon of work ahead with a short nap. I do HBOT 5x per week for one hour. The other two days, I do Compression Boots during my mid-day recharge. This is my halftime for my workday.

2 PM: Afternoon coffee & collagen jumpstart – Time to charge back in.
- 100mg Organic Coffee with Grass-Fed & Pasture Raised collagen. *Perform 20 kettle bell swings to spark blood flow to the brain, avoiding any afternoon dip. Let's go win the afternoon!*

2 PM - 5 PM: Second round of 20-min. deep work window sprints. Be a monster during this time with output. You are fully charged. This time is all about output. Win the afternoon!
- Put on Day Yellow Blocker Glasses
  *Same Deep Work Office activity rules every hour. 10 kettle bell swings after each sprint.

3 PM: Midday Outdoor Nature Ideation Walk. Use this time to think big and get outside in nature. I usually take an internal meeting while I hike when I am at my NC mountain property. If I am in the city, I still get outside. Get outside, be grounded. Fresh air to think. I even take select "walk and talks," catching up with internal employees.
- No More Caffeine After 3:00 pm

5 PM - 6 PM: My Final Tactical DEEP Work Window.
- Output, Execution, Preparation, and Task-intensive
- Finish my second 85 oz. Water for a Total of One Gallon before 5:00 pm
I stop drinking water at 5:00 pm to mitigate nighttime bathroom breaks, evoking deeper, uninterrupted sleep.

6 PM: Put on Complete Blue Blocker Glasses.

7 PM: Cognitive Rest & Personal Recharge. Begin daily pre-bedtime routine. Time to win the night so I can win tomorrow.
- Sunset Ice Bath—second ice bath, timed as the sun goes down, starts the process of getting ready for optimized sleep. For three minutes, at 39 degrees, to lower my core body temperature, reduces inflammation from the day; I use it to decompress and prepare for sleep.
- Perform my second Red Light Session—10 min, using my full body medical grade red light therapy device
- Plan The Next Day—review calendar. Set key strategic tasks. Put away cell phone.

8 PM: Bedtime. Sleep is the ultimate recovery. My restorative sleep goals focus on attaining two hours of REM, two hours of deep sleep, and reaching an optimal resting HR. An optimized night's sleep is seven to eight hours for cognitive recovery.
- Enter my Optimized Sleep Environment.
- Read a Print Book. No Blue Light.
- Turn on my Bed Cooling Sleep Pad.
- Blackout Curtains. Darkness. No Light.

- Listen to an Educational Podcast.
- 65 Degrees in the Bedroom.

I always remember to say my prayers, count my blessings, stay humble, and be present and thankful that I was given this day to actualize all my talents and purpose. Tomorrow brings you another day to build your dreams and the dreams of others. I make it a practice to be so appreciative that I can create my perfect day. Be asleep by 9:00 pm. Don't worry, nothing important happens after 9:00 pm when you are on your entrepreneurial quest. Staying up late has no ROI.

*To me there is no such thing as work hours. An entrepreneur should think about their business 24/7. So, with every activity, utilize your optimized brain to think about your business, whether you're lifting, running, recovering, showering, or eating. You should be solving issues and thinking creatively and strategically **ALL DAY**. Yes. You must be this obsessive if you truly have a passion to actualize your talents and build a business from the ground up.*

There is an independence and power that comes with being an entrepreneur and having the ability to structure your perfect and most optimized day. Corporate employees will never understand this. Build your perfect day. There is also a level of timing flexibility within the framework of my early morning. Sometimes I will take more time solving a complex problem first thing where it will slide my workouts. Some days my body will need some more rest so I will sleep a bit longer till 5:00 am.

Don't think about it as a schedule that is rigidly "time based." Think of it as key sequential biological steps that need to be taken in order. By getting up early you have freedom within a time framework to accomplish all the things you need within that time, and add some early morning flexibility. This is not a schedule; this is a practice for cognitive optimization. If all steps are executed in order, your brain will reap the benefits. As entrepreneurs we all know things come up, and when innovation hits, seize it.

No entrepreneur can tell me that they can't build their perfect day. Entrepreneurship is synonymous with independence and freedom. If you can't build your perfect day, then you have a boss.

And that is not true entrepreneurship, nor is it creating the optimal environment for innovation and, ultimately, performance. Today, too many entrepreneurs' edges are rounded. They are physically soft. They are not sharp. This Protocol sharpens your edges to become a weapon. A weapon to build dreams and create opportunities for others.

If seeing my schedule didn't scare you off, and you're still ready to move forward to do everything biologically possible to actualize your greatness, then let's move forward. You now have the "How"—all the info you need to jump into the 15-Day Jumpstart and the Next 30-Day Extreme Cognitive Plan. Feel free to jump right into the Adaptation period. GO GET IT!

Is this hard? Damn right it is. But once you start, you'll see how you feel after you adapt, how natural it is—you will wonder how you ever lived life not as the Performance CEO.

For the "why entrepreneurs" who want to go deeper, I have created Three Pillars of information that will cover Fasting/Nutrition, Strength, and Recovery in greater detail in the next chapters, so you will understand at a profound level why we are doing this to drive cognitive function.

Either path you take, you're still reading this book, and that shows me something: you may be part of the special breed of passionate entrepreneurs. Let's get started!

PILLAR I

Fasting/Nutrition

Igniting your Optimal Fuel-Burning System

It's as simple as this: fasting boosts brain power and the rate of neurogenesis.

Why do we focus on the brain and neurogenesis? Because when you focus on the brain, the body follows becoming the strongest and leanest it's ever been.

With its fusion of fasting and a cognitive performance diet, the Fasting Protocol provides the ultimate brain tools. With them, you'll have the most optimized day. And our goal is to create the right biological environment to drive energy, cognitive performance, and focus on the regeneration and capabilities for our brain and body. Every calorie you ingest is for the sole purpose of optimization.

With this Fasting Protocol, your brain, recall, memory, and mood will be your weapons. They'll allow you to build muscle at any age. They'll accelerate cognitive function. They'll help you dominate the boardroom.

This food plan has been engineered for cognitive performance. We fuse fasting with consuming the right nutrients, at the right time, to power our brains and bodies to work at an unrivaled pace.

Food choices impact brain health. There is no firewall between them. The right foods with optimal nutritional timing are twin components for making the most of your fuel-burning system. They have a symbiotic relationship. We will build muscle and lose fat, freeing up functions to help in other key areas of the body so you can run lean and mean.

Commit to this plan for 45 days, and you will reprogram your brain. It will become a must in your life, based on your body and brain signals. This is based on cutting-edge brain science.

Science tells us that the heart and brain love ketones. They are an essential part of your cognitive health journey. Utilizing ketones as fuel is the leading way to boost cognitive performance. This is proven. Even the military and government agencies are now using it to heighten brain performance.[4]

Higher ketone levels lead to better cognitive function and provide neuroprotective effects. It's an unlimited source of energy. We boost brain performance and function by following a plan where we consume only those foods that fuel body and brain.

Fasting as a Weapon

At first it might seem drastic, to go without eating for 23 hours a day, 48 hours a week, and 72 hours a month. It's not drastic, it's optimal. Our brains and bodies have been created to operate like this, we just need to reprogram our habits and outdated perceptions.

But think of it like this. What if you could acquire a battery of cognitive and physical advantages, without having to do anything in order to gain them?

Let me ask that again: *without doing anything?* Because that is what fasting can do for us. By doing nothing, we activate our systems in ways they have not been switched on before.

Fasting is good for you. It promotes major healing, increases BDNF to grow new brain cells. It's responsible for making your brain more resilient to stress, producing more brain cells, and stimulating new connections and synapses, all while boosting memory and improving mood and learning. It truly does it all. Fasting can increase your brain's BDNF by 100 to 400 percent.[5] This helps you optimize cognitive function and be all-in.

Fasting also kickstarts autophagy, which begins at 18 hours of fasting and accelerates with each hour. The longer you fast, the more powerful it gets. Autophagy is the recycling of old and damaged cells—but it's also a process that clears away old neurons to make way for new ones.

Fasting also increases natural HGH, and enables your body to retain muscle, build muscle and strength. This natural Fountain of Youth of HGH increase can be unlocked at 12 hours of fasting, and it increases with every hour. Fasting assists with anti-aging, promotes protein syntheses, eliminates inflammation of the brain and body, heals the gut, and decreases the risk of neurodegeneration.

In our plan, we fast for 23 hours daily, to get the full benefits of the practice. And it is important to understand what happens in the body at each hour, and why the Protocol has us do exact tasks when we are biologically primed to do them.

When we fast, our primal DNA gets activated. It makes us sharper, gives us energy, and uses our inborn fuel-burning systems at their maximum potential. Fasting also allows our body to heal, and it builds our resilience, discipline, and focus.

And so, although it may seem like an extreme thing to do now—something that's counterintuitive and unpleasant—when you get started you'll see how easy it truly is, and you will ask yourself, *Why did I ever eat that frequently?*

23-hour Fasts

The fasting structure is the most important part of this Protocol. It's a zero-cost tool that provides enormous healing benefits to the body that science is only now starting to appreciate and understand.

Fasting for more than 23 hours has been proven to reduce inflammation by decreasing oxidative stress in cells. We do it every day. Recent updated research and clinical trials suggest that sustained fasting regimens maintained over months or even years may also improve memory, along with executive function and overall cognition.[6] It's the silver bullet for performance, health, youth, and longevity.

And so, every day, we do a 23-hour fast. Intermittent fasting provides a good balance between eating and fasting cycles in the human body. As the body undergoes a complete internal renovation, new structures are built, and nutritive material gets redistributed.

Fasting can improve cardiovascular health.[7] In addition, it can help fight certain kinds of cancer, and even help preserve memory, as well as improve metabolic health. Your body needs a break from eating to rest and repair itself fully.

Fasting and autophagy are like Roombas that operate inside your cells, cleaning and clearing damaged parts and regenerating them. When autophagy functions optimally, it works to clear away the cellular junk that can lead to fat and external wrinkles. The 23-hour fast also triggers the generation of new white blood cells, which can reboot your whole immune system.

One study found that fasting for more than 23 hours lowered inflammation by reducing oxidative stress in cells.[8] Another study showed that both intermittent fasting and alternate-day fasting were effective at reducing insulin resistance, which is the precursor to type 2 diabetes (an inflammatory condition).

48 Hours + 72 Hours = Immeasurable Benefits

We fast for 48 hours weekly. Why? It's all about stem cells.

In a 48-hour fast, we create stem cells naturally, which can turn into anything the body needs to heal and repair. This has drastic anti-aging effects and gives your body the ultimate healing power. This healing is not only external—with skin, hair, nails—it's internal, too. When your body is not focused on digestion, it can focus on cellular repair, which will turn back the clock and give you healing that is absolutely unrivaled.

We fast for 72 hours monthly. If you think your stem cell power was great at 48…wait until 72. You will see why I have been doing this as long as I have.

A 72-hour monthly fast will be our longest-ever fast, because after that time there are no real additional benefits. With that one monthly 72-hour fast, we get tough mentally. That is when food is not the center of our existence. Our lives no longer revolve around it, and it's then that food enters the body strictly to fuel our greatness, and we can reach a higher plane of discipline and cognitive receptiveness.

During those 72 hours, the benefits of fasting firmly enhance what we gained in 23 hours—so you'll come out rejuvenated, lean, fresh, and provided with the right internal environment to solve some of the most complex business problems you're facing today.

When you have a big problem to solve, nothing works better than fasting. It gives you a level of cognitive clarity where you can tackle those issues and think big.

The 15-day Adaptation

As you begin the nutritional program, you'll begin the initial 15 days of your plan focused on getting your body to a fat-burning adapted state, and getting this new state integrated into your daily routine. During the 15-day Jumpstart, you will close your eating window, and begin to adopt the one-meal-a-day (OMAD) methodology. I can't stress enough that *what* you eat is just as important as *how much* of it you eat and *when* you eat it.

Our Fasting Protocol is essential for optimizing the brain and body, so we can work to close that window during the 15-day adaptation.

Less frequent eating means we eliminate the spiking of insulin. We provide all the nutrients our body needs to repair, heal, and fuel.

And, in case you have doubts about this, let me assure you: fasting isn't a newfangled fad. It's a well-researched modification that can help you live longer and healthier and be smarter in life. Research shows that people who practice regular intermittent fasting have lower body fat, lower resting heart rates, lower blood sugar and insulin levels, and lower unhealthy cholesterol and bad blood fats.[9]

Intermittent fasting has such a profound effect because it's the body shifting metabolic pathways from relying on blood sugar for fuel and tapping into stored body fat for energy. This is why you'll experience optimal body composition. You don't need to eat for hours, and your cells can then use your body's stored fat.

Fasting also increases levels of growth hormone, which stimulates cell growth and regeneration. The release of the neurotransmitter norepinephrine fights depression and other mood disorders. For the brain, intermittent fasting has been shown to improve memory focus, learning, and overall executive function. These habits can also reduce oxidative stress and cognitive inflammation, trigger neurogenesis, and increase neuroplasticity, or the ability for your brain to change.

Intermittent fasting can also help you become more mindful about food. We're going to create new habits, where you don't look at food as enjoyment but instead as fuel for your body or brain to attack your herculean dreams and goals.

Fasting for the Brain & Body

By simply not doing anything—through fasting—we can ignite the processes that begin healing, to create a leaner, stronger, and more powerful biology to tackle our day.

It all begins on a cellular level. Fasting can help repair previous cellular damage through autophagy—the cellular *Hunger Games*. Studies have shown that induced autophagy through fasting in hippocampal neurons is necessary to boost activity in memory and promote the stimuli needed to improve cognitive fitness.[10]

In other words, autophagy makes your brain function better at a molecular level.

The benefits of fasting, however, are not limited to creating new neuronal connections in the brain. Fasting can improve your body's health at a cellular level. By limiting your food and drink intake to only certain moments of the day, you can lower insulin and cortisol naturally, and raise your human growth hormone, or HGH, levels. This change in your molecular biology boosts energy levels and decreases inflammation in your body.

How does it do that? As you age, production of HGH in the human body declines, which then causes a hormonal imbalance. But the fasting regimen spikes HGH production naturally, to help you balance your hormones, and reverse aging processes as a byproduct.

Our 23-hour fast have been shown to naturally increase the body's HGH levels—by about 300 percent.

Balancing those hormones can also have lasting positive effects on other day-to-day activities. For example, by having a last meal at 3:00 pm, or fasting for over four hours before bed, you can optimize sleep and your natural hormone levels. Fasting can help your body grow stronger and even improve your ability to walk and breathe.

Another beneficial byproduct of fasting for mental acuity is the way fasting fights wrinkles. According to a study, intermittent fasting switches on DNA-repairing genes that help reduce inflammation in the body. This helps the skin to heal and repair, as cells are renewed more rapidly. Plus, production of a hormone called somatropin increases, helping to minimize wrinkles and fine lines, to slow the aging process and increase longevity by cleaning our cells. And so, fasting not only evokes that optimal fuel-burning, which means you think and perform at your mental peak, but you will also look amazing while doing it.[11]

Fasting to a Higher Plane

Science has shown us that the traditional three-meals-a-day approach doesn't support our biological makeup and is not necessary for performance or longevity. Science instead points to the direction of fasting. When your body is fat-adapted, you become superhuman—fast, lean, powerful, strong, and aesthetically amazing.

Fasting is God's gift to energy—you can look at it like a superpower. In addition to the physical benefits, fasting provides a huge cognitive advantage when it comes to thinking, problem-solving, and overall cerebral clarity.

Fasting has a long and storied history, too; it's nothing close to new. Throughout history, it has been known to help those who seek enlightenment reach it. In almost every religion around the world, you'll find that the practice incorporates fasting to help someone reach a higher mental plane. You'll see why, once you begin fasting. You'll feel like you've shifted into an extra gear with your brainpower. You might even see it as an unfair advantage for every big meeting.

Even as I write this book, I stay fasted to energize my brain. The primal instincts that kick in with fasting keep me laser-focused and keep my brain firing on all cylinders. I feel sharper and more ready to win, with access to boundless energy.

I always do extended fasting 23 hours or longer heading into any strategy or ideation session. Introduce caffeine and I am on a whole other level.

All you have to do is have the discipline to simply do nothing. Think about that—in a world in which working harder is praised and encouraged, one of the best things you can do for your health is *absolutely nothing*. This makes fasting the most powerful weapon in your arsenal—and possibly one of your new favorites.

If you're not tapping into those benefits and using fasting as a competitive advantage in the workplace, you might as well issue a formal apology for not doing all you can for your business, employees, shareholders, and most importantly, *clients!* It's your obligation to do this to maximize your full potential.

You have access to all the above benefits for free. Literally, from the art of doing nothing, knowing how to structure your day, and having the discipline to take on this extreme lifestyle, you can open the door to all these amazing game-changing benefits.

Fasted Workouts

Our Fasting Protocol optimizes our workouts. By promoting fat loss and building muscle, your body becomes even stronger and more able to fight off disease-causing inflammation. That extra strength builds up your body's resilience, which then burns even more fat. These lowered fat levels then help the body by producing less insulin, which can lead to a ton of other health benefits—promoting fat loss (and keeping it off) once again.

As you increase your natural HGH production, protein synthesis occurs, and you flood your muscles with mammalian target of rapamycin (mTOR). Protein synthesis is how we build muscles. You want to spike and activate mTOR to regulate the anabolic and catabolic signaling of muscle growth.

However, the science of building muscles tells us that doing it effectively is all about timing. Your body needs to be absolutely ready for that surge in protein synthesis for it to work optimally. Fortunately, the Fasting Protocol suppresses this mTOR until the right moment, which is when we consume nutrition post-workout. In other words, fasting gives your body the opportune environment to build more natural muscle.

This is why your fasted morning workouts are so important. Not only is your natural HGH boosted 200 percent from hours of fasting, but your planned eating is designed so that your mTOR bounces back up, directly after your workout, to help promote even more growth.

This is how science can help us reach otherwise unfathomable physical performance. As you learn more about your body, you'll see that it truly is an amazing science project. When you learn how to harness all of that knowledge and put it into practice, you can then truly become unstoppable.

Let's Review

Benefits of 23-hour fast

> **Enhanced autophagy:** Autophagy is a cellular process that helps remove damaged cells and waste materials from the body. The Protocol: 23-hour daily fasting periods promote autophagy, supporting cellular health and longevity.
>
> **Mental clarity:** Improved mental clarity and focus during fasting periods, due to stable blood sugar levels and the absence of energy crashes caused by frequent meals.
>
> **Health benefits**: Increased growth hormone production, reduced inflammation.

Benefits of 48-hour fast:

> **Enhanced Fat Burning:** Fasting for 48 hours can lead to significant glycogen depletion, forcing the body to turn to stored fat for

energy. This may promote more extended and more substantial fat burning compared to shorter fasting periods.

Cellular Autophagy: Extended fasting can stimulate autophagy more profoundly than shorter fasts. Autophagy is the process through which cells remove damaged components and promote cellular repair and renewal.

Improved Insulin Sensitivity: Prolonged fasting has been linked to improved insulin sensitivity, which may help regulate blood sugar levels and reduce the risk of type 2 diabetes.

Hormone Regulation: Fasting can influence various hormones related to metabolism and energy balance, potentially supporting overall hormonal health.

Brain Health: Some studies suggest that extended fasting may promote brain health by supporting the growth of new nerve cells and enhancing brain function.

Anti-inflammatory Effects: Fasting has been shown to reduce markers of inflammation in the body, potentially contributing to overall health and wellness.

Digestive Rest: Providing the digestive system with an extended break can promote gut health and reduce digestive stress.

Immune System Support: Some research indicates that fasting can enhance immune function by promoting the production of new immune cells.

Detoxification: While more research is needed, fasting may support the body's natural detoxification processes by giving organs like the liver a chance to rest and regenerate.

Mental and Emotional Clarity: We will experience mental clarity and emotional well-being during extended fasting periods.

Benefits of 72-hour fast:

Glycogen Depletion: This forces the body to rely on stored fat for energy. This can result in more substantial fat burning compared to shorter fasting periods.

Deep Autophagy: Extended fasting can trigger a deeper level of autophagy, the process through which cells remove damaged components and promote cellular repair and renewal. This intense autophagy can have potential long-term benefits for cellular health.

Insulin Sensitivity Improvement: Prolonged fasting has been associated with improved insulin sensitivity, which may aid in regulating blood sugar levels and reducing the risk of type 2 diabetes.

Hormonal Regulation: Fasting can influence various hormones related to metabolism and energy balance, potentially supporting overall hormonal health.

Brain Health: Extended fasting supports brain health by promoting the growth of new nerve cells and enhancing brain function.

Immune System Support: Fasting can enhance immune function by promoting the production of new immune cells and reducing inflammation.

Cellular Repair and Renewal: The extended fasting period allows for more comprehensive cellular repair and renewal processes to take place.

Metabolic Reset: Some proponents of extended fasting claim that it can act as a "metabolic reset," potentially aiding and improving overall metabolic health.

Cognitive performance: Promotes increased mental clarity, focus, and a sense of accomplishment during and after an extended fast.

Fasting for Women Founders

The female body and hormones have a bit of a different impact with elongated fasting. Men must adhere to the 23-48-72. Women who are on the Performance Protocol will have a bit of a fasting variation, based on their menstrual cycle.

Everything in this Protocol is the same for women, except that you'll split your food over two meals and have a longer eating window. You will still consume the max calories needed. At no time is fasting a calorie reduction, as we don't want to negatively affect your hormones.

The optimal way for women to fast can be influenced by their hormonal fluctuations throughout the menstrual cycle. Hormones play a significant role in a woman's metabolic and physiological responses, and fasting may affect women differently at different phases of their cycle. Here are some considerations for women regarding fasting and their hormones:

> **Menstrual Phase** (Days 1-5): During the menstrual phase, estrogen and progesterone levels are at their lowest. Some women may experience fatigue and increased hunger during this time. Fasting with severe calorie restriction may not be tolerated well during this phase. You must consume all your calories.
>
> **Follicular Phase** (Days 6-14): Estrogen levels gradually increase during the follicular phase, leading up to ovulation. This phase is often associated with increased energy and improved mood. Women may find it more comfortable to fast during this phase, as energy levels are generally higher.
>
> **Ovulatory Phase** (Around Day 14): Estrogen levels peak during ovulation, which may impact insulin sensitivity. Some women may experience increased hunger during this phase, so it's crucial to adjust your fasting windows accordingly.
>
> **Luteal Phase** (Days 15-28): During the luteal phase, both estrogen and progesterone levels are elevated. Some women may experience mood changes, bloating, and cravings, making fasting

more challenging. It's essential to focus on nutrient-dense foods and consider less restrictive fasting methods during this phase.

Individual Variability: Remember, while doing the Performance Protocol, individual responses to fasting can vary widely. Some women may tolerate fasting well throughout their cycle, while others may find it more challenging. Factors like stress, sleep quality, and overall health can also influence how fasting affects women hormonally.

The most important aspect of fasting for women is to listen to your bodies. Pay attention to hunger cues, energy levels, and mood throughout the menstrual cycle. Adjust fasting approaches as needed to support overall well-being and performance.

And make sure to consume all of the calories in the plan. This is *not* about caloric restriction, as it can negatively impact hormone balance and menstrual regularity. Consistency in daily caloric intake, and nourishing the body with essential nutrients, are important for hormonal health.

The Performance CEO Nutrition

So, you've fasted for the recommended number of hours. Now it's time to break your fast, and it's important that you do it with carefully chosen nutrition. This is pivotal to your quest to be the highest-performing entrepreneur.

We are selective about our schedule, the tools we use in our home, and how we approach our spartan lifestyle. In just the same way, we must be selective about what we put into our bodies, which then is absorbed as quintessential nutrients for our brains.

The fusion of elongated fasting, and consumption only of nutrients that drive cognitive performance, is paramount. It's the most powerful brain biohack I have experienced. It's like swallowing the world's strongest and most natural multivitamin. This nutrition plan increases your cerebral circulation, grows new neurons, reduces inflammation, and gives your body what it needs to build muscle and get to your optimal body fat percentage.

Eating right takes discipline. If you're not ready to commit to a strict eating lifestyle, then you're not ready to become the Performance CEO. Proper fueling means consuming the optimal nutrients, at the right time, with the foods that provide your brain with nutrients that enhance cognitive function.

Just like an elite athlete eats for performance, we entrepreneurs need to eat specifically for our brains to perform at our best. We need to tailor our fuel, to get us ready for the big stage, to crush deals, build empires, own the boardroom, and do the impossible.

90 percent of our ability to get into elite shape to support brain function at any age comes from diet and nutrition, which is why fasting and the Performance CEO Nutrition Protocol are key pillars of building an optimized body and mind.

By following an extremely disciplined biological eating window, and a Nutrition Protocol of fresh, seasonal, local, organic, real foods, consumed at the exact time, with the essential micronutrients, you will prepare your brain to become a supercomputer for what's to come—whatever that may be.

How We See Food

The Performance CEO looks at food differently than the average human. We look at our food as fuel, not as a source of enjoyment or comfort.

When we view our bodies as machines, it gives us the carefully crafted formula we can follow for every nutrient and calorie we ingest, at just the right time, to power up. By following this advice, you can reach into your optimal fuel-burning system that supplies you with clean, endless energy. Good nutrition is essential for your brain to function, and for you to outwork your competition and be the best leader for your organization.

Think of your nutrition as a technological algorithm, backed by exact science and a precise formula. The nutrients you consume help to program your body and brain to operate at an elite level. This food algorithm is easily replicable—and you will soon adopt it into your daily schedule.

Exact Nutrition for Brain & Body

The brain uses 500 calories per day. So, it's paramount we ensure our brains use the best possible calories, and consume the best possible brain nutrition—namely, neurotransmitter foods.

You need the exact nutrients that evoke the most important neurotransmitters for your brain. They come from our key staples of beef, almonds, eggs, organ meat, and wild salmon. We need to make sure to get plenty of essential fatty acids.

To build the best brain possible, you need the right building blocks—good, healthy fats. 60 percent of your brain is made up of fats, and 25 percent of it is made up of cholesterol. Yes, that's right: cholesterol.

It's essential to focus on key foods with high amounts of DHA (Docosahexaenoic acid, an essential omega-3 fatty acid), like salmon. From that 60 percent, 90 percent of the fats in the brain are DHA. So, for brain health and performance, we focus on great fats from real food. These fats are the building blocks of the brain. We eat the right foods at the right time to enhance our executive function. And we only consume the exact foods and nutrients that will increase neurogenesis and cognitive activity.

To be elite, you must consume only the best of the best.

The Benefits of OMAD

OMAD (one meal a day) is a type of intermittent fasting where an individual consumes all their daily caloric intake within a single meal, usually during a specific window of time, and fasts for the rest of the day. While OMAD is primarily associated with weight management and metabolic benefits, it may also offer some cognitive benefits for certain individuals.

And there is no such thing, for us, as a snack. We don't want to spike insulin.

Here are the cognitive benefits of OMAD:

Mental Clarity: Enhanced mental clarity and focus during fasting periods. This could be attributed to reduced fluctuations in blood sugar levels and improved brain energy utilization.

Improved Brain Health: Intermittent fasting has been studied for its potential neuroprotective effects. Animal studies suggest that intermittent fasting might support brain health and improve resistance to age-related neurodegenerative diseases.

Enhanced Autophagy: Autophagy is a cellular process that involves the removal of damaged or dysfunctional cellular components. Fasting, including OMAD, has been shown to stimulate autophagy, which may promote brain cell renewal and overall cellular health.

Neuroplasticity: Some research indicates that intermittent fasting could influence the brain's neuroplasticity, the ability to form new neural connections and adapt to changing environments.

Stress Resistance and Resilience: OMAD may induce mild stress on the body, leading to adaptations that enhance the body's ability to cope with stress. These adaptations may also extend to the brain, potentially improving stress resistance and resilience.

Enhanced Brain-Derived Neurotrophic Factor (BDNF) Production: BDNF is a protein that supports the growth and maintenance of neurons. Some studies suggest that intermittent fasting may increase BDNF production, which could have positive effects on brain health and cognitive function.

Let's look at the foods we eat and the nutrients they provide:

Grass-fed beef: A good source of protein, iron, zinc, vitamin B12, and other B-vitamins.

Liver and organs: Extremely nutrient-dense, providing essential vitamins (A, B12, riboflavin, and folate), minerals (iron, zinc, copper), and various other nutrients.

Bone broth: Contains collagen, gelatin, and some minerals like calcium and magnesium.

Sea salt: Provides essential minerals, mainly sodium and trace minerals.

Salmon: Rich in protein, omega-3 fatty acids, vitamin D, and other nutrients.

Avocado: Contains healthy monounsaturated fats, fiber, potassium, vitamin K, vitamin C, and various B-vitamins.

Raspberries: Provide fiber, vitamin C, manganese, and antioxidants.

Pecans and Almonds: A source of healthy fats, fiber, magnesium, and various other minerals. Almonds are an excellent source of vitamin E. Vitamin E is a fat-soluble antioxidant that helps protect cells from damage caused by free radicals.

Eggs: Rich in protein, healthy fats, choline, vitamin B12, selenium, and other essential nutrients.

Raw cheese: A source of protein, calcium, vitamin B12, and other nutrients found in dairy.

Fulvic minerals: Can provide trace minerals, but specific nutrient content may vary based on the source and formulation.

Vitamin C: An important antioxidant and immune-supporting nutrient.

This provides a more comprehensive array of nutrients than previous lists. This selection includes a wider range of food groups, which can contribute to meeting more of your daily nutritional needs.

Prioritizing Performance

Taking care of yourself is *the* most crucial thing you need to focus on right now. To help maximize your success in the workplace, you need to focus on every milligram of the nutrients you ingest and elongate your fasting windows to more than 20 hours. That's because every neuron, cellular repair, and micronutrient for the brain is unlocked by the power of optimal nutritional timing and fasting.

What does optimal biological timing mean? It means that by maximizing how and when a nutrient is delivered to your body, you're giving yourself the best chance to propel your body and brain to greatness. What you consume and when you consume it are seamlessly intertwined.

These details can help you judge or measure when you *should* fast, so you can produce all the essential hormones and get them to their peak states. This can help drive autophagy and optimize your body, building lean muscle and creating an impenetrable immune system.

It's all about targeting your body's natural processes. More importantly, by doing this we create the optimal biological ecosystem for our brain to thrive, repair, and evoke the power it needs, when it needs it, based on our deep work windows.

These processes work together, and the body races to optimization. First, fasting will kickstart the ideal fuel-burning system of the body. Then your body will maximize autophagy during your fasting window. It will create the perfect environment for the delivery of food and nutrients to the places where you need them the most. Lastly, now that you've opened up that highway of nutrients to your body's most important functions, you can become the unstoppable force you've always wanted to be, when you need to be it.

Fuel the brain and the body will follow.

Good nutrition, a healthy brain, and strong, healthy muscles are all connected. The mistake individuals make most often is focusing on just one aspect of these things, whether that be their nutrition, fasting, or an intense workout regimen. Performance is the result of the relationship between fueling and conditioning, giving your body all that it needs to recover and rebuild. Ultimately, it does not matter how hard you work out—or how often you work out—if your body is not getting the right nutrients to help your muscles, and most importantly your brain, to grow and repair.

The Simple, Ancient Performance Diet

An entrepreneur is a visionary, a hunter—someone who hunts goals and successes, making this Nutrition Protocol ideal for having boundless energy and elite cognitive function. It's been proven that people who follow this diet—in all different parts of the world—tend to live longer.

The Performance CEO Nutrition Protocol gets us back to our roots. It's based in part on the sort of diet people were consuming in the early days of the human race, when people were living in hunter-gatherer tribes. Only now do we live in a world of abundance.

The Nutrition Protocol turns us back to our natural state of ketosis, where we will burn fat for energy immediately rather than relying on glycogen. When combined with a daily 23-hour fasting window, with a prohibition on sugar, and consumption of the right foods, not only does it give you longevity and good health, but it also helps enhance focus, boost energy, and improve physical performance. The high-quality meat/organ meat and good fats approach is a simple formula with the biggest impact if we consume these brain foods in our eating window.

The mitochondria in your body make energy much more efficient with ketones than they do with glucose. Although the Keto Diet can help with that, I believe that the clinical Keto program gives you too much wiggle room when it comes to fat consumed. It's important to get our bodies to a state in which we are using ketones for our energy—but we still want to consume the right amounts of protein and fats with the right ratios.

When you eat the right fat and the right amount of it, your body learns to efficiently burn your stored fat for fuel. Your brain thrives on these fats (and fasting), and your mitochondria will then burn those ketones instead of glucose for fuel.

But for now, I want to talk to you about amino acids.

We all have amino acids flowing through our bloodstream that are biologically designed—no, specialized—for muscle repair, working directly with protein, and achieving nitrogen balance. To help us get that balance, we should strive to create an even intake and expenditure. There should be a very careful harmony between how much protein we consume with how much we use—input vs. output. To help build the best body for the job, we want the right equity of protein to fuel growth. We want to put on muscle, repair, and recover. We don't want excess protein left over in our system that would be turned to glycogen. We get this quality protein from our meat, cheese, and organ meat, the best natural sources.

In all areas of my life, I surround myself with the smartest people. Everything I do has a reason—and those reasons are thoroughly supported by science from some of the coolest, nerdiest people I know—even down to the littlest detail of always breaking your fast with bone broth. When you ingest just the right amount at the right time, it can help you optimize the process and get the best results.

Key Components of the Diet

We've looked at the exact nutrients we get from the components of our diet. Now let's go into some greater detail about the food we consume when we live by this Protocol. To optimize brain performance and evoke that optimal fuel, we will eat only:

Grass-Finished Beef: If you want to be the most optimized entrepreneur you can be, eat your steak. The list of all of the nutrients in steak is long. It is a true superfood, loaded with critical vitamins, minerals, and bioactives, like taurine, creatine, carnosine, and carnitine. The protein and nutrients in steak help increase synthesis of glutathione, the master antioxidant.

Organic Liver: A nutritional powerhouse, liver is packed with protein yet is low in caloric intake. It's also considered one of the most concentrated, nutrient-dense foods on the planet, because of its levels of folate, iron, vitamin B, vitamin A, and copper. With just one serving of liver, you can meet your daily recommended amount of all these vitamins and minerals. Due to its levels of B12 and folate (over 17 times more than regular ground beef), eating liver helps make learning new things easier and elevates your mood to where you can tackle any challenge.

Pasture-raised Eggs: Eggs contain choline, an excellent nutrient for the brain and the nervous system to regulate memory, mood, muscle control, and other functions. You also need choline to form the membranes surrounding your body's cells, which is beneficial to your superhuman quest at a literally cellular level. Choline is used to make acetylcholine, a neurotransmitter that is involved in memory and cognitive function.

Eggs also contain vitamins K, D, and E, which are all good for the heart and the skin; and they have omega-3 fatty acids, B vitamins, trace minerals, and carotenoids, which support the eye, lens, and retina. This combats the harmful effects of blue light from your daily devices.

The protein in eggs also builds protein tissues in your body, allowing for the highest percentage of protein conversion to directly impact your muscles and joints. What remains turns into glucose, which your body can also use for essential muscle growth. So, when you consume eggs, no carbs are needed, and eggs don't spike insulin.

Bone Broth & Grass-fed Collagen: A key component of our diet is bone broth. Collagen balances your amino acid ratios and has immense healing powers when it comes to cartilage, tissue, and joints. It also has a direct effect on keeping your skin looking young and wrinkle-free. If you haven't been making collagen a priority in your diet, it's time to start. Collagen is a key missing component of the modern diet, and as the Performance CEO it can give you that extra edge over your competition. You just want to make sure you're using grass-fed cow collagen and drinking a lot of bone broth, which is also an excellent source of collagen, along with calcium, magnesium, potassium, phosphorus, and trace minerals. Collagen brings your skin, hair, and nails a ton of benefits. If you look good and feel good, you perform at your best. We also add collagen to our afternoon coffee.

Organic Raw Dairy: Raw cheese supports a healthy gut microbiome, which has a positive impact on overall health. A great source of calcium, organic raw dairy is beneficial for you throughout your life, providing you with a source for maintaining bone density and reducing the risk of bone fractures. Not being pasteurized, it contains a wide variety of beneficial bacteria, enzymes, and nutrients. Raw cheese helps with gut health, digestion, and overall health. It can also lead to good heart health and lower blood pressure and has been found to help reduce or maintain body weight. I also think raw cheese is richer in flavor and has a softer, creamer texture than the more processed varieties. We love to produce this on the farm.

Wild-caught Seafood: A great staple in the Performance CEO diet, wild-caught seafood is full of healthy fats, micronutrients, and antioxidants. You're in luck if you're living by the water—it gives you a better chance of getting freshly caught seafood, right from its source and onto your plate. Salmon is great for the brain, because of its high omega-3 fatty acids, which play a crucial role in brain development, function, and reduction of inflammation. It also can prevent cognitive decline and neurological disorders. In addition, it's a great source of vitamin D, which plays a role in cognitive function and mood.

Organic Avocados: With high levels of unsaturated fats, this brain-boosting food improves cognitive function through its high levels of folate, omega-3, and vitamins. The essential nutrients in avocados, including vitamins K, C, E, and A, may also prevent the adverse effects of aging. This means that avocados can also help you look great through their inflammation-fighting fatty acids that promote smooth skin. Lastly, avocados are rich in potassium, fiber, vitamin B, and several plant-based nutrients, including phytosterols, which, when consumed in recommended amounts, can lower cholesterol, which at high levels is a risk factor for heart disease.

Organic Raspberries: For the brain, raspberries sharpen memory and can protect the mind from oxidative stress, which has been shown to be a major contributing factor in diseases like Alzheimer's and Parkinson's. The flavonoids in berries have also been shown to help improve coordination, memory, and mood. They are rich in antioxidants, and studies have shown that berries may improve memory and cognitive function. Berries may be the best brain food, thanks to their ability to spur neurogenesis.

For the heart, raspberries provide potassium, which is essential to heart function, and can lower blood pressure and cholesterol. The omega-3 fatty acids in raspberries can also help prevent stroke and heart disease and reduce the risk of type 2 diabetes.

For the skin and hair, raspberries contain vitamin C, antioxidants, folic acid, and ellagic acid, which can reduce the signs of aging, such as black spots, wrinkles, and acne. For those active in outdoor activities, raspberries can protect the skin from UV damage. They also host a mineral, called manganese, which helps keep your bones and skin healthy, and regulates your blood sugar. In addition, raspberries have many benefits for maintaining good hair and nail health, since they are rich in vitamin B and folic acid—which is great if you're suffering from hair loss or want to minimize grey hair.

Organic Pecans: Pecans are packed with nutrients that are beneficial for brain health. They are rich in vitamin E, which has been linked to a reduced risk of cognitive decline, containing healthy fats, fiber, and the highest levels of antioxidants among all tree nuts—and they can help fight off Alzheimer's. Pecans are considered anti-inflammatory foods because they are rich in Vitamin E, an antioxidant. They also pack a nutritional punch. Natural and neuroprotective, pecans promote a healthy memory and support cognitive function through their makeup. Made with zinc, magnesium, and potassium, pecans can help lower blood pressure and levels of bad LDL cholesterol.

Containing vitamins A and E, ellagic acid, and antioxidants, pecans can also prevent wrinkles and premature aging, fighting against free radicals and the toxins in the body, which cause skin conditions such as oily skin, dull-looking skin, and acne. The vitamins and zinc found in pecans also boost your immune system, to fight off infections and repair damage. The folate found in these nuts can also guard your body and brain against changes to your DNA that might otherwise lead to cancer.

The Performance CEO is a Performance Predator

Seeking optimal performance means seeking the best and most useful diet. Tapping into the raw habits of our ancestors—as apex predators and carnivorous people—we want to scale time *way* back, and capitalize on what our bodies are naturally designed to do. Over time, the human diet has drastically changed due to agriculture, the introduction of millions of food additives, the development of a year-round produce supply, and the hybridization of fruits and vegetables, making them higher in sugar and lower in nutrients.

This is slowly killing us, and that is the sad truth.

Another sad truth? People are working their minds and bodies to their breaking points, and then expecting them to refuel with nutrient-deficient food.

Everything is connected. In the same way that our diet and supplementation are connected to our health, we can eliminate vitamin deficiencies by approaching the quality of our diet and looking at the most minuscule ingredients.

The quality of your diet—not its quantity—is critical. We always want the highest-quality version of a nutrient, so your body can readily absorb it. This is a surefire method to biohack your way to nutrient-dense fuel, prioritizing quality over quantity.

Our bodies are built to run lean. Think about the ancient hunter who needed to feed his tribe—he had the power and strength to follow an animal for several days, running on no food. Not having that food—fasting, virtually—gave him an advantage in his hunting and tracking skills. His focus sharpened. He had more physical energy, with no muscle loss. He had the clarity he needed to stalk and kill his food.

This is in our DNA. The Protocol can help you use your body the way it was naturally intended. It will help you become all you can be. The key is to keep your diet nutrient-dense, stay fat-adapted, and let nature do the heavy lifting. By just doing these simple things, you'll be smarter, fitter, and sharp enough to stalk your prey in the business world.

Coffee Is for Closers: Morning-Fasted Caffeine

Good news: you don't have to give up drinking coffee.

Coffee consumed in a fasted state, in fact, has been proven to improve concentration and increase motivation and eagerness in the morning. A person who drinks caffeine also has higher maximal muscle strength and power, a higher metabolic rate, and a better reaction time.

Caffeine also has proven in studies to increase both aerobic and anaerobic performance. It increases serotonin and acetylcholine, which may stimulate the brain and help stabilize the blood-brain barrier. The polyphenol micronutrients in coffee may prevent tissue damage from free radicals, as well as blockage to blood vessels in the brain.

Coffee is nature's rocket fuel, antioxidant, and cognitive superfood. When coffee drinking is timed perfectly with your biological clock, it will fuel your metabolism to help you burn fat, boost your cognitive capabilities, fill you with antioxidants, lower your risk of type 2 diabetes, and even help protect your liver. In business matters, it helps increase focus, memory, recall, and cognitive performance. So, in essence, coffee is a miracle worker.

Everything we do and consume has a purpose for performance—and on top of all those benefits, I also know that I am a whole hell of a lot nicer in the morning after my first cup.

Coffee also does wonders for your metabolism, increasing it by up to 20 percent. With a medium roast blend and a smokeless roasting process, you can get all of coffee's advantages and benefit from the highest health-boosting antioxidants it provides.

My Cognitive Coffee: Choline, L-Theanine, and Vitamins B6 and B12 support energy production and alertness. L-Theanine might also affect the brain chemicals GABA, dopamine, and serotonin, while protecting brain cells and promoting cognitive function. There have been studies over the past two years that show L-theanine plays a role in supporting cognitive function and preventing its loss. Lion's Mane, one of the more popular mushrooms on the market, has been shown to stimulate neuroplastic, memory, focus, and overall brain health. Lion's Mane contains two special compounds that can stimulate growth of brain cells: hericenones and erinacine. Studies have also shown that it can improve the functioning of the hippocampus, a region of the brain responsible for the processing of memories and emotional responses.

Studies show that drinking three to five coffees a day is associated with 65 percent reduced risk of dementia. Caffeine also boosts the enzyme NNAMPT, which synthesizes NAD, a critical protective factor in the brain. It is also one of the most widely used and studied substances for both sports performance and brain function.

When it comes to fasting, introducing black coffee at 16 hours fasted has been shown to maximize cognitive skills, which is what makes it your essential morning rocket fuel. This is why the Performance CEO Protocol calls for coffee in the morning—right before we do the most important strategic and creative thinking for the day, to help us conquer any imminent business challenges.

Morning Super Water

Upon waking up, I drink 24 ounces of water with calcium ascorbate (Vitamin C), trace minerals, and Himalayan sea salt, to create a Super Water. I then consume over a gallon of water throughout the day.

Drinking water is an essential element for many bodily processes. Water assists in the communication between your brain cells, eliminates toxins that can block brain function, and brings important nutrients to your brain. When you're hydrated, you can make faster decisions and improve your cognitive performance. You will also experience a more regulated body temperature, lubricated joints, and optimal internal organ performance.

In addition, when you drink water first thing in the morning, you rehydrate your body. This not only increases your level of alertness, by fueling your brain, it helps you maintain optimal brain activity. The brain is 70 percent water, so when you're not adequately hydrated your brain operates on less fuel, and you can feel drained or even experience fatigue or mood fluctuations. It can also lead to significant reductions in memory and brain performance.

One gallon of water a day also helps you get rid of the toxins in your body, strengthens the immune system, jumpstarts your metabolism, and improves complexion and skin radiance. A gallon of water provides more energy, increased muscle mass, fat loss, improved skin, a better understanding of hunger versus thirst, and an overall feeling of having a healthy and high-functioning body.

I like to drink my water cold. When you drink cold water, thermogenesis occurs, which is the production of heat to warm up the water in your body. This not only helps you keep a healthy metabolism, but it burns calories too.

Key Vitamins

Vitamins support cognitive performance. We strive to get all these nutrients through real food and the nutrient-dense, organic foods we eat daily. If needed, there are quick ways to get the additional nutrients your body needs to keep performing well physically, aid in recovery, and fuel greatness. I have been taking my blood work quarterly, and by following this exact performance Nutrition Protocol, all of my nutrients and minerals are excellent.

When it comes to supplements, we will get almost all of our nutrition from real food. Grass-fed liver is God's multivitamin, but we add some key things to our morning water to ensure we get all the nutrients we need for our brains and to build muscle.

A general rule of thumb is that you get what you pay for. You will try to get as many vitamins as possible and minerals through your whole foods meal, but then you'll supercharge your body with carefully selected, timed, and measured quality supplements. When you follow this Protocol, you will make sure all of your nutrient levels are meeting the mark. You will see this in your quarterly bloodwork. If you consume too much of any nutrient, your body will excrete it, but you will know that you are full nutritionally and getting your daily recommended allowances.

I'm constantly traveling worldwide, trying new things; but these vitamins are staples in my everyday Nutrition Protocol that never change. I have provided a daily dosage recommendation for each vitamin and mineral, and the suggested time of day for consumption. Backed by research, these supplements work with your specific biology to get your mind and body to hit optimal levels. These natural vitamins can help you supercharge your health and mitochondria.

Please note: I am not in the business of selling supplements. I am a tech CEO, who is building the future of artificial intelligence and human performance. I have no dogs in this hunt. I'm not here to promote or sell any supplements from any company or any brand, and I'm not being compensated in any way for these suggestions. I'm here to tell you what I use and share my knowledge about a lifestyle that can help bring out the best, as I want us *all* to win. I only recommend what I use personally, and I don't do any company sponsorships. I always pay full price. If I do, down the road, enter any partnership, or launch or invest in any company, I will be transparent and let you know.

The Performance CEO needs to view nutrients at the same level of importance as a world-class athlete. Whether it's business or the Olympics, how your body performs will directly correlate to your success. To work at the tempo and output we need for success, our bodies and brains must be properly supported.

The following are the most important supplements to make sure you get daily:

Calcium Ascorbate/Vitamin C: Vitamin C is a leading natural supplement, and I consider it to be one of the most important ones—you need to max out on vitamin C. This vitamin interacts with our amino acids to build collagen, which can help promote anti-aging properties and healing processes. It also fights free radicals and boosts your immune system. In these post-COVID times, vitamin C is a key part of your daily supplements to help you stay healthy. **Dosage:** One level ¼ tsp. scoop in each morning with Super Water.

Vitamin D3: As the king of anti-aging and human performance, vitamin D3 helps us sustain and improve the health of our bones and teeth. It also aids in regulating the nervous system, cardiovascular health, and blood clot function. By positively impacting hormones like testosterone, HGH, and estrogen, it can give you more control of some of your body's processes, like your immune function and inflammation. You gain vitamin D naturally through sunlight, but getting your vitamin D3 as a supplement allows you to reach proper levels. It's also another key staple to ensure your body has optimal immunity.

I'm a huge fan of vitamin D3. It does a lot to support our bodies. It acts on over 1,000 different genes and can help produce HGH. Vitamin D3 helps your body absorb calcium and helps metabolize both calcium and phosphorus. It's also important to get actual exposure to natural sunlight.

As the Performance CEO, I know you're working hard in the office, but make it a priority to take the daily recommended vitamin D3 dose and get your ass out into the natural sunlight—at least 20 minutes of sun a day. **Dosage:** 2,000 IU per day after meal.

Ionic Trace Mineral Drops: You can benefit from ionic trace minerals, because even with a perfect diet, thanks to commercial farming, we don't get the minerals from the soil that our bodies need. Trace minerals work alongside the nutrients in our diet and supplements, to help our bodies regulate our natural biological functions. Ionic trace minerals include calcium, copper, magnesium, boron, phosphorus, potassium, silica, and zinc. Fortunately, it's easy to include these in your daily diet, as these minerals are already added to Super Water. Zinc is another important supplement to support health and your immune system. **Dosage:** Twelve drops each morning with Super Water.

Magnesium: Used in more than 300 enzymatic processes, this supplement is important to help you carry out everyday tasks—like kicking your competition's ass. So, low magnesium equals low cellular energy. If you run the data across the board, you'll find that most people will be running short on magnesium. These low levels can be life-shortening. Adding magnesium to your daily diet can help increase longevity and your quality of life. Magnesium also reverses the effects of stress on your brain to help increase memory and cognitive function. As the Performance CEO, I recommend around 500-800mg daily—best taken in the morning. **Dosage:** 500-800mg a day.

Potassium: As magnesium's better half, potassium and magnesium work synergistically to improve mind and body function. The Performance CEO should take potassium as a daily supplement through its preferred form of citrate and potassium bicarbonate. Potassium gets to the heart of things—helping keep the heartbeat at a rhythmically healthy pace. **Dosage:** 400mg of potassium per day.

Collagen Peptides: Grass-fed/pasture-raised collagen is a supplement everyone should take. It has many benefits for your joints, skin, hair, nails, bones, and overall youthful appearance. **Dosage:** One Scoop.

Creatine Monohydrate: Creatine is amazingly good for the brain. It recycles ATP from ADP, increasing energy. Its main job in the body is to store high-energy phosphate groups to form phosphocreatine, which is also great for the brain. During strength training, phosphocreatine releases the energy stored in the phosphate groups to support muscle contraction. This helps increase strength, and benefits your entire system, including the brain, bones, muscles, and the all-important liver (more on these benefits later).

Dosage: Two to five grams a day, with warm water, in the morning. I only supplement three grams, as I get the other two grams in my daily pound of meat; I consume daily to total 5g.

Stay on Track

Let's have a real talk about alcohol and socializing. I love a great time and have always enjoyed drinks with friends and a fun night out. But when I dug into the science, the evidence against these activities was overwhelming. I saw, in real numbers, how a lack of sleep and an influx of alcohol could slow and negatively impact my body, setting my performance back. I decided to eliminate alcohol from my diet.

Now, I still have a drink every now and then. But I only drink when I don't have meetings for weeks, like over a holiday period. Never compromise tomorrow's success today for a good time.

As I mentioned before, this is a lifestyle, not a program. You might not always be motivated to follow it, but you need to be disciplined to follow it and succeed. You must be willing to sacrifice. But remember, it should never *feel* like a sacrifice. This is my perfect day, and I choose to live this life of innovation.

There's a calming confidence in my abilities when my clients know that even over the weekend I am still focused, always getting better and still thinking about their businesses—and finding the best ways to help them accomplish their strategic goals. This is why my clients can engage my companies in multimillion-dollar contracts and sleep soundly. They know I am always up early, crushing workouts, optimizing my performance, and thinking about improving theirs.

When I followed this extreme Protocol, nothing became more important than my team and our goals. Looking at it from a data perspective, I eliminated anything that took my focus away from them or slowed me down. I went all-in, all the time. It is the only way to win, with 100 percent laser focus. Every detail matters. Drinking has no ROI.

Nutrition: The Bottom Line

Your nutrition input dictates your fitness output. What you put in your body helps maximize your body's potential, and helps you perform day in and day out.

In this chapter, we learned how important it is to refuel and recover so that you can kick ass the next day. Nutrition, ketosis, fasting, supplementation, and hydration are all essential pillars in creating the foundation to become the best human you can be. Taking care of business requires you to take care of your body and health first.

Here's a recap of what we learned:

- By focusing on developing your **Premium Food Plan for Performance,** you have learned how to home in on the benefits of cognitive performance, fasting for autophagy and its brain cell-cleaning properties.
- By putting your brain first, you can maximize the connection between good nutrition and strong, healthy muscles while engaging in **optimal timing.**
- You know the components of the **Nutrition Protocol** and how it can help reshape your relationship with food. We eat only for fuel.
- You know that the **key principles** are the building blocks of everything you need to make yourself a Predator CEO.
- **Fasting is an essential tool** to reach higher mental and physical planes.
- To perform optimally, you'll need grass-finished **beef** and **organs** to bring out the best nutrients in your daily diet. You've learned which ones are best—opt for **grass-fed beef,**

pasture-raised eggs, grass-fed collagen, wild-caught seafood, full-fat nuts, organic berries, organic avocado, and raw dairy and cheese.
- We get our carbs only from avocados, nuts, and raspberries.
- As nature's rocket fuel, antioxidant, and superfood, **coffee** can be timed perfectly with your biological clock to burn fat, boost your cognitive capabilities, fill you with antioxidants, and keep you sharp in the boardroom.

PILLAR II

Strength

Lift Heavy Shit, Sprint, Get Smarter

To keep our brains at peak performance, our bodies have to work hard. Physical activity is crucial to the way we think, feel, and make executive decisions. So, let's use our bodies to help our brains, and let's keep it simple.

The biggest surge of new neurons comes from sprints and high-intensity training. Lifting weights and running fast are two of the most powerful ways to biohack your brain.

Lifting heavy things and sprinting evoke neurogenesis, the ability to grow new brain cells. We lift for the brain, but our bodies will benefit as we build muscle and strength. Exercise influences the brain at the cellular level, improving its potential to log and process new information. Who doesn't want that?

Extreme, intense workouts make you smarter; science shows their physiological merit. Exercise promotes the production of neurotrophins, which are proteins that aid neuron survival and function. This leads to greater brain plasticity and, therefore, better memory and learning. Intense exercise also spikes BDNF, which, as we know, grows new brain cells.

Exercise is the most transformative activity you can do for your brain. Your brain is only two percent of your bodyweight, yet it consumes 50 percent of the glucose and 20 percent of the oxygen available in the body. High-intensity exercise increases blood flow. So, while you are doing those deadlifts, blood flow will deliver all these essentials to the brain. It's that simple.

Physical prowess creates cognitive mastery. The evidence for this is incontrovertible.

One of the most important stimuli for muscle growth and the brain is the intensity of the exercise. I am lifetime "Natural"—never enhanced—so to do things the right way we need to work hard and have optimal workouts that evoke hypertrophy and build strength and muscle naturally.

We never take shortcuts. We always do things the right way—just like in business.

Lifting heavy weights or engaging in resistance training in a scientific order can have several positive effects on the brain and cognitive function. These benefits are primarily attributed to the physiological and neurochemical changes that occur in response to the physical demands of heavy lifting. Some of the reasons why lifting heavy can be good for the brain include:

Increased Blood Flow: Heavy lifting increases blood flow to the brain. This enhanced blood circulation can improve the delivery of oxygen and nutrients to brain cells, supporting their optimal function.

Neurotransmitter Release: Intense physical exercise, triggers the release of various neurotransmitters, such as dopamine, serotonin, and norepinephrine. These chemicals are associated with improved mood, reduced stress, and enhanced cognitive performance.

Brain-Derived Neurotrophic Factor (BDNF) Production: Heavy lifting can stimulate the production of Brain-Derived Neurotrophic Factor (BDNF), a protein that promotes the growth, survival, and plasticity of brain cells. BDNF is essential for learning, memory, and overall brain health.

Neuroplasticity: Resistance training, particularly high-intensity exercises, can increase brain plasticity, which refers to the brain's ability to reorganize and form new connections between neurons. This neuroplasticity is vital for learning and adapting to new challenges.

Stress Reduction: Engaging in heavy lifting can help reduce stress by triggering the release of endorphins, which are natural mood elevators and stress reducers. Lower stress levels are associated with improved cognitive function.

Hormone Regulation: Heavy lifting can positively influence hormone levels, including testosterone and growth hormone, which play essential roles in brain health and cognitive function.

Enhanced Executive Function: Studies have shown that resistance training can improve executive functions, such as attention, working memory, and decision-making.

Improved Sleep: Regular heavy lifting has been associated with better sleep quality, which is crucial for optimal brain function and overall well-being.

Protection Against Cognitive Decline: Regular resistance training has been linked to a reduced risk of age-related cognitive decline and neurodegenerative conditions like Alzheimer's disease.

We automate our entire workout with the clock and timer, so that we can think big and strategically as we spike our BDNF during our fasted workout. With every set and rest set timing, your brain can go into the depths to solve problems and think strategically. Let's be process driven and smart about our training. Automating every one of our workouts with a timer offers us a transformative approach that liberates our mind from the minutiae of exercise logistics, allowing us to think big about our businesses. By pre-setting rest intervals and repetitions, for Strength, Accessory, Volume, Burnout, GPP, and our Cognitive Walk/Sprint, we create a structured framework that optimizes our training efficiency. This streamlined process eliminates the need to constantly monitor the clock, calculate rest periods, or count reps, enabling you to redirect your focus towards what matters. The freedom from these distractions cultivates a deeper engagement with your body and brain and the exercise itself, enhancing mindfulness and concentration. With a timer managing the timing and sequencing, you can invest your mental energy into visualizing goals, fine-tuning form, and embracing the empowering sensation of pushing your limits. In essence, automating your workouts serves as a gateway to a more immersive, innovative, and rewarding strength training sessions.

As we engage in our Strength Protocol with this automation, it provides a unique opportunity to unleash the power of creativity and create the impossible. As your body surges with energy and endorphins, your mind becomes primed for expansive thinking and innovative ideas. The surge of oxygen and nutrient-rich blood to our brains enhances cognitive function and stimulates the neural networks responsible for creativity. In this unburdened state, we can traverse uncharted mental territories, ideate novel solutions, and envision ambitious goals. Physical exertion ignites a synergy between body and mind, where the endorphins fuel enthusiasm and determination, and the kinetic motion invites free-flowing thoughts. Harnessing this dynamic synergy, strength training has become not just a means to performance, but a gateway to ideas and big thinking.

I solve most of my daily tasks during my workouts. I go into a cognitive zone where I am crushing things physically, but I am thinking deeply. I wrote this book, in fact, on my iPhone Notes app during my early morning strength sessions, where my brain is at my best.

We will use daily physical activity to improve brain function. Studies from the Harvard Medical School of Neurology have proven that physical exercise improves memory and problem-solving and reduces dementia. Dr. Alvaro Pascual-Leone, Ph.D., MD, states, "To gain the benefits for the brain, we need to push ourselves more than cardiovascular health and beyond limits." Net physical exercise is important for the brain as it increases its blood supply.

Lifting for the Brain

If you look at the best professional athletes, they spend an inordinate amount of time doing something other than their actual sport. As the Performance CEO, you'll emulate them. You'll spend time fine-tuning your mental and physical abilities, to be at your best and seize the most important moments—those make-or-break business opportunities.

You need to train so you can capitalize on that big interview, that client meeting—even that company holiday party speech. You never know when these moments will come, but you need to crush them, and the hard work you've already put in will allow you to do so. Following the Performance CEO Protocol will have you primed and ready to earn your victory.

Lifting is not done only for muscles and strength. It's to build lean muscle at any age, improve mitochondrial function, increase insulin sensitivity, reduce cardiac risk, improve bone density, mood, and sleep, melt away stress, and boost metabolism for days; having more muscle mass also makes you more resilient to fatigue, diseases, pathogens, and toxins, and allows you to perform with more confidence daily.

Never underestimate a boost in confidence. When you are in great shape and look your best, it can turn you into an unstoppable force. When you are at your best, look your best, and feel your best—when you walk into a boardroom to crush a deal—you feel invincible.

Cognitively, our specific type of exercise boosts your rate of neurogenesis by increasing blood flow to your brain and putting your body under short-term, healthy stress. It triggers the release of nerve growth factors that help the activation, protection, and survival of neurons in your brain. So, not only do you get stronger lifting heavy things, but your brain can also get smarter. Aren't we biologically amazing?

By stimulating the muscles and nervous system together, through a combination of sprinting and weight training, you can build new muscle, to help you experience less inflammation, reduce oxidative stress, increase mental clarity, improve your ability to think, and improve recall.

All of this is done while slowing down the cognitive aging process. It sounds like a no-brainer to me. Pun intended.

High-intensity activity cranks up neuronal growth and releases important growth factors that build up the brain. High-intensity anaerobic exercise (a.k.a. lifting heavy shit) causes the pituitary gland in your brain to unleash the human growth hormone (HGH), which is the Fountain of Youth. Loss of brain volume happens when you age, so increasing HGH is like doping the natural way.

Sprinting and interval training keep HGH naturally elevated for up to four hours. It normally stays in the bloodstream for only a few minutes, increasing the heart rate that pumps more oxygen to the brain. In the brain, HGH balances neurotransmitter levels and boosts the production of all growth factors.

Exercise also increases levels of dopamine, and with our set schedule, the brain cells in your motivation center will sprout new dopamine receptors, giving you an unrivaled initiative to get things done that day.

Our body and brain are naturally programmed so we can push through heavy weights, be sharp cognitively, and, like a primal human, be ready for the kill. So, get under a heavy load, to provide all the benefits from the strength the body needs, and everything else that benefits an entrepreneur.

The Workout

Our early a.m. training is like a meeting. Give it the proper respect. You wouldn't look at your phone when you are meeting with the CEO of your top client. Give your workouts the same type of attention.

We create a two-hour window for morning workouts. This is the reason we wake up early. Your success is worth the investment in your time.

Our workouts are organized in a simple, structured manner, so we can take this time to think about our business while we work out. It's when our bodies and brains are primed to do their best work.

Everyone should have a whiteboard in their weight room or use the Notes section of their cell phones to write down ideas during the workout. We time everything from rep time to recovery, so you don't need to think about what you're doing. The physical work is automatic. You just show up and lift heavy things and continue to think big.

We start with core, to focus on strength. We spike neurogenesis and BDNF. The harder we work our bodies, the more our brains get to work.

It's no secret that working out leads to mental, physical, and even emotional benefits. Exercise increases serotonin, norepinephrine, and dopamine, which are neurotransmitters that traffic thoughts and emotions. However, while researching scientific data to build the ultimate Protocol of becoming the best biological human, I have found that lifting heavy weights and running fast are, quite literally, the most powerful ways to biohack your brain.

Deadlift is king. We train hard. We train smart. Research shows that the fitter you are, the stronger you are, the more resilient your brain becomes, and the better it functions both cognitively and psychologically.

With our Fasting Protocol, our approach is to spike HGH to its highest levels during a workout. We are using our stored body fat and ketones for fuel, and lifting heavy weights with explosive lifts.

I am asking you to commit 12 hours a week, which is only ten percent of your waking hours, to do the hard strength work so you have the energy to attain your dreams and be the best leader possible.

The Performance CEO Training Protocol is not a life balancing workout to find your Chi or center. It's a clang-and-bang workout where the weak will be gutted out very quickly. I've said it before and will say it again and again—this lifestyle is not for everyone. It is only for those who want an unrivaled competitive advantage. Heavyweights, big lifts, early mornings, crushing shit. Become indomitable.

We place heavier and heavier loads on our bodies, and our bodies respond by increasing the size of our muscles to bear the weight of their environment—literally. This natural process makes gaining strength a formula—as adaptive creatures, we are wired to be the smartest and strongest we can be. It's primal.

The Performance CEO works out for strength, power, speed, balance, mobility, and endurance. Lifting weights is a metabolism booster. By building lean muscle, you will burn more calories and add definition to your body. The right strength training plan can also prevent injury by improving your posture, building core strength, and helping with joint alignment to keep you healthy and kicking ass.

Your singular focus should be to gain strength on essential foundational lifts. Sprint training and anaerobic bursts are scientifically proven to be the best types of training for building muscle and lean mass. They are essential to lowering inflammation and gaining overall health. By adding a few anaerobic interval workouts once or twice a week to this lifting Protocol, you will boost the production of natural growth hormones and increase insulin sensitivity. Put briefly, you will be indomitable.

The Performance CEO Training Protocol

Head into every workout 16 to 17 hours fasted. This makes for the perfect environment for muscle growth and fat burning; it's when your HGH levels are elevated naturally enough to maximize performance.

By the end of your morning workout, your HGH, due to working out in a fasted state, will have increased 1,000 percent—yes, you've read that right. Fasting boosts your body naturally, where it will be running like a fine-tuned sports car and become a fat-burning, muscle-building machine. Optimizing your workout schedule, and training in this window, can help you utilize this spike in your body's natural levels. This is essential to the Performance CEO Training Protocol. Always be fasted.

You begin with eight sets of abs, with 30 seconds of rest in between sets. I like to do incline weighted sit-ups and leg raises. We want to build our foundation and a strong core. By now, our blood flow is at an optimal cognitive level. This is why I have a whiteboard in my gym.

The first component is the **Strength 5x5** Component, with heavy weights and compound movements that will stimulate neurogenesis and get your neurons firing while gaining muscle size and density. The heavy weight training will consist of major muscle groups via compound movements, such as the Deadlift, Incline Bench Press, Squat, and Overhead Press.

You will perform these five sets of five reps at your heaviest weight capability—heavy weight and low reps translate to building muscle. With this kind of intensity, you'll need longer rest periods of two to three minutes between each of the five complete sets. Take a three-minute rest between sets.

The next segment of the workout is **Accessory Exercises 4x6**. This is doing a second variation of the compound movement for strength. This will consist of four sets for six to eight reps. Between each set you'll have a two-minute rest period.

Next is the **Volume Component.** The Volume Component consists of exercises focused on hitting the major muscle groups and the minor muscle groups, with higher repetitions and lighter weight, and shorter rest periods of one minute between sets. You'll do four sets of ten reps each with only 30 seconds' rest in between, with four different exercises each set. This type of training creates muscle shape, definition, and tone. It is not by some magical effect that muscles become defined, but rather, it is simply this type of training that burns fat and strengthens muscle.

The fourth component is **Burnout** and includes sets for the designated individual muscle groups. This component focuses on both volume and burnout. This should be done at the end of your workout.

We select specific muscle groups and do fifty reps for each muscle group in the fewest sets possible. In the end, your body should feel like it is earning greatness with every rep, with every sprint, and every Endurance Burnout set. No one said this would be easy, but it is rewarding.

The Last Component is **GPP (General Physical Preparedness)**. This is general conditioning to spark blood flow to the brain and improve strength, speed, endurance, flexibility, structure, and skill. We will do exercises, such as Sled Push, Farmer's Walk, Sled Pull, Rogue Echo Bike, Box Jumps, Medicine Ball Throws, and Sled Sprints with the vest, for 30 seconds on, 30 seconds rest, three times. This is where we functionally lift very heavy things to build real-world strength.

In the Performance Strength Protocol, we only do Incline bench. It offers distinct advantages over flat bench pressing due to its unique biomechanics and muscle engagement. The incline bench targets the upper portion of the chest (pectoralis major) to a greater extent, contributing optimal and balanced chest development. This variation places more emphasis on the clavicular head of the pectoral muscles, enhancing the appearance of a fuller and more sculpted upper chest. Moreover, incline bench pressing also engages the anterior deltoids and triceps to a greater degree than flat bench pressing, promoting overall upper body strength and stability. The inclined angle of the bench also tends to place less stress on the shoulders and may reduce the risk of shoulder strain or impingement, making it safer for individuals with any shoulder issues. The key is to lift heavy things while staying healthy.

Squats are a foundational component of the Protocol to gain our functional strength. As a compound movement, squats engage numerous muscle groups simultaneously, primarily targeting the quadriceps, hamstrings, glutes, and lower back. This comprehensive activation promotes muscle development and enhances lower body strength, contributing to improved athletic performance and everyday movements like lifting and walking. Squats also stimulate the release of anabolic hormones, such as testosterone and growth hormone, fostering muscle growth and overall metabolic rate. Furthermore, squats engage the core muscles and promote stability, enhancing posture and reducing the risk of lower back pain. Beyond muscle and strength gains, squats promote bone density by subjecting the skeletal system to a weight-bearing load, supporting long-term bone health. We build a strong and resilient foundation that translates into enhanced strength and function.

Deadlifts are a cornerstone of our strength training, offering a multitude of benefits that extend beyond mere muscle development. This compound exercise engages a vast array of muscle groups, including the hamstrings, glutes, lower back, core, and grip muscles. As a result, deadlifts foster overall functional strength, making routine activities more manageable and improving athletic performance. This movement's demand for full-body coordination enhances proprioception and balance, which are crucial for injury prevention and optimal movement patterns. Moreover, deadlifts stimulate the release of growth-promoting hormones, such as testosterone and growth hormone, amplifying muscle growth and metabolism. In addition to its physical advantages, deadlifting contributes to robust bone health by imposing a weight-bearing load on the skeletal system. Proper deadlift form requires a neutral spine and engaged core, leading to improved posture and decreased risk of lower back pain. This is important for an entrepreneur who sits at their computer.

My personal favorite compound exercise is the overhead press, as it offers a host of advantages that extend beyond sculpting a strong upper body. This movement primarily targets the deltoid muscles, engaging the front, middle, and rear portions, which contributes to well-rounded shoulder development and enhanced shoulder stability. The overhead press also activates the triceps and upper chest, promoting balanced muscle growth across the upper body. Beyond aesthetics, this exercise cultivates functional strength by simulating movements like lifting objects overhead, making it highly applicable to daily tasks. As a weight-bearing exercise, the overhead press stimulates bone density in the spine, shoulders, and arms, supporting long-term skeletal health. Furthermore, the core muscles engage to stabilize the body throughout the movement, promoting better posture and reducing the risk of lower back discomfort. By incorporating the overhead press into our Strength Protocol, we build a foundation of stability, mobility, and practical strength that contributes to overall physical prowess.

Living in Eastern Europe for over a decade has left an indelible mark on me with my view of strength training. The countries that I lived in contributed a rich legacy of methodologies renowned for their emphasis on systematic and disciplined training. I absorbed like a sponge. Eastern European countries where I lived, like Bulgaria, Ukraine, and Romania, have been instrumental in shaping modern strength training practices. Their rigorous and science-driven approaches, often rooted in weightlifting and powerlifting traditions, have produced some remarkable feats of strength and performance. These nations have pioneered innovative training techniques, periodization models, and coaching philosophies that have not only elevated their own athletes to international prominence but have also contributed to the global evolution of strength training strategies. I have blended these principles into the Performance Strength Protocol you will be doing for the next 45 Days.

HIIT Training: The Cognitive Walk/Sprint

We want to be fast—physically, mentally, and in the boardroom. We want to get our nervous systems primed to optimize our brain function. We can do this through HIIT, high-intensity interval training.

Remember, this is not a diet or workout book. This is a business book, solely for optimizing your physical and cognitive capabilities. By incorporating HIIT sprints with cognitive walk/sprints into your day, and focusing on fast, explosive movements, you can optimize your brain-body coordination.

We sprint hard for 30 seconds, rest for two minutes and 30 seconds, and repeat ten times. Do this and you'll see your stored body fat begin to melt off. HIIT will also produce more human growth hormone (HGH)—which can keep you young through its anti-aging properties. It helps your heart *and* your lungs.

The Performance CEO needs time efficiency, and with sprints we trade intensity for time, making the most out of your workouts.

The total benefits of HIIT include:

- increased blood flow, which delivers more oxygen and nutrients to brain cells
- Release of neurotransmitters such as dopamine and endorphins
- Brain-derived neurotrophic factor (BDNF) production
- Enhanced neuroplasticity
- Improved executive function
- Stress reduction
- Positive influence on hormone levels, including an increase in growth hormone
- Cardiovascular health
- Better regulation of blood sugar levels and improved insulin sensitivity

And, as you saw in my "A Day in the Life," an afternoon nature walk is just as powerful as sustained aerobic activity, like in our run/walk. This activity has been found to boost the size of the hippocampal volume, promoting cognitive health that is related to memory, and reducing the risk of dementia. The longer walk also triggers the sympathetic nervous system, which can speed up your heartrate, bringing all the benefits of exercise, as well as delivering more blood and oxygen to your brain.

Lastly, and most importantly, movement reduces stress. We all know it, but incorporating movement into your everyday schedule will help you address higher levels of stress, which can adversely impact your memory, mood, inflammation, and anxiety levels.

Bringing it All Together

The CEO Performance Training Protocol schedule consists of three straight days of working out, and then we repeat that formula. With this Protocol we work out every single day because the brain needs blood to perform, and we need the benefits daily that lifting hard and sprinting provide. Our body has a large capacity and adaptability to handle this. The human body is highly adaptable and stronger than we even know. We get out of the comfort zone and push ourselves every day. Why? Because we use our brains every day, and the blood flow from working out optimizes our cognitive functions. Linear Progression is a fundamental principle in the Performance Strength Protocol, characterized by a systematic and incremental increase in weight lifted over successive training sessions. It forms the bedrock of structured strength development, guiding you through a gradual and sustainable journey toward increased muscle mass and power. The essence of Linear Progression lies in its simplicity—each workout aims to surpass the previous one by adding a small, manageable amount of weight to the bar. This consistent, linear increase in resistance challenges the body to adapt and grow stronger over time. Focusing on steady and measurable advancements, Linear Progression serves as a powerful tool for you to forge a resilient foundation of strength and lay the groundwork for building strength.

In the first week, we will determine your One Rep Max (1RM) for each exercise. After warming up with a spotter or the appropriate safety equipment, you will keep adding weight to see what is the most you can get to for three to five reps. Once you have that number, use a conversion chart to figure out the 1RM, and your first set to begin the program will be at 65-75 percent of your 1RM. This is a solid starting point for your strength lifts and you will keep adding weight through linear progression after you are able to complete all five reps for all sets of the exercise.

Every aspect of this Performance CEO Training Protocol is based on science and structure. As an efficient hack for all of your workouts, I recommend downloading a boxing timer app. With this app, you can set all of your workout sets, rep times, and rest times for each of the four components.

Set a HIIT setting for ten rounds, three minutes each. Set the timer for two minutes and 30 seconds to walk/run, and a 30-second timer right after that for sprinting, with no rest time. After you're finished with the 30-second sprint, you'll immediately resume walking/running for two minutes and 30 seconds, and then, again, a 30-second sprint until you've completed this ten times. We are all about the automation of our workouts.

You will use the same format with the Strength 5x5, Accessory, Volume, and Endurance Burnout Components with Sets/Rounds/Reps/Rest.

Thinking about your business as a 24/7 job. By having a timer, I am able to have some of my best business ideation sessions while I am crushing heavy weights. I am able to think strategically and respond to the sounds that keep me operating like clockwork.

You will never work out again without a timer app. This is work time.

Lift big. Think big.

The detailed action plans, which appear later in this book, provide different variations of ab exercises that you can plug in. The most important factors are core strength and ab activation.

Remember, we are doing all of this for the brain, but in addition to cognitive performance, having more muscle mass is positively correlated with higher natural HGH, the Fountain of Youth your body provides you. You'll train progressively by adding weight every time you train, so your body adapts to higher and higher tension levels. You'll lift explosively.

Moving weight quickly has a great effect on all of your body's systems. By using compound lifts, your body naturally activates large amounts of muscle mass. By focusing on body parts that have a higher density of androgen receptors, like in the chest, shoulders, and legs, you'll see major gains. By doing interval sprints to maximize force production in minimal time, you can fully activate your fast-twitch muscle fibers. Deadlift and squat are the top exercises for boosting the right hormones.

Our three days of training are divided into:

> Day One: Chest, Shoulders, Triceps
> Day Two: Deadlift, Bicep, Back
> Day Three: Legs
> On Day Four, we are back to Day One.

On Day One, our core lifts are the Incline Bench Press and the Overhead Press. On Day Two, our core lift is the Deadlift and Row, and on Day Three, we do Squat and Bulgarian Split Squat. These are the Strength 5x5 foundational lifts along with the 4x6 (six to eight) Accessory lifts that will turn any workout into a Performance CEO Training Session. Do these things to become the most powerful executive you know.

When you work out at 4:00 am, you will work out alone. The only person who will know how much effort you give is going to be the only one in the room—you. Be honest with yourself, and you'll know immediately if you have what it takes. When you follow this Protocol and you see the Performance CEO, you'll know you are in the presence of an incredibly unique breed of human.

You will have the daily journal that is included in this book, which will show you exactly what to do each day and how to do it. All you need to do is execute it. It's simple, but powerful. Plan the work, work the plan.

Real talk: if you can't go through with this Training Protocol, then you simply don't have the mental toughness to be the great Performance CEO entrepreneur you yearn to be. Building a company from zero is a lot harder than this workout and 15 days. This test of your toughness could save you a lot of hours and lost money.

I am going to assume you have an established level of fitness heading into this book. I am going to assume you have lifted weights and are in good foundational shape. This is a book about accelerating cognitive performance. This is for people to take their entrepreneurial capabilities to the next level, not to get in shape.

See if you have the grit to pick yourself up when you get knocked down, or the obsession possessed by every person who has achieved greatness. If you can't do this…I am sorry, but this book wasn't for you all along. Maybe entrepreneurship isn't either. Think hard on that. This life is not for the weak.

Our Performance Strength Protocol focuses on hypertrophy which is a physiological process that describes the enlargement or growth of skeletal muscle fibers. It occurs as a response to sustained resistance training, where muscles are repeatedly subjected to mechanical tension. This tension leads to a series of cellular and molecular adaptations within the muscle fibers, resulting in an increase in size, cross-sectional area, and overall mass of the muscle. Hypertrophy involves the synthesis of new proteins, specifically myofibrillar proteins, which make up the contractile units of the muscle. Over time, these adaptations lead to stronger and more voluminous muscles, enhancing functional strength. Hypertrophy can be achieved through following our exact Strength Protocol. Through lifting progressively heavier weights, hitting our different rep ranges, manipulating repetitions and sets, and incorporating appropriate rest and recovery periods. It is the foundational component of our strength training.

After the Workout

Think you're done? Nope! Go knock out your Cognitive Walk/Sprint and then off to post-workout recovery (we will get into more of this in the next chapter).

For post-workout benefits, I use the infrared sauna and stay there for 25 to 30 minutes. This is both the end of the workout and the start of your recovery.

The power of post-strength training sauna is to amplify the benefits of our strength workouts, creating a fusion between our training and heat-induced stress. Emerging research suggests that engaging in a sauna session after strength training can enhance muscle recovery and growth. The sauna's heat promotes vasodilation, increasing blood flow to recovering muscles and delivering essential nutrients and oxygen more efficiently. This process may expedite the removal of metabolic waste products, reducing muscle soreness and accelerating healing. Moreover, post-training saunas can stimulate the release of heat shock proteins, which play a pivotal role in protecting and repairing cells. Combined with the muscle stress induced by strength training, saunas might trigger a hormetic response—where a controlled stressor results in enhanced adaptability and resilience.

Adding time in the sauna to your routine will give you the time to sweat and fight through the heat. This is great for building mental toughness—if you don't physically feel the pain of the struggle daily, or you forget what it is like, you will never work consistently to taste that sweet, sweet victory. After the Performance CEO morning, the rest of the day is easy.

There will be naysayers who say that dedicating two hours to workouts in the morning is too much. You might be one of them. But I'd like to point out that when you are done it's still only 6:00 am. Your competition is still sleeping, the sun might not even be up yet, and a new day is dawning. The ball is in your court—so get up and grind.

Or do you want to do what everyone else does? If you don't, you will feel a pride that you never felt, now that you know unequivocally that you will never be outworked.

You get to make the decision of whether you're going to make yourself unstoppable. Look in the mirror at the person you're building. Impressed? You should be! You are from the one percent of the 100 percent.

Afternoon Ideation Nature Walk

I included this in training, as it's an essential part of keeping the blood flowing and also assisting with staying active. This is an important time, when you can think big about your business and get outside in nature.

Science has proven the benefits of a 30- to 60-minute postprandial walk after your meal in sunlight and nature. Consider it the second workout of your day. Get outside, get air in your lungs, get that sunshine on your face, walk, and breathe.

Studies have shown that both walking and running are optimal ways to spike these levels (it's hard to get mice to lift weights). And it feels good to be out in the fresh air. Human beings weren't made to be inside all day and all night.

Go back far enough in our history, and you'll find that people were always outdoors, or in shelters that were still pretty exposed to the elements. As a species we adapted to that, and it takes a long time for biology to shake that adaptation. Our bodies, and our brains, want our skin to be exposed to sunlight and cool breezes. It's good for us.

So, if you don't already enjoy the outside, learn to. It's important. Connect with nature. Enjoy the sun coming up, take deep breaths, and be blessed.

To be efficient, I build my business activities into my walk. It could be an internal call, an interview, a press conference, talking to partners, or a simple conference call I need to attend. It can even be the time when I call my mom. You choose what you do with that time—it's just important that you always choose to do something productive. We can now work and be healthy at the same time to help us and our businesses grow. Isn't technology wonderful?

Strength Lifts Technique Refresher

The 5x5 Strength Component of the Strength Protocol Technique is very important. So, I am just going to take a little time for a technique refresher, for these four important lifts.

The Deadlift

Deadlifting is a compound exercise that targets multiple muscle groups, including the lower back, glutes, hamstrings, and core. Performing the deadlift with proper form is crucial for safety and effectiveness. Here's a step-by-step guide on how to deadlift properly:

1. Setup:
   - Place the barbell on the ground in front of you. It should be positioned over the middle of your feet.
   - Stand with your feet hip-width apart, toes pointing forward or slightly outward.
   - The barbell should be close to your shins but not touching them. Your shins should be perpendicular to the floor.
2. Grip:
   - Bend at the hips and knees to reach down and grip the barbell. You can use either a double overhand grip (both palms facing you) or a mixed grip (one palm facing you, one palm facing away).
   - Your hands should be just outside your knees.
3. Set your back:
   - Before lifting, engage your core and set your back in a neutral position. Avoid rounding or arching your back. Keep it flat with a natural curve in your lower back.
4. Lift-off:
   - Take a deep breath, brace your core, and push through your heels to lift the barbell off the ground. Focus on driving your hips forward while keeping your chest up and shoulders back.
5. Lift the bar:
   - As the bar passes your knees, continue extending your hips and stand up straight. Keep the barbell close to your body throughout the movement.
6. Lockout:
   - Once you are in the fully upright position, squeeze your glutes and stand tall, making sure to avoid leaning back excessively.

7. Lowering the bar:
    - To lower the bar, push your hips back and hinge at the hips while maintaining a flat back. Lower the bar along the same path you used to lift it.
    - The bar should touch the ground gently between each rep, but do not relax your form during the descent.
8. Repeat:
    - Perform the desired number of repetitions while maintaining proper form.

Additional tips:
- Keep the bar close. Throughout the lift, the bar should remain close to your body. This minimizes the strain on your lower back and keeps the weight centered.
- Don't rush. Deadlift with control and avoid jerking motions. Lift the weight in a smooth, steady manner.
- Breathe properly. Take a deep breath before lifting and exhale at the top of the movement or during the lowering phase.
- Use an appropriate weight. Start with a weight that allows you to maintain proper form. Gradually increase the weight as you become more comfortable and confident with the movement.

Incline Bench Press

This is a variation of the traditional bench press that primarily targets the upper chest and shoulders. Here's a step-by-step guide on how to perform the incline bench press properly:

1. Setup:
    - Adjust the incline bench to a 30- to 45-degree angle. The exact angle can vary depending on your preference and equipment availability.
    - Sit on the bench with your feet flat on the floor, and your back and head firmly pressed against the bench.

2. Grip:
    - Reach for the barbell on the rack, slightly wider than shoulder-width apart. Your palms should be facing away from you (overhand grip).
    - Alternatively, you can use dumbbells for this exercise. Hold one in each hand with your palms facing forward.
3. Positioning:
    - Engage your core and keep your shoulder blades retracted (squeezed together) throughout the exercise.
    - Plant your feet firmly on the floor for stability.
4. Unracking the bar/dumbbells:
    - If using a barbell, lift it off the rack and hold it above your upper chest with your arms fully extended.
    - If using dumbbells, start with them held above your upper chest, with your arms fully extended.
5. Lowering the weight:
    - Inhale and slowly lower the barbell or dumbbells towards your upper chest in a controlled manner. Keep your elbows at a 90-degree angle relative to your torso.
    - The barbell should touch your chest lightly, and with dumbbells, lower them until your elbows are just below the bench level.
6. Pressing the weight:
    - Exhale and push the barbell or dumbbells back up to the starting position, fully extending your arms but not locking out your elbows.
    - Focus on using your chest and shoulder muscles to press the weight, avoiding excessive arching of your back.
7. Repeat:
    - Perform the desired number of repetitions while maintaining proper form.

Tips for a safe and effective incline bench press:
   - Choose an appropriate weight: Start with a weight that allows you to perform the exercise with proper form. As

you become more comfortable and confident, gradually increase the weight.
- Keep your back and head in contact with the bench: Maintaining proper contact with the bench provides stability and helps prevent injury.
- Avoid using excessive momentum: Focus on a controlled and steady movement throughout the exercise. Avoid using your legs to help lift the weight.
- Don't lock out your elbows: Fully extend your arms during the pressing phase, but avoid hyperextending or locking out your elbows, as this can strain the joints.
- Perform the exercise at a controlled speed: Avoid bouncing the weight off your chest or allowing it to drop rapidly during the lowering phase.

Overhead Press

The overhead press, also known as the shoulder press or military press, is a great compound exercise that targets the shoulders, triceps, and upper chest. Here's a step-by-step guide on how to perform the overhead press properly:

1. Setup:
    - Stand with your feet shoulder-width apart or slightly narrower for stability.
    - Hold the barbell or dumbbells at shoulder height with your palms facing forward and your elbows slightly in front of the bar/dumbbells.
2. Grip:
    - For a barbell overhead press, grip the bar slightly wider than shoulder-width apart. For dumbbells, hold one in each hand at shoulder level.
3. Positioning:
    - Brace your core to stabilize your spine. Your head should be in a neutral position, looking forward.
    - Keep your chest up and your shoulders back.

4. Pressing:
   - Take a deep breath, and as you exhale, push the barbell or dumbbells directly overhead.
   - Press the weight in a straight line, directly above your head. Avoid pushing the weight forward or backward; it should move in a vertical line.
   - Fully extend your arms without locking out your elbows at the top.
5. Lowering the weight:
   - In a controlled manner, lower the barbell or dumbbells back to the starting position at shoulder height.
   - Maintain tension in your core and control the weight throughout the descent.
6. Breathing:
   - Inhale as you lower the weight to your shoulders.
   - Exhale as you press the weight overhead.
7. Repeat:
   - Perform the desired number of repetitions while maintaining proper form.

Tips for a safe and effective overhead press:
- Start with an appropriate weight: If you're new to the exercise, begin with a weight that allows you to perform the movement with proper form. Gradually increase the weight as you gain strength and confidence.
- Engage your core: Keeping your core muscles engaged throughout the movement will help stabilize your spine and prevent excessive arching in your lower back.
- Avoid using momentum: Focus on a controlled and steady movement. Avoid using your legs or hips to help lift the weight, as this can take away from the effectiveness of the shoulder press.
- Don't lock out your elbows: While it's essential to fully extend your arms, avoid hyperextending or locking out your elbows at the top of the movement. This can strain the joints.

- Keep the bar or dumbbells in line with your ears: To maintain proper balance and prevent strain on your shoulders, make sure the weight moves in a straight line above your head.

Squat

Set your feet: Stand with your feet shoulder-width apart or slightly wider, toes pointing slightly outward. Keep your weight evenly distributed across your feet.

1. Engage your core: Tighten your abdominal muscles to stabilize your spine and protect your lower back during the movement.
2. Initiate the movement: Begin the squat by pushing your hips back as if you are sitting in a chair. Simultaneously, start bending your knees to lower your body.
3. Maintain proper alignment: Keep your chest up and your back straight throughout the movement. Avoid rounding your back, as this can lead to injury.
4. Go down: Continue lowering your body until your thighs are at least parallel to the ground. Ideally, aim to get your thighs parallel to the floor or go slightly below that point. It's important not to let your knees cave inward but keep them aligned with your toes.
5. Watch your knees: Ensure that your knees are tracking over your toes, not extending too far forward past them, or caving inward.
6. Keep a neutral spine: Be cautious not to let your back arch or round during the squat. A neutral spine will help protect your lower back.
7. Maintain balance: Keep your weight on your heels and midfoot. Avoid shifting too far forward onto your toes, as it can strain your knees and lead to instability.
8. Breathing: Inhale as you lower yourself down, and exhale as you push back up to the starting position. Proper breathing helps stabilize your core and provides more power during the movement.

9. Push through your heels: As you begin to rise back up, focus on pushing through your heels to engage your glutes and hamstrings effectively.
10. Fully extend your hips and knees: Stand up completely until your hips and knees are fully extended, but avoid locking your knees at the top.
11. Repeat: Perform the desired number of repetitions while maintaining proper form.

Why Do You Need to Be Strong?

Physical strength is one of the most important capabilities anyone can build. Not only is it necessary in everyday life, but strength also plays a huge role in longevity. Now I want you to direct your laser-like focus on building pure strength.

The Performance CEO definition of strength:
- "Strong" refers to both muscular and inner strength. The building of physical strength is used to spike neurogenesis and cognitive performance.
- Strength builds muscle and physical symmetry, to create an unrivaled CEO presence in the boardroom. An athletic physical stature can lead to a strong business and leadership presence. It matters.
- Lifting weights to gain strength is the best fat-burning mechanism, and helps you become lean and full of energy. Strength training can help you master your metabolism.
- Lifting heavy strengthens your DNA, mitochondria, and fast-twitch muscle fibers.
- Doing the hard lifting leads to confidence in all scenarios—not only do you look confident, but you also feel it. Remember, survival of the fittest—this will make you harder to kill.
- Lifting in a fasted state boosts natural HGH, taps into your stored body fat for energy, and makes you lean and strong while naturally optimizing your body. It's nature's performance-enhancing formula.

- Strength is also waking up and crushing 4:00 am workouts, to give you the energy to outwork the competition and give you the resolve to win. Your body is primed to do its hardest work based on fasting and a nutritional schedule.
- Lifting heavy things is one of the most potent tactics for defying age and avoiding sarcopenia, the process of losing muscle. Keeping strength is essential for longevity.
- Lifting gives you the perfect combination of performance, aesthetics, and longevity.

The Performance CEO understands a workout is not just a slow jog in the park. The Training Protocol is not for the weak-hearted. It is a solitary, hard-charging time to challenge yourself by lifting heavy, sprinting, and pushing your mind and will to win.

With this Protocol, I want to show you the best way to build lean, functional muscle in the cleanest, most efficient way possible. I want to not only get you from point A to point B—I want to give you the map that can get you there the fastest.

Performance is all about seizing moments, and you will want to make sure you are ready, powerful, and able to seize the moment and win. It is the ultimate preparation for business.

Daily wins, even if one is just a micro weight increase on an exercise, put confidence in your bank to seize upcoming moments. We revel in every inch, every half-pound, every rep. And by jumping on every opportunity and following the exact Lifting Heavy Protocol, to think like the Performance CEO and feel like a professional athlete, you will achieve the most unstoppable combination.

While strength refers to how much force your muscles can exert, power refers to how quickly that force can be exerted. Power is the ability to generate lots of force in a short period. As the Performance CEO, you want your workouts to create the perfect balance between strength and power to generate high amounts of force in short periods. You will do workouts that will turn your cells into tiny muscle-building machines—so you can reap the benefits in a big way. The devil is in the detail, and the Incline Press, Squat, Overhead Press, Deadlift, and Row are your key workout movements. We focus on these big movements with an Upper Push, Lower Push, Upper Pull, and Lower Pull.

To stay successful, you can never be content, never be satisfied, and must always push for more weight, better performance times, and more reps. This directly correlates to more deals, more clients, and the growth of your business. The two go hand in hand. You must be hungry for strength and for growth.

Doing the hard, early work also sets a tempo for employees, investors, partners, and even family members, which builds your reputation as a doer. If you're willing to do the 4:00 am workouts, you're sending a message: you're not scared of a hard day's work. This will translate to all areas of your life.

Leadership is about showing that you'll be in the trenches and stay in the grind with your team—no matter how early in the day it is. This 4:00 am workout not only sets the tone for your day, but can also help strengthen your persona based on real, physical work. It is okay to be extreme with a singular focus. It's okay to be viewed as obsessed with greatness. It's okay to be a boss. To become a legend, you need to do real-world, herculean things.

Where Confidence Comes From

When we feel and look our best, we perform at our best. So, to take a deeper look at the reasons behind that phenomenon, I researched the human brain on confidence.

The feeling of confidence in yourself activates "value areas" of the brain, including the striatum and the prefrontal cortex, often brought on by pleasure and reward. And when you are physically picking up heavy things, pushing them, and sprinting as fast as you humanly can, you are triggering that activation. You are gaining confidence in your body and in yourself, convincing yourself that you are capable of becoming stronger and reaching new levels of speed and fitness.

Consequently, the emergence and continuation of confidence are key factors in boosting your brain. Since the brain is ever-changing, we are realigning our synaptic connections all the time at a cellular level.

Therefore, reinforcing confidence in yourself through lifting heavy shit and running fast can be done at every workout.

When you do hard things, like a tough workout, you become neuronally more confident to take on whatever challenge comes your way—it literally becomes ingrained in your brain.

And to be at your best, you need to be faster, stronger, fitter, and more confident than you ever were before. As you are enroute to becoming the Performance CEO, know that you will be part of a unique breed of human. Fittingly, you need a workout that sets you apart from the rest. This routine may seem over the top, it may be obsessive, but it protects your cognitive function and will make you smarter and sharper through the chemical reactions in your body.

It's simple: the more blood you pump to your brain, the more oxygen and nutrients your brain receives. And when you have more blood flow and nutrients, your brain will become faster and more effective in performance. That enhanced speed, in your brain's electrical synapses, is key to thinking at the highest level, solving pivotal problems, and outperforming your competitors.

As you work on your startup, working out hard helps you react, think, remember, learn, and focus better. As you pump your muscles, you also pump blood to your brain, optimizing cerebral circulation, boosting brain volume, strengthening synaptic connections, and helping manufacture vital proteins and hormones, while growing new brain cells.

Who knew you could get jacked and get smarter at the same time?

Strength Training: The Bottom Line

A strong body facilitates a strong mind, and the **Performance CEO Strength Protocol** places heavier and heavier loads on our bodies. This forces our bodies to respond by increasing in size to bear the weight of their environment.

In this chapter, you learned that everything we do is done with intent and purpose. It requires physical and mental strength. It's all part of the path to achieving greatness, to being healthy, and to becoming your best.

Here's a recap of what we learned:

- The seven components of the Performance CEO Strength Protocol
  - Core
  - Strength: 5x5 five sets of heavy weights and just five reps (3 Minutes rest).
  - Accessory: 4x6-8 (2 Minutes rest).
  - Volume: Four exercises, four rounds of ten reps (30 Sec rest).
  - Burnout: fifty reps for each body part.
  - GPP: Three rounds of 30 seconds on, 30 seconds rest.
  - Cognitive Walk/Sprint: where your body becomes an efficient, fat-burning machine (2:30 sec walk, 30 sec sprint).
- Lifting heavy helps the body in so many ways. Getting stronger, both physically and mentally, with the essential foundational lifts can help you get better in the gym and in the boardroom.
- The Performance CEO focuses on low reps and key lifts for each muscle group to build strength. Lifting heavy at a low repetition number *increases strength* and builds lean muscle.
- Lifting not only pushes you in a physically demanding way—but it also boosts your rate of neurogenesis and stimulates your nervous system, bringing you a ton of benefits for your physical and mental health.
- Lifting heavy triggers the release of nerve growth factors that have a strong fighting purpose for your brain—to protect neurons and control hormones.
- Weightlifting as the Performance CEO can also be a high-quality source of anti-aging miracles.
- 3:00 pm: Afternoon Ideation Nature Walk—bringing you the benefits of a 30- to 60-minute walk in nature as the second workout of your day.

PILLAR III

Recovery

Recover Like a Boss

In the fast-paced world of entrepreneurship, cognitive performance is paramount to success, making daily recovery practices crucial for optimizing mental acuity and overall productivity. As entrepreneurs we juggle countless responsibilities, our brains undergo tremendous strain, leading to potential reduction of cognitive function. Incorporating a holistic approach to daily recovery—including methods such as Red Light therapy, Hyperbaric Oxygen Therapy (HBOT), Ice Baths, prioritized sleep, and intermittent fasting—can significantly enhance brain health and cognitive abilities. By nurturing their minds with these scientifically-backed techniques, entrepreneurs can not only sustain peak mental performance but also foster the resilience needed to tackle challenges and seize opportunities in the ever-evolving business landscape.

In the CEO Recovery Protocol, we look at every day as recovery day. The Protocol will optimize the tools and techniques around you to support your body so you can get back at it with the gas pedal to the floor. Our bodies and brains are so reliant. We can build that adaptation over time to increase our output. Every day my goal is to tire out my body and brain, and always focus on daily recovery to be at my best.

Up to this point, you have learned about the mindset, daily schedule, the training, and the nutrition that will fuel your output. Now we're going to go deep into the third pillar of optimizing your entrepreneurial success. We'll get into some cutting-edge technology that will give you a seemingly unfair advantage, to ensure you attain all your dreams and ambitions. It will help get you across the finish line first every time. But remember, the core fundamentals of this Protocol are free. The investment in recovery should be made only when you know you are going to adopt this Performance CEO lifestyle.

In the past, recovery was an area I often neglected—but when I looked at the science of human performance and recovery, I made sure to slot it into my everyday schedule, to fully support the recovery of my body and mind.

After you finish your ideation, meetings, strength, and walk/sprints, your brain and body will discover that following the daily plan to recovery is essential for performance.

Why Recovery Matters

Recovery is more than just not being sore the day after a hard workout. Recovery is a comprehensive Protocol to help you be at your best inside and out, by speeding up your rate of cognitive and physical recovery every single day. The brain for an entrepreneur has no days off. It is designed to optimize the processes of your neurons, cells, muscles, joints, nervous system, and brain, to get them ready to attack the next day. Through the Performance CEO Protocol, you are truly changing yourself into an entrepreneurial superhero.

You work and work out hard, consuming the perfect nutrients at the right times, but you must recover hard as well. Every part of this Protocol is full on. Professional athletes understand that a comprehensive recovery plan is critical to make sure they are ready to attack each day, every day. As the Performance CEO, you need to take that same approach, to ensure you're at your best, no matter how hard you worked or how late you stayed up working the day before. We need to normalize using the tools of professional athletes to drive entrepreneurial performance.

An array of tools is available to help you continue to work at a frenetic pace, day in and day out. Each and every one of these tools will be a check on the list of what every Performance CEO needs to have to be at their best. I have tried all of the tools in the space, and what I talk about in this chapter are the modalities I have whittled down that support my recovery, and recharge where I can operate at the highest level. This will save you a decade of experimentation and investment. I only use modalities that really work.

Recovery is often the limiting factor for all levels of performance. You will learn to recover from both physical and mental stress at a quicker pace, so you're able to do more and be the leader your business needs. The goal here is to learn how to optimize every day with active recovery. It's just as important as anything we do in this Protocol. It's not a buffet, everything works together in a symbiotic relationship.

The speed with which you can recover and attack another day—and flourish—ultimately determines how best you can seize the moment for that big meeting that can close your most important deal. The ability to recover both physically and mentally is critical in overcoming the stresses of running a business, training, and extreme competition, all of which you encounter on a daily basis. Here we go.

How We Recover

I have worked tirelessly (pun intended) to find a way to rebuild my mind and body to their optimal state with proper rest through sleep and active regeneration recovery. As the Performance CEO, you'll want to optimize your sleep to get into the most rejuvenating stages and make sure they make up at least 50 percent of your night's sleep. The Performance CEO Recovery Protocol will show you how to engineer the perfect night's sleep in the most measurable ways.

How will you continuously perform at such a high level? Essentially, by biohacking your recovery, you will never have to slow down, working optimally in peak shape, always. This is why we can work at an unrivaled pace every day, 365 days a year. We create the daily time and space to recharge, recover, and refuel. You'll want the right volume and intensity to create the optimal response to having another successful day of goal-crushing.

Although technology has accelerated in all areas of our lives, recovery is an interesting fusion of the new and old, using techniques that are both modern and from ancient times. From a traditional massage to relax your body and mind, to a modern bed cooling system pad to optimize your sleep, the fusion of both spectrums can help create the optimal environment for your cognitive and physical regeneration. As the Performance CEO, I like knowing I've done everything in my power—even creating the optimal recovery and sleep environment—to get the edge over my competition. My goal is to wake up more refreshed, focused, and driven than anyone else in the tech space. My home has become a complete Performance and Recovery Center. I invested the money in my recovery—it my highest ROI.

The Performance CEO builds Recovery Protocol into their daily workday. As an entrepreneur, you recognize the true value of success as freedom—the freedom to build out your optimal day to accomplish every task you put your mind to. To do this, you might take a conference call from the sauna, use a standing desk while rolling a ball on the arches of your feet, think strategically during your cold bath, call your top employee on your nature walk, and take your quick afternoon recharge in your hyperbaric chamber. You will build your life around your business to maximize performance, to always be ready to seize moments and win—and that mindset continues throughout the recovery.

Let's also remember that we are doing this all for our brains—so the physical benefits (though amazing) are not the main goal. It's all about cognitive performance. I will say it once, then I will say it again. The body is a biproduct of a powerful brain.

Our brain contains approximately 100 billion neurons, or brain cells, which are the oldest and longest-living cells in the body. Some of those cells have been in our brains since the day of our birth. In the hippocampus, however, our recovery modalities are able to evoke neurogenesis, which is the process of growing new brain cells.

Neurogenesis is the process we want to unlock for optimal brain function with our entrepreneurial tasks. I have learned, through my extensive research, that recovery, fasting, dieting, exercising, minimizing stress, and optimizing sleep can stimulate new neuron growth. We will also include information not only on recovery but key optimization tools that are built into each day of the Protocol.

The great news is that by following this Protocol and these specific recovery modalities, we can continue to grow new neurons, even as we age. Therefore, we can run hard as entrepreneurs well into our seventies, eighties, and even nineties. So, as you recover physically and eliminate stress, know that our real objective is to create healthier cells to hone our focus and memory, as well as improve our overall executive function. These recovery modalities all focus on the higher-level cognitive skills that control our behavior. These modifications to our daily habits and adaptations in how we handle stress can ultimately create new neuron growth and bio-hack our recovery.

Invest in Yourself: Daily Scientific Recovery

As the Performance CEO, I have shown that a lot of the best parts of this Protocol are free. But I do believe that when it comes to recovery you should spare no expense in world-class modalities. I have tested and invested in them, and they have proven to keep me up and running, such that I can attack each day recharged and use the best methods on the planet to fuel our optimization and recovery to do more and become more. There is no better financial investment than your own brain.

As I mentioned earlier, I want to normalize having an HBOT in every CEO's bedroom. I want us to turn away from decadence and adopt a spartan lifestyle. For those who are not ready or able to make these investments, there are businesses popping up all over the world that offer use of their HBOT, red light, ice baths, sauna, and other modalities for a nominal cost.

Let me walk you through some of the recovery modalities we use as Performance CEOs, with the how and the why:

Fasting for Recovery

We have talked about fasting already, but it's important enough that its correlation to recovery bears mentioning. It's a modality—a free one you can access every single day, remember—that aids in recovery as much as it does performance.

Why: Fasting for 23 hours daily doubles the regenerative abilities of stem cells, according to MIT research. Short-term calorie restriction also increases stem cell activity, even if you are not fully fasted. We've already reviewed the important role nutrition plays in optimizing your power, strength, and growth. Now we'll take some time to divulge how important nutrition is to recovery—and that begins with fasting. The ability to incite autophagy and cellular rejuvenation is the start of the benefits that fasting for recovery provides.

Red Light Therapy

Why: From enhancing mental sharpness and boosting memory, to improving thinking skills, red light therapy can benefit the brain in innumerable ways. Red light is one of the sensory stimuli our brains is always processing. Light exposure plays a central role in the biological processes affecting our mental acuity, sleep, and other circadian rhythms. I have learned that red light has also proven to be beneficial for treating brain injuries and degenerative brain disorders. It is used for these ailments because it has been studied to improve memory, motor skills, and recognition.

For the body, when applied before exercise, it can improve performance and endurance and can prevent future muscle damage. This means longer, more powerful workouts with less soreness afterward. Pre-workout red light therapy appears to be most effective for weight loss as well. Red light therapy can also reduce inflammation, stimulate tissue regeneration, boost recovery, and promote healing, leading to a better night's sleep. The treatment can also repair sun damage, reduce wrinkles, heal scarring, reduce joint inflammation and stretch marks, reduce internal inflammation, boost testosterone levels, and enhance collagen production.

Our internal biological clock—or circadian rhythm—relies on light cues to regulate various physiological processes. Excessive blue light exposure during the evening can disrupt this rhythm, leading to sleep disturbances and other health issues. Blue light filtering glasses can help mitigate this disruption.

How: Every morning for ten minutes. Every night for ten minutes.

Cold Water Immersion: Ice Bath

Why: In the pursuit of peak cognitive performance, ice baths activate our sympathetic and parasympathetic nervous system, stress response, and recovery process, all of which contribute to a natural high and boost in mood and attitude. Daily ice baths eliminate inflammation by working on the way your blood flows. Your blood vessels will begin to contract almost immediately when you submerge yourself in the cold water, and afterward vessels will gradually dilate when you get out. The ice bath will train your circulatory system to bring more oxygen to your tissues. It also trains your stress response, to increase resilience in your daily life by bringing you into a stressful environment, where your body evokes a natural fight-or-flight response and helps you to be adaptable. An ice bath has also been found to create a stronger immune system, to help you stay healthy and keep kicking ass.

When done pre-exercise, cold water immersion significantly increases your peak performance output. It provides a delayed rise in core body temperature and spares muscle glycogen depletion. It also boosts your plasma volume, oxygen uptake by muscle, and power output, helping your body lift stronger and longer.

When done before bedtime, an ice bath can improve your sleep quality by dropping your body temperature to initiate sleep onset at a faster rate. So, icing before bed mimics this natural rhythm and will allow you to sleep more deeply and more quickly. This can be done via a cold shower or putting your face in a bowl of ice. I never miss my Sunset Ice Bath.

When done every day, an ice bath can improve your immune system and help you fight off illnesses. Studies done in the Netherlands found that cold showers were linked to a 29 percent reduction in people taking sick leave from work. Another study even connected cold showers to improved cancer survival.

How: Twice daily for three minutes
- In the morning, after red light therapy and before your workout
- Before red light therapy and bed, to evoke deep sleep optimization and lower your core body temperature

HBOT (Hyperbaric Oxygen Therapy)

Why: Hyperbaric oxygen therapy triggers the body's ability to heal itself. Therefore, a hyperbaric chamber can increase energy rejuvenation at the cellular level. When it comes to brain recovery, HBOT improves brain function and can improve cerebral blood flow, brain metabolism, and brain microstructure, leading to improved cognitive functions, physical functions, and sleep. The Performance CEO uses the chamber for the afternoon recharge nap after the day's one meal.

HBOT significantly increases the amount of oxygen dissolved in the blood, allowing more oxygen to reach tissues and organs throughout the body. This oxygen saturation can promote healing and support the body's natural regenerative processes.

HBOT has also been shown to accelerate wound healing in various conditions, such as diabetic foot ulcers, non-healing surgical wounds, and radiation-induced tissue damage. It can help reduce inflammation, by modulating immune responses and decreasing the production of pro-inflammatory molecules. As for athletic performance, HBOT boosts your recovery and longevity by aiding in the circulation of oxygen in the body, to fix damaged blood vessels or trigger collagen growth, leading to healing at a faster pace. It also helps promote new blood vessel formulation, mobilizes stem cells, and reduces inflammation.

As for the skin, HBOT aids in the formation of new collagen. This means that with your chamber, you can look younger by regenerating skin cells, connective tissue, and blood vessels. Receiving regular treatments of HBOT increases skin elasticity and stimulates collagen production, leading to the reduction of wrinkles and fine lines, and improvement in skin texture. It also makes the skin smooth and clear.

How: Five days a week for one hour. Two days off. I like to do this during my midday recharge.

Infrared Sauna

Why: As a part of your daily Recovery Protocol, I recommend maximizing health benefits by getting your sweat on in an infrared sauna. The Performance CEO always uses the sauna post-workout to enhance training benefits, increase blood flow, and decrease recovery time. You can also prevent the loss of muscle mass by using a sauna. Heat stress prevents muscle loss by triggering the release of Heat Shock Proteins (HSPs), which eliminate free radicals, support antioxidant production, and repair proteins in the muscles. Heat stress also has significant anti-aging effects—which, as you know by now, I'm all about.

HGH is also key for muscle growth—and studies have shown that with a 20-minute sauna session, you can dramatically increase your HGH levels. You can also combine heat stress and exercise with isometrics, yoga, pushups, and squats, and create a similar spike. Sauna exposure increases blood flow to skeletal muscles, to help them with glucose, amino acids, fatty acids, and oxygen production, while removing lactic acid. It can also increase the production of *new* red blood cells at the same speed and rate that illegal drugs like EPO can. This is why if you do the right things, you can always be lifetime Natural. This simple 20-minute sauna session can induce both HGH and IGF-1 release, which also results in increased longevity. We will find the key balance of HGH, and we will do it naturally. The Performance CEO is 100 percent natural, and we use our God-given bodies and science to enhance our efficiency.

How: 30 minutes every day. Try taking an internal call during this daily session—but you'll want to keep your phone outside the sauna.

Compression Gear

Why: Wearing compression boots and compression gear helps you achieve your ultimate Recovery Protocol. Compression apparel can help your body minimize soreness after exercising, by reducing the muscle pain and inflammation that often come directly after a workout. It reduces the lactic acid in your muscles (the excess amount of lactate causes muscle soreness) by issuing a graduated tightness that gets the lactic acid moving throughout your body, dissipating its negative effects.

How: You can wear compression boots while you do a number of business activities. Operating at a high performance is about multitasking in all business activities. I do it two times a week for 45 minutes.

Percussion Therapy Gun

Why: Percussion therapy, via a handheld device that pulses pressure over the muscle tissue to trigger recovery, provides a simple way to give yourself a deep tissue massage. Doing this daily for recovery can alleviate post-workout pain and relieve any restriction in flexibility you may be feeling. It's such a powerful tool that it can even help break down scar tissue.

How: Daily pre-workout.

PMB Photobiomodulation

Why: This uses low-level light therapy to simulate cellular function. PMB has shown to increase blood flow to the brain, which can improve the delivery of oxygen and nutrients to brain cells, leading to improved cognitive function. It has also been shown to stimulate the production of neurotrophic factors, which are proteins that support growth and survival of neurons in the brain. PMB is also shown to increase the production of serotonin, a neurotransmitter that plays a key role in regulating mood and reducing symptoms of depression and anxiety. When the brain absorbs light energy within the NIR wavelength range, it stimulates your brain to improve cognition, memory, and mood.

How: Two sessions per week using my light headset.

20 Minutes of Daily Morning Sun

Why: Sunrises can trigger the release of serotonin, a neurotransmitter that contributes to feelings of happiness and well-being. Starting your day with a beautiful sight like a sunrise can positively influence your mood and set a positive tone for the rest of the day. Watching the sunrise can boost your energy levels and promote alertness, making you feel more awake and focused for the day ahead.

Exposure to natural light, especially in the morning, can help regulate your body's internal clock, known as the circadian rhythm. This can improve sleep-wake cycles and overall sleep quality. Early morning sunlight is a natural source of vitamin D, which is essential for bone health, immune function, and various other physiological processes in the body.

Since our bodies produce vitamin D when exposed to sunlight, just 15 to 20 minutes a day of morning sun is essential to maximizing your health. I have never missed a sunrise in over three years. The morning sunshine zone between 8:00 and 10:00 am is ideal.

Just 15 minutes of natural light in the morning will help you sleep better at night. The sun regulates your circadian rhythm by letting your body know when it's time to raise and lower your levels of melatonin to help you sleep. Therefore, when you get your daily sun, you'll sleep better at night, and it can also reduce stress.

Soaking in the sun is essential for longevity and has recovered from getting a bad rap over the years. Vitamin D is also critical for your immune system, and with consistent exposure to sunlight you can help strengthen it. A healthy immune system will reduce the risk of illness, infections, and some cancers, as well as handle the stress of your workload and travel schedule.

For men, the daily morning sun boosts testosterone levels by up to 69 percent. Studies have shown that levels of testosterone in men's blood rise when the doses of Vitamin D also rise.

How: Each day, find time after a workout to get 20 to 25 minutes of morning sunshine. This modality has many vital components for the optimal functioning of the body.

Office Movement Rules

Why: Working hours from a sitting desk is too sedentary. Sitting is the new smoking. For every hour of sitting, you need ten minutes of activity. Brief walks, push-ups, crunches, and kettle bell swings—even when done for just a few minutes—can help reactivate the brain.

Unfortunately, the worst time of day for your brain is typically around 1:00 to 3:00 pm in an afternoon crash. Our afternoon nature walk eliminates this slump as that brief rest time recharges and reinvigorates.

An afternoon reset nap is important, whether you are doing HBOT for one hour or simply lying down. Harvard Medical School reported that a midday nap is more effective than sleeping at night in improving cognitive performance, physical recovery, alertness restoration to morning levels, performance enhancement, and mistake reduction in the afternoon.

NASA pilots take in-flight naps as short as 26 minutes to one hour, to enhance performance and alertness by 34 percent and also experience a 16 percent increase in reaction time, attention, reduction in errors, and increased productivity.

If the nap is timed at the natural mid-afternoon dip, the body will come out of the hour-long session with the same cognitive performance levels and recall as your prime working hours of 9:00 am to 11:00 am. Post-nap, consume one cup of black coffee with collagen.

How: Following the Protocol, we do ten kettle bell swings every 20 minutes. Make sure you are getting up every hour for five minutes or so and do the mini-cognitive workouts. Even after you sit back down or go back to your desk, the benefits in your brain will stick around for a little while—allowing for better concentration and improved creativity. If you can, getting outside for a breath of fresh air can also boost your mood, your memory, and your focus.

Morning Walk/Sprint

Why: Although this is a workout, it is also a powerful tool for recovery and health. It always gets the blood flowing to the brain, sparking BDNF and neurogenesis. Watching the sunrise can have several benefits for both the body and the brain, fostering a positive impact on overall well-being. It encourages you to be present in the moment and experience a sense of calm and relaxation. It can serve as a form of mindfulness, allowing you to disconnect from daily stressors and immerse yourself in the beauty of nature.

How: Get outside and do your walk/sprint at the right time to experience both the great benefits of physical activity and what it does for the recovery of your brain.

Afternoon Recharge

Why: Taking a midday recharge can offer several benefits for the brain and overall cognitive function. Napping has been shown to improve memory, attention, and problem-solving abilities. It can help recharge the brain, leading to better mental clarity and alertness. Napping can aid in memory consolidation, which is the process of stabilizing and strengthening memories formed during wakefulness. It can help solidify new information, making it easier to recall later.

Taking a brief nap can help reduce stress and promote relaxation. It gives the brain a chance to rest and recover, which can be particularly beneficial for individuals experiencing high levels of mental or emotional stress. Some studies suggest that napping can boost creativity and problem-solving skills. It may help the brain form new connections and facilitate "out-of-the-box" thinking.

A short nap can rejuvenate the brain and improve focus and productivity, making it easier to concentrate on tasks and maintain attention to detail. Napping can have mood-enhancing effects, furthermore, contributing to a more positive and balanced emotional state. Napping allows the brain to rest and recover, similar to the way sleep at night rejuvenates the body and mind.

A brief nap can even boost wakefulness and alertness, making it an effective strategy for combating drowsiness and fatigue during the day. Taking a nap can help replenish energy levels and enhance overall physical and mental performance, especially during long or demanding work or study sessions.

How: Rest your eyes, your brain, and your body for up to an hour, after your OMAD. Remember, you are an entrepreneur, and you build your perfect day.

Afternoon Nature Walks

Why: Walking in nature, often referred to as "nature walks" or "forest bathing," can have significant positive effects on the brain and overall mental well-being. Benefits to the brain include lower cortisol levels, which are associated with stress, and can lead to an improvement in mood and a reduction in symptoms of anxiety and depression. Nature's calming effect can help elevate mood and increase feelings of happiness.

Nature walks can stimulate creativity and problem-solving abilities. Being in a natural setting can inspire new thoughts and ideas. Time spent in nature has been shown to improve focus and attention. It may help reduce mental fatigue and restore cognitive abilities.

Nature walks provide an opportunity to disconnect from everyday demands and allow the brain to rest and recharge. Exposure to nature has been associated with improved cognitive function, memory, and learning abilities. Spending time in nature can decrease rumination, the repetitive and negative thought patterns that can contribute to stress and anxiety. Nature walks foster a sense of connection to the environment, which can lead to feelings of purpose and well-being.

How: To maximize the benefits of nature walks, try to be present and mindful during the experience. Engage your senses, notice the sounds, smells, and sights around you, and let go of distractions from electronic devices.

Deep Tissue Massage

Why: I really learned the true healing power of massage when I moved to Thailand to fight professional Muay Thai.

In that program, we would have two training/pads/sparring sessions a day, running a 5K before each session. I was running a 10K six days a week and training/sparring Muay Thai for four hours a day.

That kind of training regimen takes a dramatic toll on the body. This was when I started to investigate the healing power of massage, and how it could work out the pain and stiffness before heading back to do it all again the next day. A traditional Thai massage is uncomfortable, but I could get up and do it all over again, because the massage would do its job of working out all the toxins, keeping me healthy and fresh.

Since that experience, no matter where I am in the world, I have at least one deep tissue massage a week. It is essential to staying young, being flexible, and minimizing stress and cortisol levels. I earn my massage weekly through hard work.

How: One 60- to 90-minute deep tissue massage a week.

Standing Desk

Why: Not only does it help strengthen the muscles in your core and legs, but it also helps prevent spinal injury and can aid in recovery post-workout. It can improve circulation and blood flow to your muscles, and aid in keeping your hips flexible and uninjured. Standing desks also help maintain or lose weight, as your body will burn more calories standing than sitting. We want our bodies to get used to always being in motion, as the human body will adapt to what it needs to do. Standing and movement keep you healthy and on top of your game.

How: Try and work half of your day from a standing desk.

Sleep to Win: The Ultimate Recovery Modality

Sleep is a critical yet often overlooked aspect of recovery and success. Amidst endless to-do lists and round-the-clock responsibilities, entrepreneurs may find themselves sacrificing precious hours of rest in favor of work. However, understanding the profound impact of sleep on cognitive function, creativity, and overall well-being is crucial for those seeking peak performance. In this discussion, we explore why sleep stands as the ultimate recovery tool for entrepreneurs, offering them the key to unlocking their full potential and achieving sustainable success in the dynamic business landscape.

Sleep is not merely a passive state of inactivity; it is a dynamic and essential process that plays a fundamental role in consolidating memories, restoring the body, and optimizing cognitive function. For entrepreneurs, who often face complex problem-solving and decision-making challenges, sufficient sleep is the cornerstone of mental acuity and creativity. During sleep, the brain undergoes critical processes, such as memory consolidation, where the day's experiences and information are organized and integrated into the neural framework. This consolidation enhances learning and problem-solving abilities, allowing entrepreneurs to tackle challenges with increased efficiency and innovative thinking. Moreover, sleep is intrinsically linked to emotional regulation, and a well-rested mind is better equipped to navigate stress, maintain composure during high-pressure situations, and make level-headed decisions. By recognizing sleep as the ultimate recovery mechanism, entrepreneurs can harness the power of restful slumber to not only optimize their cognitive prowess but also cultivate the mental resilience required to thrive in their entrepreneurial endeavors.

During deep sleep stages, the brain consolidates and strengthens memories, helping to retain information and experiences learned during the day. The brain's glymphatic system becomes more active, allowing for the removal of waste products and toxins that accumulate during waking hours. This process is vital for maintaining brain health.

Sleep supports neuroplasticity, the brain's ability to reorganize and form new neural connections. This process is essential for learning, adapting new experiences, and memory formation. Sufficient sleep helps regulate emotions and supports emotional resilience. Lack of sleep can lead to increased emotional reactivity and mood disturbances.

A well-rested brain performs better on cognitive tasks, such as problem-solving, decision-making, attention, and creativity. Adequate sleep improves sustained attention and the ability to stay focused on tasks, leading to increased productivity and reduced errors. During sleep, the brain's energy consumption decreases, allowing it to conserve energy for essential restorative processes.

During deep sleep stages, the brain engages in repair and growth processes, including the production of new nerve cells and synapses.

Overall, getting enough high-quality sleep is essential for brain health, cognitive function, emotional well-being, and overall physical health.

Keeping your sleep schedule consistent every day is critical to entering the necessary sleep stages regularly. Try to get to bed at the same time each night and allow for at least seven hours of rest before you need to wake up. Over time, your body will acclimate to this schedule. It will be easier to fully experience the light, deep, and REM stages. You may even find it easier to wake up.

REM Sleep

Staying focused on the quality of REM and deep sleep—which is the magic zone for ultimate recovery, both cognitively and physically—is essential. Our goal is to focus on attaining two hours of each.

Throughout the night, the sleep cycle repeats multiple times, with REM sleep becoming longer and more prevalent in the latter part of the night. Each sleep cycle lasts about 90 to 120 minutes. You will maximize the quality of your sleep in the REM and deep sleep stages to best recover and regenerate.

Metabolism in the brain increases during deep sleep, supporting short-term and long-term memory and overall learning. Deep sleep is also when the pituitary gland secretes important hormones, like HGH, which leads to the growth and development of the body. The benefits of deep sleep also include energy restoration, cell regeneration, increased blood supply to muscles, immune system fortification, growth promotion, and tissue and bone repair.

Look at your bedroom as a sleep lab, where you will be creating the best environment to get the most out of your sleep. Working hard begins with sleeping hard, and sleep quality comes down to the details.

Adjusting Our Attitude toward Sleep

I used to think sleep was for losers. I prided myself on always working long hours, always having early mornings, and always having my light on, so to speak. However, when I started to truly dig into the science, I learned that sleep shouldn't be avoided—it should be crafted, used, and cherished as one of the most amazing things we *all* can do to supercharge our bodies.

When I realized that the quality of my sleep could enhance my performance, I was in—all-in. I began monitoring my sleep and found that the days I was not as strong, fast, or intellectually sharp had a direct correlation to my sleep patterns. So now I make my daily decisions about which physical and cognitive tasks I perform and when, or if at all, based on my sleep data. This way, I don't overtax my nervous system or tear my body down.

With just a few small changes in your sleep habits, you too can create a routine that will help you crush every day and have the energy to reach your dreams. Sleep is the greatest secret weapon for greatness.

The highest-performing people who are under the most pressure are the most likely to avoid or have trouble sleeping—leading them to pay the highest cost. You cannot kick ass when you are tired. I don't care who you are. We are all still human. Sleep is not optional. However, using our human DNA, we can instead find better ways to optimize our minds and bodies by using sleep to our best benefit.

The goal of your sleep routine is to spend as much time in deep or slow-wave delta sleep as possible. This is when your breathing and heartrate drop to their lowest levels, brainwaves slow down, and your mind and body will truly find recovery. Slow-wave sleep helps the brain recover from all that it has learned and thought about during the day. It helps memory—both short- and long-term—and can help you run your business. Slow-wave sleep also impacts your muscles by reducing the stress hormone cortisol and triggering the release of prolactin and HGH.

Science shows adults need 1.7 to two hours of deep sleep each night. The more time you spend in REM, the more restorative your time sleeping will be—you will wake up refreshed, energetic, smarter. By following the hacks in this book, I have been consistently getting—and tracking—over two hours of deep sleep nightly.

Optimize your Sleep Routine

Focus on creating the perfect sleep environment so you can attain your two hours of REM and two hours of deep sleep every night. Take an ice bath before bed to lower core body. I have taken my sunset ice bath for almost a year, and my sleep data is irrefutable: my sleep is deeper, my heart rate is lower, and I have attained my goal of two hours each of REM and deep Sleep on a nightly basis.

Here are some other ways you can optimize sleep.

Reduce Blue Light

One of the most overlooked ways to enhance your sleep is to take control of your light exposure. Nothing disturbs a good night's sleep worse than bright blue and traditional white light. Blue light can really throw off your circadian rhythm. Blue light is everywhere—we get it from the sun, TVs, computers, tablets, and even our smartphones. Blue light has a short wavelength, so it produces more energy than other light and can create a huge disruption to your sleep cycle and quality.

Your biological clockwork (circadian biology) requires a strong rhythmic light/dark cycle for optimal functioning. Unfortunately, blue-enriched light at night and a lack of natural light during the day can create erratic sleep and light cycles. You can destroy your chance of a good night's sleep without even knowing it.

Not only are our bodies placed under a great deal of stress with external factors, but internally they are always fighting to maintain a stable rhythm, which entails creating a routine and monitoring light exposure from your actual environment.

Blue light is not all bad. It is what wakes you up in the morning, improves your mood, and makes you more alert. But it can also disrupt your sleep as you are winding down for bed. When taken in through your photoreceptors, the effect is truly counterproductive. The blue light will shift your circadian rhythm by suppressing melatonin, the hormone that tells your brain when it is time to sleep. This tricks your body into thinking it's daytime—24/7. If you hadn't noticed this before, there's no wondering anymore—blue light can be one of the major reasons why your sleep quality is bad.

The pineal gland in the brain starts to release melatonin a couple of hours before your body realizes it's time to go to bed. But blue light can interrupt this process by causing stimulation in the retina. To make things worse, the amount of blue light you are exposed to has also been linked to rapid aging. So, between blue light and bad sleep quality, you'll be looking and feeling older—which is not exactly optimal for the Performance CEO.

Blue Light Glasses

Blue light glasses have been developed to filter out the most disruptive wavelengths of light and create a virtual darkness that allows your body to naturally transition to sleep and restoration mode. I recommend these glasses, to help you block those harmful lights that can disrupt your sleep quality. They help to protect you best from blue light, so your body can begin the natural process of getting ready for sleep by releasing natural melatonin.

Full disclosure: it is hard to look cool in these glasses. However, when your skin looks amazing, you have no bags under your eyes, when your sleep is deep and restorative, and when people start to make comments about how great you look, it's worth wearing the nerd specs at night.

At least they don't look horrible, and they are comfortable enough to wear around the house. The Performance CEO wears these glasses at the same time every evening. If you wake up in the middle of the night, and need to check your phone, make sure you put your glasses on first. Studies have shown that even brief pulses of light can throw off your clock. When worn, the body starts its natural night process, and soon you'll find that you are maximizing your sleep and attaining your best sleep scores with them.

One last thing: get as much light as possible during the daytime and keep your room dark at night. I use blackout curtains at night and during the day. I recommend wearing yellow lens glasses when looking at computer screens. This will limit your blue light exposure and keep your body in rhythm.

The Perfect Bedroom Temperature

If you have control over your room temperature, you have a key to open the door to optimal sleep. Studies have shown that the ideal environment for the highest quality of sleep is 65 degrees Fahrenheit—so set your room temperature to match that.

It's not all about room temperature, though. By optimizing your body temperature, you can also help take control of your sleep quality. I would recommend taking a three- to five-minute cold shower around one hour prior to bed. Cold is an effective signal to help your body prepare for the onset of sleep. By taking a cold shower, you can cool the body down with a natural tranquilizer that will put you right to sleep.

Early Morning Power

After a night of sleep, the brain is well-rested and refreshed in the morning, leading to increased alertness and mental clarity. This enhanced state of alertness can promote better cognitive function and productivity throughout the day. The early morning hours are in sync with the body's natural circadian rhythm, which regulates various physiological processes, including sleep-wake cycles. Exposure to natural light in the morning helps regulate the internal clock, leading to improved sleep quality and wakefulness during the day.

During sleep, the brain consolidates and processes memories from the previous day. Waking up early allows the brain to take advantage of this period of memory consolidation and start the day with a fresh mental slate. Some research suggests that the brain is more receptive to learning and information processing in the morning. Cognitive functions such as attention, focus, and problem-solving may be at their peak during this time.

In the early morning, cortisol (the stress hormone) levels tend to be naturally higher, which contributes to increased alertness and preparedness for the day's activities. Moderate cortisol levels are essential for maintaining energy and focus.

Starting the day early provides an opportunity to get a head start on tasks and goals. The brain is often at its sharpest in the morning, making it an excellent time to tackle challenging projects or engage in creative activities. The morning hours are typically characterized by a quieter environment and fewer distractions. This can create a conducive environment for improved mental clarity and focus. The early morning offers a peaceful time for reflection, goal setting, and planning for the day ahead. Engaging in mindfulness practices or setting intentions can positively influence the brain's state and emotional well-being.

Early morning sunlight exposure helps regulate the body's internal clock and provides a natural boost in mood and energy levels. Sunlight stimulates the release of serotonin, a neurotransmitter that promotes feelings of happiness and well-being. Establishing a morning routine can create a sense of structure and predictability, reducing stress and contributing to a more organized and disciplined mindset throughout the day.

Deep Work: 20-Minute Sprints

A deep work window is a dedicated period of time during which an individual focuses exclusively on high-concentration, cognitively demanding tasks without distractions or interruptions. The goal is to achieve a state of flow, where deep focus and concentration lead to increased productivity and higher-quality work output.

For the best results in a deep work window, try these practices:

1. Time Blocking: Allocate a specific period in your schedule solely for deep work. This time is often dedicated to work on tasks that require intense focus, problem-solving, creativity, or learning.
2. Minimal Distractions: During the deep work window, individuals minimize or eliminate distractions that could disrupt their concentration. This may involve turning

off notifications, silencing phones, or working in a quiet environment.
3. Extended Periods: Deep work windows are typically longer blocks of uninterrupted time, often lasting for several hours. This extended focus allows individuals to dive deeply into complex tasks and make significant progress.
4. Single-Tasking: Deep work encourages single-tasking rather than multitasking. By focusing on one task at a time, individuals can maintain better concentration and deliver more focused and high-quality results.
5. Scheduled Regularly: To make deep work a habit, individuals often schedule these dedicated time blocks regularly throughout their workweek. Consistency helps to develop the discipline and focus required for deep work.

The concept of a deep work window is especially valuable in today's world, in which distractions and interruptions from technology and the digital environment can significantly impact productivity and cognitive performance. By deliberately setting aside distraction-free time to work deeply on important tasks, individuals can make significant strides in their professional endeavors and achieve a higher level of productivity and success.

For most people, sustaining focused attention on a single task for about 20 minutes is considered typical. This time frame aligns with the "Pomodoro Technique," a popular time management method that involves breaking work into 25-minute intervals (known as Pomodoros) followed by short breaks. The idea behind this technique is that working in short bursts can improve focus and productivity while preventing mental fatigue and burnout.

However, the ability to concentrate for 20 minutes is not strictly defined and can vary depending on the factors mentioned earlier. Some individuals may be able to maintain focus for more extended periods, while others might find it challenging to concentrate for even shorter intervals.

Kettle Bell Swings

We do ten kettle bell swings after every 20-meeting deep window session. Engaging in kettle bell swings can have several benefits for the brain and overall cognitive function. Benefits of ten of these swings include increased blood flow to the brain; release of neurotransmitters like dopamine, serotonin, and norepinephrine; and production of BDNF, the protein that supports the growth, survival, and plasticity of brain cells.

Monitoring and understanding key health biomarkers is vital for our performance. These indicators provide insights into various aspects of health and can guide preventive measures. Blood pressure and cholesterol levels offer essential cardiovascular health information, while blood sugar levels help assess metabolic health. Body Mass Index (BMI) and waist circumference provide insight into weight-related risks. Resting heart rate and testosterone levels impact cardiovascular fitness and reproductive health. Prostate-specific antigen (PSA) levels and liver enzymes offer insights into prostate and liver health. Kidney function, inflammation markers, and vitamin D levels are crucial for evaluating overall wellness. Thyroid hormones affect metabolism, and bone density indicators assess bone health. Additionally, cognitive function and stress hormone levels contribute to optimizing your performance.

*Following the Performance Protocol, we have DEXA scans and comprehensive blood work every quarter to show results and take a proactive approach to performance management. DEXA scans provide precise measurements of body composition, bone density, and fat distribution, offering insights into changes over time. Comprehensive blood work, including biomarkers such as cholesterol, blood sugar, and hormones, provides a comprehensive overview of internal health, helping identify potential issues before they escalate. Regular monitoring allows for early detection of trends and the effectiveness of biohacking modifications, aiding in the prevention and management of conditions such as cardiovascular disease, diabetes, and hormonal imbalances. By adopting a quarterly assessment routine, we gain a dynamic understanding of our health, enabling us to make informed decisions, track progress, and proactively address any concerns, ultimately to enhance our entrepreneurial output and energy.

Don't let biohackers tell you that you need to spend Two Million Dollars on a Protocol. Like in life, the best things are free. Rest and sleep stand as the most accessible and essential recovery methods, allowing the body to naturally heal and regenerate. Hydration, often overlooked, plays a vital role in recovery by aiding nutrient transportation and waste elimination. Fasting is the best way to recover, and we know that is free. There are also breathing exercises and mindfulness practices. Activities in the Recovery Protocol like walking, sprinting, morning sun, cold showers are potent tools for fostering optimal physical recovery and cognitive rejuvenation, ensuring we attain consistent progress in your entrepreneurial pursuits even when on a start-up budget.

Recovery: The Bottom Line

In this chapter, you learned the **Recovery Protocol**, designed to optimize the regeneration processes of your cells, muscles, joints, nervous system, and brain, and how to get them ready to attack the next day. We repair our bodies *and* brains.

Here's a quick recap:

- **Recovery Protocol** for your daily workday is about recovering both your body and brain. It includes fasting and feeding to create better HGH responses to heal and activate tissue growth.
- Science-based hacks that have uncovered the data allow you to master sleep and optimize your resting periods.
- Make yourself your top investment and use all the recovery modalities that you can from Red light therapy, Ice Bath, Sauna, HBOT, PMB, Percussion Gun therapy and Compression boots. Just always remember it is worth it to recover. There is no price you can put on your dreams.
- **The Performance CEO Sleep Protocol** has shown you the importance of *spending as much time as possible in deep or slow-wave delta sleep*—because it's not about the quantity but the quality.

- Optimize your bedroom to become the ultimate sleeping and recovery laboratory:
  1. Engage in daily exercise to reach the highest peaks of sleep at night.
  2. Keep your sleep schedule consistent with regulating your circadian clock.
  3. Find creative outlets for stress, which can impede sleep quality.
  4. Be mindful of beverage intake—both alcoholic and non—and stop drinking at 5:00 pm.
  5. Invest in blue light-blocking glasses or reduce blue light from your devices (especially in your bedroom).
  6. Optimize your bedroom's perfect room temperature, around 65 degrees Fahrenheit.
  7. Fasting for recovery and autophagy/cellular rejuvenation.
  8. Deep tissue massage to lower cortisol and stress levels.
  9. Cold therapy/shower to decrease body temperature and get all the benefits of a cold plunge.
  10. Wear compression gear to minimize soreness.
  11. Sauna to improve blood flow and decrease recovery time by releasing so many good hormones for your body and brain.
  12. A foot-rolling ball can loosen your plantar fascia, reducing the risk of injury or irritation.
  13. A standing desk at work to improve circulation and blood flow.
  14. A hyperbaric chamber can heal at the cellular level.

HERE WE GO!

15-DAY JUMPSTART PLAN

Welcome the 15-Day Jumpstart—a pivotal adaptation period that will pave the way for your success as the Performance CEO. During these two weeks, you will immerse yourself in a dynamic fusion of cutting-edge practices that encompass waking up at 4:00 am, elongated fasting, strength training, consuming specific cognitive foods, embracing ice baths, and mastering the art of restful sleep. This intensive adaptation phase is designed to synchronize these elements seamlessly, empowering you to unlock the full potential of your mind and body. By the end of this empowering journey, you will emerge ready to embrace the full 30-day Extreme Cognitive Protocol, as a seasoned leader destined to thrive in the ever-changing landscape of entrepreneurship.

As the 15-Day Jumpstart commences, you will experience the transformative power of your brain—an interconnected harmony of practices that elevate your cognitive prowess. Waking up at 4:00 am creates an empowering foundation for productivity, allowing you to seize the early hours and accomplish tasks with unparalleled focus. Embracing intermittent fasting cultivates mental clarity and sharpness, preparing your body to embrace the cognitive benefits of the Extreme Cognitive Protocol. Coupled with strategic strength training, your physical and mental resilience will flourish, providing you with the stamina and determination needed to overcome any challenge that comes your way.

During these two weeks, you will delve into the world of cognitive nutrition, where specific foods fuel your brain's potential. You will unlock the secrets of nourishing your mind, boosting creativity, and optimizing cognitive function. Alongside this, you will embrace the invigorating power of ice baths, discovering the profound impact of controlled cold exposure on your mental acuity and overall well-being. These elements, when harnessed in harmony, will solidify your foundation as the Performance CEO, equipped with a razor-sharp mind and an unyielding drive to succeed.

As the 15-Day Jumpstart draws to a close, you will stand at the threshold of the full 30-day Extreme Cognitive Protocol, ready to embark on the full optimization journey of entrepreneurial success. The adaptation period will have seamlessly integrated the practices that constitute the Performance Protocol, optimizing your brain for peak performance. You will unveil the unlimited potential within you—a potent combination of resilience, adaptability, and innovation. As you step into the 30-day Extreme Cognitive Protocol, rest assured that you are poised to rewrite the narrative of your success, harnessing the force of the Performance CEO within to create a pace and tenacity that will be felt throughout your industry.

15-DAY JUMPSTART

DAY 1   **Wednesday**

> "The speed of the leader determines
> the rate of the pack."
> - Michael Koch

We start the program on a Wednesday, so that your body has a few days before a weekend to begin the process of becoming fat-adapted, as it moves from utilizing glycogen to the optimal fuel source—ketones—for energy. This way, your most difficult, low energy adapting days will be over the weekend when you can have the appropriate time to rest and recover. We will build the nutritional and strength baseline and start adapting behaviors to win the morning. Focus on just today, following today's performance protocol. This is the beginning of creating the best entrepreneurial you. This adaptation process of combining exercise with the consumption of the right brain foods will create clean energy and the optimal fuel-burning system for your body and brain. Let's get it!

Wake Up_____am   Sleep: 7+ hrs Optimized Sleep ☐ Deep_____REM_____

Weight_____lbs   Ketones______mmol/L   Super Water ☐   Cognitive Coffee ☐ ☐

Red light* ☐   Ice Bath/Cold Shower ☐   Prayer/Meditation/Gratitude ☐

---

* Optional

DEEP WORK WINDOW 1: Be Brilliant.   ☐

Morning Strength Workout: Adaptation					
Core: 4x15 (30-sec Rest)					
Incline Sit-up					x
Leg Raises					x
Strength Warmup 20-20-10 Compound Movement					

DAY 1   **Wednesday**   (Continued)

Strength: Mogul Maker: 4x5 each exercise 4 sets x 5 reps (1-min rest between each exercise)					
Incline Bench					x
Deadlift					x
Overhead Press					x
Squat					x
Cognitive Walk/Sprint: 2:30 min walk, 30-sec Sprint, 10 rounds					☐
GPP: Farmer's Walk: 3 rounds - 30 secs on, 30 secs off					☐

Complete First 85oz Water (Morning)	☐

Post-Workout Recovery	
20 Minutes Sauna*	☐
20 Minutes of Morning Sun	☐
Cold Shower: Adaptation Protocol - 30 Seconds of Cold, 10 Seconds of Warm, 6 times through (rounds) for a total of 3 Min. Cold	☐

DEEP WORK WINDOW 2: Six to Eight 20-minute deep work window sprints, 10-min break, 10 Kettle bell swings and look outside in the distance 1 minute to adjust eyes.	☐

Adaptation Nutrition Plan: Do the .8 calculation to understand the exact amount of grass fed beef you must consume today. For the Adaptation Jumpstart, you will be splitting these foods into two meals initially. First Meal at 11am and the second meal at 2:50pm.	
Organic Bone Broth (2 cups)	☐
Grass-Fed Beef	g
2oz Liver or Organ Meat	☐
4 Eggs Men, 2 Eggs Women	☐
1 large Avocado	☐
40 Raspberries	☐

DAY 1 Wednesday   (Continued)

20 Pecans or 23 Almondss	☐
50g of Raw Cheese	☐

Afternoon Recharge: HBOT*, Compression* or Cognitive Reset Rest: No more than 1 hour.	☐
Post Recharge: Cognitive Coffee & Collagen	☐

DEEP WORK WINDOW 3: Output ☐

Afternoon Nature Ideation Walk: 30 Min. – 1 hour. Think Big, Walk & Work, Dream Big. Call an Employee	☐

DEEP WORK WINDOW 4: Tactical ☐

Begin Optimized Nighttime Routine

Complete Second 85oz Water	☐
Blue Light Blocker Glasses	☐
No Water after 5 PM for uninterrupted sleep	☐
Sunset Ice Bath* or Cold Shower (2-3 hours before sleep)	☐
Red light*	☐
Prayer & Gratitude	☐
Create Optimal Sleep Environment: 65 degrees, No Cell Phone/EMF	☐

Completed Perfect Day	☐

Notes: How I win tomorrow.

DAY 2 — Thursday

> "The question isn't who is going to let me;
> it's who is going to stop me."
> - Ayn Rand

If you're new to working out with lower reps or just getting started again, you might be feeling a little sore today—but we have recovery built into our day to optimize the physical, cognitive, and physiological aspects of regeneration. Push through! Build a strong foundation today for greatness. You will be 16 hours fasted by the time you wake so your neurons, natural HGH, and autophagy will be firing. Embrace the benefits of the healing effects and clarity fasting provides. You must be mentally strong as you are detoxing your body of sugar and there will be signs of hunger and cravings. Ignore them, be tough—your body has all the nutrition it needs to thrive. It's now a mental game. Are you strong enough?

Wake Up_____am   Sleep: 7+ hrs Optimized Sleep ☐ Deep_____REM_____

Weight_____lbs   Ketones_____mmol/L   Super Water ☐   Cognitive Coffee ☐ ☐

Red light* ☐   Ice Bath/Cold Shower ☐   Prayer/Meditation/Gratitude ☐

---

* Optional

DEEP WORK WINDOW 1: Be Brilliant. ☐

Morning Strength Workout: Adaptation					
Core: 4x15 (30-sec Rest)					
Incline Sit-up					x
Leg Raises					x
Strength Warmup 20-20-10 Compound Movement					

DAY 2   Thursday   (Continued)

Strength: Mogul Maker: 4x5 each exercise 4 sets x 5 reps (1-min rest between each exercise)					
Incline Bench					x
Deadlift					x
Overhead Press					x
Squat					x
Cognitive Walk/Sprint: 2:30 min walk, 30-sec Sprint, 10 rounds					☐
GPP: Farmer's Walk: 3 rounds - 30 secs on, 30 secs off					☐

Complete First 85oz Water (Morning)	☐

Post-Workout Recovery	
20 Minutes Sauna*	☐
20 Minutes of Morning Sun	☐
Cold Shower: Adaptation Protocol - 30 Seconds of Cold, 10 Seconds of Warm, 6 times through (rounds) for a total of 3 Min. Cold	☐

DEEP WORK WINDOW 2: Six to Eight 20-minute deep work window sprints, 10-min break, 10 Kettle bell swings and look outside in the distance 1 minute to adjust eyes.	☐

Adaptation Nutrition Plan: Do the .8 calculation to understand the exact amount of grass fed beef you must consume today. For the Adaptation Jumpstart, you will be splitting these foods into two meals initially. First Meal at 11am and the second meal at 2:50pm.	
Organic Bone Broth (2 cups)	☐
Grass-Fed Beef	g
2oz Liver or Organ Meat	☐
4 Eggs Men, 2 Eggs Women	☐
1 large Avocado	☐
40 Raspberries	☐

DAY 2   Thursday   (Continued)

20 Pecans or 23 Almonds	☐
50g of Raw Cheese	☐

Afternoon Recharge: HBOT*, Compression* or Cognitive Reset Rest: No more than 1 hour.	☐
Post Recharge: Cognitive Coffee & Collagen	☐

DEEP WORK WINDOW 3: Output ☐

Afternoon Nature Ideation Walk: 30 Min. – 1 hour. Think Big, Walk & Work, Dream Big. Call an Employee	☐

DEEP WORK WINDOW 4: Tactical ☐

Begin Optimized Nighttime Routine

Complete Second 85oz Water	☐
Blue Light Blocker Glasses	☐
No Water after 5 PM for uninterrupted sleep	☐
Sunset Ice Bath* or Cold Shower (2-3 hours before sleep)	☐
Red light*	☐
Prayer & Gratitude	☐
Create Optimal Sleep Environment: 65 degrees, No Cell Phone/EMF	☐

Completed Perfect Day	☐

Notes: How I win tomorrow.

DAY 3

Friday

> "If you can't fly then run, if you can't run then walk, if you can't walk then crawl, but whatever you do you have to keep moving forward."
>
> - Martin Luther King Jr.

You'll notice that on Day 3, your body will start going through changes as it shifts your primary fuel-burning system to help you get clean, optimized energy. You have been lifting the core lifts, getting outside, taking your cognitive walk/sprint. You may feel tired, and you may have cravings. **Stay. The. Course.** The other side of this is incredible and life-changing mental clarity and clean, limitless energy. Keep grinding. Fight through it.

Wake Up_____am   Sleep: 7+ hrs Optimized Sleep ☐   Deep_____REM_____

Weight_____lbs   Ketones___.___mmol/L   Super Water ☐   Cognitive Coffee ☕☕

Red light* ☐   Ice Bath/Cold Shower ☐   Prayer/Meditation/Gratitude ☐

* Optional

DEEP WORK WINDOW 1: Be Brilliant.   ☐

Morning Strength Workout: Adaptation					
Core: 4x15 (30-sec Rest)					
Incline Sit-up					x
Leg Raises					x
Strength Warmup 20-20-10 Compound Movement					
Strength: Mogul Maker: 4x5 each exercise 4 sets x 5 reps (1-min rest between each exercise)					
Incline Bench					x

DAY 3 Friday   (Continued)

Deadlift					x
Overhead Press					x
Squat					x
Cognitive Walk/Sprint: 2:30 min walk, 30-sec Sprint, 10 rounds					☐
GPP: Farmer's Walk: 3 rounds - 30 secs on, 30 secs off					☐

Complete First 85oz Water (Morning)	☐

Post-Workout Recovery	
20 Minutes Sauna*	☐
20 Minutes of Morning Sun	☐
Cold Shower: Adaptation Protocol - 30 Seconds of Cold, 10 Seconds of Warm, 6 times through (rounds) for a total of 3 Min. Cold	☐

DEEP WORK WINDOW 2: Six to Eight 20-minute deep work window sprints, 10-min break, 10 Kettle bell swings and look outside in the distance 1 minute to adjust eyes.	☐

Adaptation Nutrition Plan: Do the .8 calculation to understand the exact amount of grass fed beef you must consume today. For the Adaptation Jumpstart, you will be splitting these foods into two meals initially. First Meal at 11am and the second meal at 2:50pm.	
Organic Bone Broth (2 cups)	☐
Grass-Fed Beef	g
2oz Liver or Organ Meat	☐
4 Eggs Men, 2 Eggs Women	☐
1 large Avocado	☐
40 Raspberries	☐
20 Pecans or 23 Almonds	☐
50g of Raw Cheese	☐

DAY 3   Friday   (Continued)

Afternoon Recharge: HBOT*, Compression* or Cognitive Reset Rest: No more than 1 hour.	☐
Post Recharge: Cognitive Coffee & Collagen	☐

DEEP WORK WINDOW 3: Output ☐

Afternoon Nature Ideation Walk: 30 Min. – 1 hour. Think Big, Walk & Work, Dream Big. Call an Employee	☐

DEEP WORK WINDOW 4: Tactical ☐

Begin Optimized Nighttime Routine	
Complete Second 85oz Water	☐
Blue Light Blocker Glasses	☐
No Water after 5 PM for uninterrupted sleep	☐
Sunset Ice Bath* or Cold Shower (2-3 hours before sleep)	☐
Red light*	☐
Prayer & Gratitude	☐
Create Optimal Sleep Environment: 65 degrees, No Cell Phone/EMF	☐

Completed Perfect Day	☐

Notes: How I win tomorrow.

DAY 4 — Saturday

> "The man who moves a mountain begins by carrying away small stones."
> - Confucius

Today is going to be your most taxing day mentally, which is why we've scheduled it to fall on a Saturday. Your body is changing to your optimal fuel-burning system. You may feel dips in energy or feel tired, and you may experience cravings. Some people feel amazing because fat adaptation is very individual. Keep pushing through—once you get through these initial stages, you will feel like a new person physically and cognitively in just a few days. Your day is built around optimization and recovery. You are building your foundation every single day.

Wake Up _____ am   Sleep: 7+ hrs Optimized Sleep ☐   Deep _____ REM _____

Weight _____ lbs   Ketones ___.___ mmol/L   Super Water ☐   Cognitive Coffee ☕☕

Red light* ☐   Ice Bath/Cold Shower ☐   Prayer/Meditation/Gratitude ☐

* Optional

DEEP WORK WINDOW 1: Be Brilliant. ☐

Morning Strength Workout: Adaptation

Core: 4x15 (30-sec Rest)					
Incline Sit-up					x
Leg Raises					x
Strength Warmup 20-20-10 Compound Movement					
Strength: Mogul Maker: 4x5 each exercise 4 sets x 5 reps (1-min rest between each exercise)					
Incline Bench					x

DAY 4   Saturday   (Continued)

Deadlift					x
Overhead Press					x
Squat					x
Cognitive Walk/Sprint: 2:30 min walk, 30-sec Sprint, 10 rounds					☐
GPP: Farmer's Walk: 3 rounds - 30 secs on, 30 secs off					☐

Complete First 85oz Water (Morning)	☐

Post-Workout Recovery	
20 Minutes Sauna*	☐
20 Minutes of Morning Sun	☐
Cold Shower: Adaptation Protocol - 30 Seconds of Cold, 10 Seconds of Warm, 6 times through (rounds) for a total of 3 Min. Cold	☐

DEEP WORK WINDOW 2: Six to Eight 20-minute deep work window sprints, 10-min break, 10 Kettle bell swings and look outside in the distance 1 minute to adjust eyes.	☐

Adaptation Nutrition Plan: Do the .8 calculation to understand the exact amount of grass fed beef you must consume today. For the Adaptation Jumpstart, you will be splitting these foods into two meals initially. First Meal at 11am and the second meal at 2:50pm.	
Organic Bone Broth (2 cups)	☐
Grass-Fed Beef	g
2oz Liver or Organ Meat	☐
4 Eggs Men, 2 Eggs Women	☐
1 large Avocado	☐
40 Raspberries	☐
20 Pecans or 23 Almonds	☐
50g of Raw Cheese	☐

DAY 4   Saturday   (Continued)

Afternoon Recharge: HBOT*, Compression* or Cognitive Reset Rest: No more than 1 hour.	☐
Post Recharge: Cognitive Coffee & Collagen	☐

DEEP WORK WINDOW 3: Output	☐

Afternoon Nature Ideation Walk: 30 Min. – 1 hour. Think Big, Walk & Work, Dream Big. Call an Employee	☐

DEEP WORK WINDOW 4: Tactical	☐

Begin Optimized Nighttime Routine	
Complete Second 85oz Water	☐
Blue Light Blocker Glasses	☐
No Water after 5 PM for uninterrupted sleep	☐
Sunset Ice Bath* or Cold Shower (2-3 hours before sleep)	☐
Red light*	☐
Prayer & Gratitude	☐
Create Optimal Sleep Environment: 65 degrees, No Cell Phone/EMF	☐

Completed Perfect Day	☐

Notes: How I win tomorrow.

DAY 5

Sunday

> *"Discipline is choosing between what you want now and what you want most."*
> — Abraham Lincoln

On Day 5, you'll test your ketone levels in the morning. If you followed this plan exactly, you most likely would have entered ketosis. Each person has their own adaptation rate. Day 5 is when you'll start to feel better—your energy is starting to come alive with mental clarity, focus, and the beginning stages of boundless energy. Cravings will likely have disappeared. If you don't feel that way, keep going. It's coming. All our bodies adapt differently. Let's go crush a strong workout and let's keep on progressing with adding weight to our Foundational Mogul Maker Circuit.

Wake Up _____ am   Sleep: 7+ hrs Optimized Sleep ☐   Deep _____ REM _____

Weight _____ lbs   Ketones _____ mmol/L   Super Water ☐   Cognitive Coffee ☕☕

Red light* ☐   Ice Bath/Cold Shower ☐   Prayer/Meditation/Gratitude ☐

* Optional

DEEP WORK WINDOW 1: Be Brilliant.   ☐

Morning Strength Workout: Adaptation					
Core: 4x15 (30-sec Rest)					
Incline Sit-up					x
Leg Raises					x
Strength Warmup 20-20-10 Compound Movement					
Strength: Mogul Maker: 4x5 each exercise 4 sets x 5 reps (1-min rest between each exercise)					
Incline Bench					x

DAY 5   Sunday   (Continued)

Deadlift					x
Overhead Press					x
Squat					x
Cognitive Walk/Sprint: 2:30 min walk, 30-sec Sprint, 10 rounds					☐
GPP: Farmer's Walk: 3 rounds - 30 secs on, 30 secs off					☐

Complete First 85oz Water (Morning)	☐

Post-Workout Recovery	
20 Minutes Sauna*	☐
20 Minutes of Morning Sun	☐
Cold Shower: Adaptation Protocol - 30 Seconds of Cold, 10 Seconds of Warm, 6 times through (rounds) for a total of 3 Min. Cold	☐

DEEP WORK WINDOW 2: Six to Eight 20-minute deep work window sprints, 10-min break, 10 Kettle bell swings and look outside in the distance 1 minute to adjust eyes.	☐

Adaptation Nutrition Plan: Do the .8 calculation to understand the exact amount of grass fed beef you must consume today. For the Adaptation Jumpstart, you will be splitting these foods into two meals initially. First Meal at 11am and the second meal at 2:50pm.	
Organic Bone Broth (2 cups)	☐
Grass-Fed Beef	g
2oz Liver or Organ Meat	☐
4 Eggs Men, 2 Eggs Women	☐
1 large Avocado	☐
40 Raspberries	☐
20 Pecans or 23 Almonds	☐
50g of Raw Cheese	☐

DAY 5   Sunday   (Continued)

Afternoon Recharge: HBOT*, Compression* or Cognitive Reset Rest: No more than 1 hour.	☐
Post Recharge: Cognitive Coffee & Collagen	☐

DEEP WORK WINDOW 3: Output	☐

Afternoon Nature Ideation Walk: 30 Min. – 1 hour. Think Big, Walk & Work, Dream Big. Call an Employee	☐

DEEP WORK WINDOW 4: Tactical	☐

Begin Optimized Nighttime Routine	
Complete Second 85oz Water	☐
Blue Light Blocker Glasses	☐
No Water after 5 PM for uninterrupted sleep	☐
Sunset Ice Bath* or Cold Shower (2-3 hours before sleep)	☐
Red light*	☐
Prayer & Gratitude	☐
Create Optimal Sleep Environment: 65 degrees, No Cell Phone/EMF	☐

Completed Perfect Day	☐

Notes: How I win tomorrow.

DAY 6 — Monday

> "It always seems impossible until it's done."
> - Nelson Mandela

Test ketone levels. We are not wasting time getting your body to the full benefits of autophagy. Today you start a 23-hour fast. This might even be the first 23-hour fast you've ever done. It may seem daunting, but use your mental strength, stay the course, and your body will thank you. We will eat one meal, all the same amounts of food, in just one sitting. We are beginning OMAD. Longer term fasting will spike HGH, evoke cellular repair with autophagy, cognitive repair, and use your stored body fat for fuel. Trust your body to adjust to fasting—you need to know your body has the nutrients it needs from the previous day's food. You will consume your one meal at 12pm and you will not eat again until 12pm Tuesday. Let's start healing your body, mind, and drive cellular regeneration. This is the ultimate tool for repair and cognitive performance.

Wake Up_____am   Sleep: 7+ hrs Optimized Sleep ☐   Deep_____REM_____

Weight_____lbs   Ketones_____mmol/L   Super Water ☐   Cognitive Coffee ☐ ☐

Red light* ☐   Ice Bath/Cold Shower ☐   Prayer/Meditation/Gratitude ☐

Optional

DEEP WORK WINDOW 1: Be Brilliant. ☐

Morning Strength Workout: Adaptation					
Core: 4x15 (30-sec Rest)					
Incline Sit-up					x
Leg Raises					x
Strength Warmup 20-20-10 Compound Movement					

DAY 6   Monday   (Continued)

Strength: Mogul Maker: 4x5 each exercise 4 sets x 5 reps (1-min rest between each exercise)					
Incline Bench					x
Deadlift					x
Overhead Press					x
Squat					x
Cognitive Walk/Sprint: 2:30 min walk, 30-sec Sprint, 10 rounds					☐
GPP: Farmer's Walk: 3 rounds - 30 secs on, 30 secs off					☐

Complete First 85oz Water (Morning)	☐

Post-Workout Recovery	
20 Minutes Sauna*	☐
20 Minutes of Morning Sun	☐
Cold Shower: Adaptation Protocol - 30 Seconds of Cold, 10 Seconds of Warm, 6 times through (rounds) for a total of 3 Min. Cold	☐

DEEP WORK WINDOW 2: Six to Eight 20-minute deep work window sprints, 10-min break, 10 Kettle bell swings and look outside in the distance 1 minute to adjust eyes.	☐

Jump Start Nutrition Plan: Do the .8 calculation to understand exactly the amount of Wild-caught salmon you must consume today.	
Organic Bone Broth (2 cups)	☐
Wild-caught salmon	g
2oz Liver or Organ Meat	☐
4 Eggs Men, 2 Eggs Women	☐
1 large Avocado	☐
40 Raspberries	☐

DAY 6 Monday   (Continued)

20 Pecans or 23 Almonds	☐
50g of Raw Cheese	☐

Afternoon Recharge: HBOT*, Compression* or Cognitive Reset Rest: No more than 1 hour.	☐
Post Recharge: Cognitive Coffee & Collagen	☐

DEEP WORK WINDOW 3: Output	☐

Afternoon Nature Ideation Walk: 30 Min. – 1 hour. Think Big, Walk & Work, Dream Big. Call an Employee	☐

DEEP WORK WINDOW 4: Tactical	☐

Begin Optimized Nighttime Routine	
Complete Second 85oz Water	☐
Blue Light Blocker Glasses	☐
No Water after 5 PM for uninterrupted sleep	☐
Sunset Ice Bath* or Cold Shower (2-3 hours before sleep)	☐
Red light*	☐
Prayer & Gratitude	☐
Create Optimal Sleep Environment: 65 degrees, No Cell Phone/EMF	☐

Completed Perfect Day	☐

Notes: How I win tomorrow.

DAY 7

Tuesday

> *"The sun has not caught me in bed in fifty years."*
> - Thomas Jefferson

As you wake up this morning, your body is going to be in an amazing place of healing and strength through the 23-hour fast. Your body is healing, recharging, repairing, and your brain is thriving with regeneration of neurons. Not only are you completing your first 23-hour fast, but you are advancing your strength protocol. Embrace this early morning workout during which you are fasted for the longest. Your brain will be laser sharp, natural HGH is at peak levels, autophagy is accelerating cellular regeneration, and your stored body fat will be used as clean energy to perform your workout. You have fully introduced your body to the benefits of being in a state of ketosis—strength for body and mind. Let's go crush the Mogul Maker. **Your brain is on its way to being a supercomputer.**

Wake Up_____ am   Sleep: 7+ hrs Optimized Sleep ☐ Deep_____ REM_____

Weight_____ lbs   Ketones_____ mmol/L   Super Water ☐   Cognitive Coffee ☐ ☐

Red light* ☐   Ice Bath/Cold Shower ☐   Prayer/Meditation/Gratitude ☐

* Optional

DEEP WORK WINDOW 1: Be Brilliant.   ☐

Morning Strength Workout: Adaptation					
Core: 4x15 (30-sec Rest)						
Incline Sit-up					x
Leg Raises					x
Strength Warmup 20-20-10 Compound Movement						

DAY 7   Tuesday   (Continued)

Strength: Mogul Maker: 4x5 each exercise 4 sets x 5 reps (1-min rest between each exercise)					
Incline Bench					x
Deadlift					x
Overhead Press					x
Squat					x
Cognitive Walk/Sprint: 2:30 min walk, 30-Sec Sprint, 10 rounds					☐
GPP: Farmer's Walk: 3 rounds - 30 secs on, 30 secs off					☐

Complete First 85oz Water (Morning)	☐

Post-Workout Recovery	
20 Minutes Sauna*	☐
20 Minutes of Morning Sun	☐
Cold Shower: Adaptation Protocol - 30 Seconds of Cold, 10 Seconds of Warm, 6 times through (rounds) for a total of 3 Min. Cold	☐

DEEP WORK WINDOW 2: Six to Eight 20-minute deep work window sprints, 10-min break, 10 Kettle bell swings and look outside in the distance 1 minute to adjust eyes.	☐

Jump Start Nutrition Plan: Do the .8 calculation to understand exactly the amount of grass fed beef you must consume today.	
Organic Bone Broth (2 cups)	☐
Grass-Fed Beef	g
2oz Liver or Organ Meat	☐
4 Eggs Men, 2 Eggs Women	☐
1 large Avocado	☐
40 Raspberries	☐

DAY 7   Tuesday   (Continued)

20 Pecans or 23 Almonds	☐
50g of Raw Cheese	☐

Afternoon Recharge: HBOT*, Compression* or Cognitive Reset Rest: No more than 1 hour.	☐
Post Recharge: Cognitive Coffee & Collagen	☐

DEEP WORK WINDOW 3: Output ☐

Afternoon Nature Ideation Walk: 30 Min. – 1 hour. Think Big, Walk & Work, Dream Big. Call an Employee	☐

DEEP WORK WINDOW 4: Tactical ☐

Begin Optimized Nighttime Routine	
Complete Second 85oz Water	☐
Blue Light Blocker Glasses	☐
No Water after 5 PM for uninterrupted sleep	☐
Sunset Ice Bath* or Cold Shower (2-3 hours before sleep)	☐
Red light*	☐
Prayer & Gratitude	☐
Create Optimal Sleep Environment: 65 degrees, No Cell Phone/EMF	☐

Completed Perfect Day	☐

Notes: How I win tomorrow.

DAY

Wednesday

"The distance between insanity and genius is measured only by success."
- Bruce Fierstein

Congratulations on blasting through the baseline of the Performance CEO Protocol—not an easy feat. This week, prepare to lift heavier, sprint faster, and work even harder. You know you can do it. You'll begin to you'll experience real, impactful change in your body evoking neurological change. Yes, we'll be turning up the physical intensity, but it is going to spark neuronal connections in your brain. Let's go spark neurogenesis, BNDF, and amplify autophagy which will start turning back the clock and build the optimal biological environment in which you will thrive. Today let's really push Incline Bench, Shoulder Press, and triceps—to build our strength both physically and mentally.

Wake Up_____am   Sleep: 7+ hrs Optimized Sleep ☐   Deep_____REM_____

Weight_____lbs   Ketones_____mmol/L   Super Water ☐   Cognitive Coffee ☐ ☐

Red light* ☐   Ice Bath/Cold Shower ☐   Prayer/Meditation/Gratitude ☐

* Optional

DEEP WORK WINDOW 1: Be Brilliant. ☐

Day 1 Workout					
Core: 30 rest between sets (6:20)	15 reps				
Incline Sit-up					
Leg Raises					
Strength Warmup 20-20-10 Compound Movement					
Strength: 5 sets x 5 reps (3-min rest)	5 reps				
Incline Bench Press					

DAY 8   Wednesday   (Continued)

Accessory: 4 sets x 6-8 reps (2-min rest)	6-8 reps				
Overhead Press					x
Volume: 4 sets x 10 reps of 4 exercises (30-sec rest)	10 reps				
Side Raises					x
Front Raises					x
Dips					x
Deltoid Flys					x
Burnout: 2 exercises x 50 reps each (Side Raises, Triceps Press downs)					☐
GPP: Farmer's Walk: 3 rounds - 30 secs on, 30 secs off					☐
Cognitive Walk/Sprint: 30 Minutes (HIIT Sprint) 2:30 walk, 30 Second Sprint 10 Rounds					☐

Complete First 85oz Water (Morning)	☐

Post-Workout Recovery	
20 Minutes Sauna*	☐
20 Minutes of Morning Sun	☐
Cold Shower: Adaptation Protocol - 30 Seconds of Cold, 10 Seconds of Warm, 6 times through (rounds) for a total of 3 Min. Cold	☐

DEEP WORK WINDOW 2: Six to Eight 20-minute deep work window sprints, 10-min break, 10 Kettle bell swings and look outside in the distance 1 minute to adjust eyes.	☐

Jump Start Nutrition Plan: Do the .8 calculation to understand exactly the amount of grass fed beef you must consume today.	
Organic Bone Broth (2 cups)	☐
Grass-Fed Beef	g
2oz Liver or Organ Meat	☐
4 Eggs Men, 2 Eggs Women	☐

DAY 8   Wednesday   (Continued)

1 large Avocado	☐
40 Raspberries	☐
20 Pecans or 23 Almonds	☐
50g of Raw Cheese	☐

| Afternoon Recharge: HBOT*, Compression* or Cognitive Reset Rest: No more than 1 hour. | ☐ |
| Post Recharge: Cognitive Coffee & Collagen | ☐ |

| **DEEP WORK WINDOW 3:** Output | ☐ |

| Afternoon Nature Ideation Walk: 30 Min. – 1 hour. Think Big, Walk & Work, Dream Big. Call an Employee | ☐ |

| **DEEP WORK WINDOW 4:** Tactical | ☐ |

Begin Optimized Nighttime Routine	
Complete Second 85oz Water	☐
Blue Light Blocker Glasses	☐
No Water after 5 PM for uninterrupted sleep	☐
Sunset Ice Bath* or Cold Shower (2-3 hours before sleep)	☐
Red light*	☐
Prayer & Gratitude	☐
Create Optimal Sleep Environment: 65 degrees, No Cell Phone/EMF	☐

| Completed Perfect Day | ☐ |

| **Notes: How I win tomorrow.** |

DAY 9 — Thursday

> "Success is the sum of small efforts, repeated day in and day out."
> - Robert Collier

Today you're going to focus on your explosiveness, power, and strength with a strong deadlift and back work. With the Strength segment of the workout, push through, be strong, and get in those five reps. You will record the weight used, and look to keep getting stronger every day, every week to be the strongest, leanest, driven person you can be. We will increase the weight of each workout to drive progressive overload with Strength and Accessory components of the strength protocol.

Wake Up _____ am   Sleep: 7+ hrs Optimized Sleep ☐   Deep _____ REM _____

Weight _____ lbs   Ketones _____ mmol/L   Super Water ☐   Cognitive Coffee ☕☕

Red light* ☐   Ice Bath/Cold Shower ☐   Prayer/Meditation/Gratitude ☐

* Optional

DEEP WORK WINDOW 1: Be Brilliant.   ☐

Day 2 Workout					
Core: 30 rest between sets (6:20)		15 reps			
Incline Sit-up					
Leg Raises					
Strength Warmup 20-20-10 Compound Movement					
Strength: 5 sets x 5 reps (3-min rest)		5 reps			
Dead Lift					
Accessory: 4 sets x 6-8 reps (2-min rest)		6-8 reps			
Row					x

DAY 9   Thursday   (Continued)

Volume: 4 sets x 10 reps of 4 exercises (30-sec rest)	10 reps				
Lat Pulldown/Pullup					x
Hammer Curl					x
Row					x
Individual Bicep Curl					x
Burnout: 2 exercises x 50 reps each (50 Rows, 50 Bicep Curls)					☐
GPP: 3 rounds - 30 sec on, 30 sec off: Sled Pulls					☐
Cognitive Walk/Sprint: 30 Minutes (HIIT Sprint) 2:30 walk, 30 Second Sprint 10 Rounds					☐

Complete First 85oz Water (Morning)	☐

Post-Workout Recovery

20 Minutes Sauna*	☐
20 Minutes of Morning Sun	☐
Cold Shower: Adaptation Protocol - 30 Seconds of Cold, 10 Seconds of Warm, 6 times through (rounds) for a total of 3 Min. Cold	☐

DEEP WORK WINDOW 2: Six to Eight 20-minute deep work window sprints, 10-min break, 10 Kettle bell swings and look outside in the distance 1 minute to adjust eyes.	☐

Jump Start Nutrition Plan: Do the .8 calculation to understand exactly the amount of grass fed beef you must consume today.	
Organic Bone Broth (2 cups)	☐
Grass-Fed Beef	g
2oz Liver or Organ Meat	☐
4 Eggs Men, 2 Eggs Women	☐
1 large Avocado	☐
40 Raspberries	☐

DAY 9   Thursday   (Continued)

20 Pecans or 23 Almonds	☐
50g of Raw Cheese	☐

Afternoon Recharge: HBOT*, Compression* or Cognitive Reset Rest: No more than 1 hour.	☐
Post Recharge: Cognitive Coffee & Collagen	☐

DEEP WORK WINDOW 3: Output ☐

Afternoon Nature Ideation Walk: 30 Min. – 1 hour. Think Big, Walk & Work, Dream Big. Call an Employee	☐

DEEP WORK WINDOW 4: Tactical ☐

Begin Optimized Nighttime Routine	
Complete Second 85oz Water	☐
Blue Light Blocker Glasses	☐
No Water after 5 PM for uninterrupted sleep	☐
Sunset Ice Bath* or Cold Shower (2-3 hours before sleep)	☐
Red light*	☐
Prayer & Gratitude	☐
Create Optimal Sleep Environment: 65 degrees, No Cell Phone/EMF	☐

Completed Perfect Day	☐

Notes: How I win tomorrow.

DAY 10 — Friday

> "Believe you can and you're halfway there."
> — Theodore Roosevelt

Let's build a strong foundation today with focus on your legs. Just as with yesterday's workout, focus on building strength and increasing weight in the Strength and Accessory components of the Strength Protocol. Don't you love the cognitive clarity that comes with your 23-hour daily fast? Let's crush those squats.

Wake Up _____ am   Sleep: 7+ hrs Optimized Sleep ☐   Deep _____ REM _____

Weight _____ lbs   Ketones _____ mmol/L   Super Water ☐   Cognitive Coffee ☐ ☐

Red light* ☐   Ice Bath/Cold Shower ☐   Prayer/Meditation/Gratitude ☐

Optional

DEEP WORK WINDOW 1: Be Brilliant. ☐

Day 3 Workout					
Core: 30 rest between sets (6:20)	15 reps				
Incline Sit-up					
Leg Raises					
Strength Warmup 20-20-10 Compound Movement					
Strength: 5 sets x 5 reps (3-min rest)	5 reps				
Squat					
Accessory: 4 sets x 6-8 reps (2-min rest)	6-8 reps				
Bulgarian Split Squats					
Volume: 4 sets x 10 reps of 4 exercises (30-sec rest)	10 reps				
Hip Thrusts					

DAY 10 Friday   (Continued)

Squat Jumps					
Calf Raises					
Bulgarian Split Squats					
Burnout: 2 exercises x 50 reps each (Air Squats, Calf Raises)					☐
GPP: 3 rounds - 30 sec on, 30 sec off: Sled Push					☐
Cognitive Walk/Sprint: 30 Minutes (HIIT Sprint) 2:30 walk, 30 Second Sprint 10 Rounds					☐

Complete First 85oz Water (Morning)	☐

Post-Workout Recovery	
20 Minutes Sauna*	☐
20 Minutes of Morning Sun	☐
Cold Shower: Adaptation Protocol - 30 Seconds of Cold, 10 Seconds of Warm, 6 times through (rounds) for a total of 3 Min. Cold	☐

DEEP WORK WINDOW 2: Six to Eight 20-minute deep work window sprints, 10-min break, 10 Kettle bell swings and look outside in the distance 1 minute to adjust eyes.	☐

Jump Start Nutrition Plan: Do the .8 calculation to understand exactly the amount of grass fed beef you must consume today.	
Organic Bone Broth (2 cups)	☐
Grass-Fed Beef	g
2oz Liver or Organ Meat	☐
4 Eggs Men, 2 Eggs Women	☐
1 large Avocado	☐
40 Raspberries	☐
20 Pecans or 23 Almonds	☐
50g of Raw Cheese	☐

DAY 10 Friday   (Continued)

Afternoon Recharge: HBOT*, Compression* or Cognitive Reset Rest: No more than 1 hour.	☐
Post Recharge: Cognitive Coffee & Collagen	☐

DEEP WORK WINDOW 3: Output	☐

Afternoon Nature Ideation Walk: 30 Min. – 1 hour. Think Big, Walk & Work, Dream Big. Call an Employee	☐

DEEP WORK WINDOW 4: Tactical	☐

Begin Optimized Nighttime Routine	
Complete Second 85oz Water	☐
Blue Light Blocker Glasses	☐
No Water after 5 PM for uninterrupted sleep	☐
Sunset Ice Bath* or Cold Shower (2-3 hours before sleep)	☐
Red light*	☐
Prayer & Gratitude	☐
Create Optimal Sleep Environment: 65 degrees, No Cell Phone/EMF	☐

Completed Perfect Day	☐

Notes: How I win tomorrow.

DAY 11

Saturday

> *"The early morning has gold in its mouth."*
> - Benjamin Franklin

Weekend work!!! Let's get after it with a strong Chest, Shoulders, and Triceps day. Now that your have your body operating like a fine-tuned machine, focus on all the modalities for recovery. Loss of sleep over the years, and then gaining all the sleep back is a process. You must refill your sleep cup while optimizing both recovery from your challenging workouts, as well as fasting for cognitive performance. Embrace the simplicity of your meals, and the convenience of not having to worry about what and when you need to eat. You are on nutritional autopilot and can focus on the things that really matter.

Wake Up_____am   Sleep: 7+ hrs Optimized Sleep ☐   Deep_____REM_____

Weight_____lbs   Ketones_____mmol/L   Super Water ☐   Cognitive Coffee ☕☕

Red light* ☐   Ice Bath/Cold Shower ☐   Prayer/Meditation/Gratitude ☐

---

* *Optional*

DEEP WORK WINDOW 1: Be Brilliant.   ☐

Day 1 Workout					
Core: 30 rest between sets (6:20)	15 reps				
Incline Sit-up					
Leg Raises					
Strength Warmup 20-20-10 Compound Movement					
Strength: 5 sets x 5 reps (3-min rest)	5 reps				
Incline Bench Press					
Accessory: 4 sets x 6-8 reps (2-min rest)	6-8 reps				
Overhead Press					x

DAY 11   Saturday   (Continued)

Volume: 4 sets x 10 reps of 4 exercises (30-sec rest)	10 reps				
Side Raises					x
Front Raises					x
Dips					x
Deltoid Flys					x
Burnout: 2 exercises x 50 reps each (Side Raises, Triceps Press downs)					☐
GPP: Farmer's Walk: 3 rounds - 30 secs on, 30 secs off					☐
Cognitive Walk/Sprint: 30 Minutes (HIIT Sprint) 2:30 walk, 30 Second Sprint 10 Rounds					☐

Complete First 85oz Water (Morning)	☐

Post-Workout Recovery	
20 Minutes Sauna*	☐
20 Minutes of Morning Sun	☐
Cold Shower: Adaptation Protocol - 30 Seconds of Cold, 10 Seconds of Warm, 6 times through (rounds) for a total of 3 Min. Cold	☐

DEEP WORK WINDOW 2: Six to Eight 20-minute deep work window sprints, 10-min break, 10 Kettle bell swings and look outside in the distance 1 minute to adjust eyes.	☐

Jump Start Nutrition Plan: Do the .8 calculation to understand exactly the amount of grass fed beef you must consume today.	
Organic Bone Broth (2 cups)	☐
Grass-Fed Beef	g
2oz Liver or Organ Meat	☐
4 Eggs Men, 2 Eggs Women	☐
1 large Avocado	☐

DAY 11 Saturday   (Continued)

40 Raspberries	☐
20 Pecans or 23 Almonds	☐
50g of Raw Cheese	☐

Afternoon Recharge: HBOT*, Compression* or Cognitive Reset Rest: No more than 1 hour.	☐
Post Recharge: Cognitive Coffee & Collagen	☐

DEEP WORK WINDOW 3: Output ☐

Afternoon Nature Ideation Walk: 30 Min. – 1 hour. Think Big, Walk & Work, Dream Big. Call an Employee	☐

DEEP WORK WINDOW 4: Tactical ☐

Begin Optimized Nighttime Routine

Complete Second 85oz Water	☐
Blue Light Blocker Glasses	☐
No Water after 5 PM for uninterrupted sleep	☐
Sunset Ice Bath* or Cold Shower (2-3 hours before sleep)	☐
Red light*	☐
Prayer & Gratitude	☐
Create Optimal Sleep Environment: 65 degrees, No Cell Phone/EMF	☐

Completed Perfect Day	☐

Notes: How I win tomorrow.

DAY 12 — Sunday

"Great things never come from comfort zones."
— Roy T. Bennett

You are putting in the work, and you are getting very close to completing the 15-Day Jumpstart. Keep your laser focus, enjoy the solitude of the early morning, master the ability to focus on your deep work windows, and weaponize your business output to do all the things you need to do. As it is Sunday, always take a moment to show appreciation that you have the ability to go chase your dreams and build the future you desire.

Wake Up _____ am   Sleep: 7+ hrs Optimized Sleep ☐   Deep _____ REM _____

Weight _____ lbs   Ketones _____ mmol/L   Super Water ☐   Cognitive Coffee ☐ ☐

Red light* ☐   Ice Bath/Cold Shower ☐   Prayer/Meditation/Gratitude ☐

* Optional

DEEP WORK WINDOW 1: Be Brilliant. ☐

Day 2 Workout					
Core: 30 rest between sets (6:20)	15 reps				
Incline Sit-up					
Leg Raises					
Strength Warmup 20-20-10 Compound Movement					
Strength: 5 sets x 5 reps (3-min rest)	5 reps				
Dead Lift					
Accessory: 4 sets x 6-8 reps (2-min rest)	6-8 reps				
Row					x

DAY 12 Sunday   (Continued)

Volume: 4 sets x 10 reps of 4 exercises (30-sec rest)	10 reps				
Lat Pulldown/Pullup					x
Hammer Curl					x
Row					x
Individual Bicep Curl					x
Burnout: 2 exercises x 50 reps each (50 Rows, 50 Bicep Curls)	☐				
GPP: 3 rounds - 30 sec on, 30 sec off: Sled Pulls	☐				
Cognitive Walk/Sprint: 30 Minutes (HIIT Sprint) 2:30 walk, 30 Second Sprint 10 Rounds	☐				

Complete First 85oz Water (Morning)	☐

Post-Workout Recovery	
20 Minutes Sauna*	☐
20 Minutes of Morning Sun	☐
Cold Shower: Adaptation Protocol - 30 Seconds of Cold, 10 Seconds of Warm, 6 times through (rounds) for a total of 3 Min. Cold	☐

DEEP WORK WINDOW 2: Six to Eight 20-minute deep work window sprints, 10-min break, 10 Kettle bell swings and look outside in the distance 1 minute to adjust eyes.	☐

Jump Start Nutrition Plan: Do the .8 calculation to understand exactly the amount of grass fed beef you must consume today.	
Organic Bone Broth (2 cups)	☐
Grass-Fed Beef	g
2oz Liver or Organ Meat	☐
4 Eggs Men, 2 Eggs Women	☐
1 large Avocado	☐

DAY 12 Sunday   (Continued)

40 Raspberries	☐
20 Pecans or 23 Almonds	☐
50g of Raw Cheese	☐

Afternoon Recharge: HBOT*, Compression* or Cognitive Reset Rest: No more than 1 hour.	☐
Post Recharge: Cognitive Coffee & Collagen	☐

DEEP WORK WINDOW 3: Output ☐

Afternoon Nature Ideation Walk: 30 Min. – 1 hour. Think Big, Walk & Work, Dream Big. Call an Employee	☐

DEEP WORK WINDOW 4: Tactical ☐

Begin Optimized Nighttime Routine

Complete Second 85oz Water	☐
Blue Light Blocker Glasses	☐
No Water after 5 PM for uninterrupted sleep	☐
Sunset Ice Bath* or Cold Shower (2-3 hours before sleep)	☐
Red light*	☐
Prayer & Gratitude	☐
Create Optimal Sleep Environment: 65 degrees, No Cell Phone/EMF	☐

Completed Perfect Day	☐

Notes: How I win tomorrow.

DAY 13 — Monday

> *"Opportunities are usually disguised as hard work, so most people don't recognize them."*
>
> — Ann Landers

Monday, the day of limitless possibilities. Utilize your ideation time today to really think big about your business, goals, where you need to be and how to get there. You want to leverage the full cognitive benefits of your early AM time, as by Day 13 you should be feeling unstoppable. Physically and cognitively. Let's go attack the week!

Wake Up _____ am   Sleep: 7+ hrs Optimized Sleep ☐   Deep _____ REM _____

Weight _____ lbs   Ketones _____ mmol/L   Super Water ☐   Cognitive Coffee ☕☕

Red light* ☐   Ice Bath/Cold Shower ☐   Prayer/Meditation/Gratitude ☐

* Optional

DEEP WORK WINDOW 1: Be Brilliant. ☐

Day 3 Workout					
Core: 30 rest between sets (6:20)	15 reps				
Incline Sit-up					
Leg Raises					
Strength Warmup 20-20-10 Compound Movement					
Strength: 5 sets x 5 reps (3-min rest)	5 reps				
Squat					
Accessory: 4 sets x 6-8 reps (2-min rest)	6-8 reps				
Bulgarian Split Squats					

DAY 13 Monday   (Continued)

Volume: 4 sets x 10 reps of 4 exercises (30-sec rest)	10 reps			
Hip Thrusts				
Squat Jumps				
Calf Raises				
Bulgarian Split Squats				
Burnout: 2 exercises x 50 reps each (Air Squats, Calf Raises)	☐			
GPP: 3 rounds - 30 sec on, 30 sec off: Sled Push	☐			
Cognitive Walk/Sprint: 30 Minutes (HIIT Sprint) 2:30 walk, 30 Second Sprint 10 Rounds	☐			

Complete First 85oz Water (Morning)	☐

Post-Workout Recovery	
20 Minutes Sauna*	☐
20 Minutes of Morning Sun	☐
Cold Shower: Adaptation Protocol - 30 Seconds of Cold, 10 Seconds of Warm, 6 times through (rounds) for a total of 3 Min. Cold	☐

DEEP WORK WINDOW 2: Six to Eight 20-minute deep work window sprints, 10-min break, 10 Kettle bell swings and look outside in the distance 1 minute to adjust eyes.	☐

Jump Start Nutrition Plan: Do the .8 calculation to understand exactly the amount of Wild-caught salmon you must consume today.	
Organic Bone Broth (2 cups)	☐
Wild-caught salmon	g
2oz Liver or Organ Meat	☐
4 Eggs Men, 2 Eggs Women	☐
1 large Avocado	☐

DAY 13 Monday   (Continued)

40 Raspberries	☐
20 Pecans or 23 Almonds	☐
50g of Raw Cheese	☐

Afternoon Recharge: HBOT*, Compression* or Cognitive Reset Rest: No more than 1 hour.	☐
Post Recharge: Cognitive Coffee & Collagen	☐

DEEP WORK WINDOW 3: Output ☐

Afternoon Nature Ideation Walk: 30 Min. – 1 hour. Think Big, Walk & Work, Dream Big. Call an Employee	☐

DEEP WORK WINDOW 4: Tactical ☐

Begin Optimized Nighttime Routine

Complete Second 85oz Water	☐
Blue Light Blocker Glasses	☐
No Water after 5 PM for uninterrupted sleep	☐
Sunset Ice Bath* or Cold Shower (2-3 hours before sleep)	☐
Red light*	☐
Prayer & Gratitude	☐
Create Optimal Sleep Environment: 65 degrees, No Cell Phone/EMF	☐

Completed Perfect Day	☐

Notes: How I win tomorrow.

DAY 14   **Tuesday**

> "Risk-taking is the cornerstone of empires."
> - Estée Lauder

You are on the next level. From building strength, mastering time management, and fostering resilience, to cultivating innovative thinking and honing your communication skills – you've tackled each day with unwavering enthusiasm, pushing yourself beyond limits you once thought impossible.

In this final stretch of the 15-Day Jumpstart, stay focused, stay determined, and stay true to the passion that led you here. Believe in yourself and your unique ability to make a difference. You are armed with the skills and mindset of a true entrepreneur – adaptable, resourceful, and ready to take on whatever comes your way today.

Wake Up_____am   Sleep: 7+ hrs Optimized Sleep ☐   Deep_____ REM_____

Weight_____lbs   Ketones_____mmol/L   Super Water ☐   Cognitive Coffee ☐☐

Red light* ☐   Ice Bath/Cold Shower ☐   Prayer/Meditation/Gratitude ☐

* Optional

DEEP WORK WINDOW 1: Be Brilliant.   ☐

Day 1 Workout					
Core: 30 rest between sets (6:20)	15 reps				
Incline Sit-up					
Leg Raises					
Strength Warmup 20-20-10 Compound Movement					
Strength: 5 sets x 5 reps (3-min rest)	5 reps				
Incline Bench Press					

DAY 14 Tuesday   (Continued)

Accessory: 4 sets x 6-8 reps (2-min rest)	6-8 reps				
Overhead Press					x
Volume: 4 sets x 10 reps of 4 exercises (30-sec rest)	10 reps				
Side Raises					x
Front Raises					x
Dips					x
Deltoid Flys					x
Burnout: 2 exercises x 50 reps each (Side Raises, Triceps Press downs)	☐				
GPP: Farmer's Walk: 3 rounds - 30 secs on, 30 secs off	☐				
Cognitive Walk/Sprint: 30 Minutes (HIIT Sprint) 2:30 walk, 30 Second Sprint 10 Rounds	☐				

Complete First 85oz Water (Morning)	☐

Post-Workout Recovery

20 Minutes Sauna*	☐
20 Minutes of Morning Sun	☐
Cold Shower: Adaptation Protocol - 30 Seconds of Cold, 10 Seconds of Warm, 6 times through (rounds) for a total of 3 Min. Cold	☐

DEEP WORK WINDOW 2: Six to Eight 20-minute deep work window sprints, 10-min break, 10 Kettle bell swings and look outside in the distance 1 minute to adjust eyes.   ☐

Jump Start Nutrition Plan: Do the .8 calculation to understand exactly the amount of grass fed beef you must consume today.	
Organic Bone Broth (2 cups)	☐
Grass-Fed Beef	g
2oz Liver or Organ Meat	☐
4 Eggs Men, 2 Eggs Women	☐

DAY 14 Tuesday   (Continued)

1 large Avocado	☐
40 Raspberries	☐
20 Pecans or 23 Almonds	☐
50g of Raw Cheese	☐

Afternoon Recharge: HBOT*, Compression* or Cognitive Reset Rest: No more than 1 hour.	☐
Post Recharge: Cognitive Coffee & Collagen	☐

DEEP WORK WINDOW 3: Output ☐

Afternoon Nature Ideation Walk: 30 Min. – 1 hour. Think Big, Walk & Work, Dream Big. Call an Employee	☐

DEEP WORK WINDOW 4: Tactical ☐

Begin Optimized Nighttime Routine

Complete Second 85oz Water	☐
Blue Light Blocker Glasses	☐
No Water after 5 PM for uninterrupted sleep	☐
Sunset Ice Bath* or Cold Shower (2-3 hours before sleep)	☐
Red light*	☐
Prayer & Gratitude	☐
Create Optimal Sleep Environment: 65 degrees, No Cell Phone/EMF	☐

Completed Perfect Day	☐

Notes: How I win tomorrow.

DAY 15 — Wednesday

> *"If you want something new, you have to stop doing something old."*
>
> - Peter F. Drucker

You've crushed of the first 15 days of the **Performance CEO Protocol**. Congratulations! By completing the 15-Day Jumpstart, you've affirmed—not to me but to yourself—how committed you are to the **Performance CEO Protocol**. Keep the momentum going. It's time to move the next phase of optimization and follow the next 30 days of the Performance CEO Protocol exactly. Focus on today and close out the 15 days with the best workout so far. Go push your deadlifts with power. **The Performance CEO needs to get smarter and stronger every day.**

Wake Up_____am Sleep: 7+ hrs Optimized Sleep ☐ Deep_____REM_____

Weight_____lbs Ketones_____mmol/L Super Water ☐ Cognitive Coffee ☕☕

Red light* ☐   Ice Bath/Cold Shower ☐   Prayer/Meditation/Gratitude ☐

* Optional

DEEP WORK WINDOW 1: Be Brilliant. ☐

Day 2 Workout					
Core: 30 rest between sets (6:20)	15 reps				
Incline Sit-up					
Leg Raises					
Strength Warmup 20-20-10 Compound Movement					
Strength: 5 sets x 5 reps (3-min rest)	5 reps				
Dead Lift					

DAY 15 Wednesday   (Continued)

Accessory: 4 sets x 6-8 reps (2-min rest)	6-8 reps				
Row					x
Volume: 4 sets x 10 reps of 4 exercises (30-sec rest)	10 reps				
Lat Pulldown/Pullup					x
Hammer Curl					x
Row					x
Individual Bicep Curl					x
Burnout: 2 exercises x 50 reps each (50 Rows, 50 Bicep Curls)					☐
GPP: 3 rounds - 30 sec on, 30 sec off: Sled Pulls					☐
Cognitive Walk/Sprint: 30 Minutes (HIIT Sprint) 2:30 walk, 30 Second Sprint 10 Rounds					☐

Complete First 85oz Water (Morning)	☐

Post-Workout Recovery	
20 Minutes Sauna*	☐
20 Minutes of Morning Sun	☐
Cold Shower: Adaptation Protocol - 30 Seconds of Cold, 10 Seconds of Warm, 6 times through (rounds) for a total of 3 Min. Cold	☐

DEEP WORK WINDOW 2: Six to Eight 20-minute deep work window sprints, 10-min break, 10 Kettle bell swings and look outside in the distance 1 minute to adjust eyes.	☐

Jump Start Nutrition Plan: Do the .8 calculation to understand exactly the amount of grass fed beef you must consume today.	
Organic Bone Broth (2 cups)	☐
Grass-Fed Beef	g
2oz Liver or Organ Meat	☐
4 Eggs Men, 2 Eggs Women	☐

DAY 15 Wednesday   (Continued)

1 large Avocado	☐
40 Raspberries	☐
20 Pecans or 23 Almonds	☐
50g of Raw Cheese	☐

Afternoon Recharge: HBOT*, Compression* or Cognitive Reset Rest: No more than 1 hour.	☐
Post Recharge: Cognitive Coffee & Collagen	☐

DEEP WORK WINDOW 3: Output ☐

Afternoon Nature Ideation Walk: 30 Min. – 1 hour. Think Big, Walk & Work, Dream Big. Call an Employee	☐

DEEP WORK WINDOW 4: Tactical ☐

Begin Optimized Nighttime Routine	
Complete Second 85oz Water	☐
Blue Light Blocker Glasses	☐
No Water after 5 PM for uninterrupted sleep	☐
Sunset Ice Bath* or Cold Shower (2-3 hours before sleep)	☐
Red light*	☐
Prayer & Gratitude	☐
Create Optimal Sleep Environment: 65 degrees, No Cell Phone/EMF	☐

Completed Perfect Day	☐

Notes: How I win tomorrow.

30-DAY EXTREME COGNITIVE PROTOCOL

Congratulations on completing the Fifteen-Day Jumpstart! Your body and brain are ready for more after this adaptive period to ignite your cognitive and biological capabilities. As you embark on the next 30 Days, get ready to take the extraordinary journey of peak performance and cognitive mastery. In this phase, we delve deeper into the intricacies of the Extreme Cognitive Protocol, harnessing longer fasting, strength training, and resiliency-building recovery modalities to unlock the full potential of your mind and body.

During these next 30 days, you will embrace the power of fasting like never before, adopting a bold approach of 23-hour fasts daily, supplemented 48-hour fasting periods each week, and culminating with 72-hour fasting intervals each month. By nourishing your body with bioavailable cognitive foods during your one daily meal, you will propel your brain to new heights of acuity, focus, and creativity.

In tandem with fasting, we will accelerate your strength training journey, following a linear progression that ensures constant growth and physical empowerment. Each workout will lead you to new levels of strength and energy, aligning your physical prowess with your cognitive brilliance.

The next 30 Days will emphasize the importance of exact resiliency-building recovery modalities. Strategic practices such as twice daily ice baths, mindful rest, and targeted sleep optimization will become integral to your daily routine, enabling you to recharge, rejuvenate, and be at your absolute best cognitively as an entrepreneur. It's time to take it to the next level and complete the 45-day Cognitive Protocol.

Attack this next 30 Days with unwavering determination and a commitment to unlocking your true potential. The next 30 days hold the promise of unparalleled growth, fortitude, and innovation. Are you ready to rise to the occasion, make your mark as a visionary leader, and lead the future of optimized entrepreneurs?

The journey awaits—get ready to unleash the Performance CEO within.

30-DAY EXTREME COGNITIVE PROTOCOL

DAY 16 — Thursday

> "The only way to discover the limits of the possible is to go beyond them into the impossible."
>
> - Arthur C. Clarke

Wake Up _____ am   Sleep: 7+ hrs Optimized Sleep ☐   Deep _____ REM _____

Weight _____ lbs   Ketones _____ mmol/L   Super Water ☐   Cognitive Coffee ☐ ☐

Red light* ☐   Ice Bath/Cold Shower ☐   Prayer/Meditation/Gratitude ☐

* Optional

DEEP WORK WINDOW 1: Be Brilliant. ☐

Day 3 Workout					
Core: 30 rest between sets (6:20)	15 reps				
Incline Sit-up					
Leg Raises					
Strength Warmup 20-20-10 Compound Movement					
Strength: 5 sets x 5 reps (3-min rest)	5 reps				
Squat					
Accessory: 4 sets x 6-8 reps (2-min rest)	6-8 reps				
Bulgarian Split Squats					
Volume: 4 sets x 10 reps of 4 exercises (30-sec rest)	10 reps				
Hip Thrusts					
Squat Jumps					
Calf Raises					
Bulgarian Split Squats					

DAY 16 Thursday (Continued)

Burnout: 2 exercises x 50 reps each (Air Squats, Calf Raises)	☐
GPP: 3 rounds - 30 sec on, 30 sec off: Sled Push	☐
Cognitive Walk/Sprint: 30 Minutes (HIIT Sprint) 2:30 walk, 30 Second Sprint 10 Rounds	☐

Complete First 85oz Water (Morning)	☐

Post-Workout Recovery	
20 Minutes Sauna*	☐
20 Minutes of Morning Sun	☐
Cold Shower	☐

DEEP WORK WINDOW 2: Six to Eight 20-minute deep work window sprints, 10-min break, 10 Kettle bell swings and look outside in the distance 1 minute to adjust eyes.	☐

Jump Start Nutrition Plan: Do the .8 calculation to understand exactly the amount of grass fed beef you must consume today.	
Organic Bone Broth (2 cups)	☐
Grass-Fed Beef	g
2oz Liver or Organ Meat	☐
4 Eggs Men, 2 Eggs Women	☐
1 large Avocado	☐
40 Raspberries	☐
20 Pecans or 23 Almonds	☐
50g of Raw Cheese	☐

Afternoon Recharge: HBOT*, Compression* or Cognitive Reset Rest: No more than 1 hour.	☐
Post Recharge: Cognitive Coffee & Collagen	☐

DAY 16 Thursday   (Continued)

DEEP WORK WINDOW 3: Output	☐

Afternoon Nature Ideation Walk: 30 Min. – 1 hour. Think Big, Walk & Work, Dream Big. Call an Employee	☐

DEEP WORK WINDOW 4: Tactical	☐

Begin Optimized Nighttime Routine	
Complete Second 85oz Water	☐
Blue Light Blocker Glasses	☐
No Water after 5 PM for uninterrupted sleep	☐
Sunset Ice Bath* or Cold Shower (2-3 hours before sleep)	☐
Red light*	☐
Prayer & Gratitude	☐
Create Optimal Sleep Environment: 65 degrees, No Cell Phone/EMF	☐

Completed Perfect Day	☐

Notes: How I win tomorrow.

DAY 17 — Friday

> "Dreams don't work unless you do."
> - John C. Maxwell

Wake Up _____ am   Sleep: 7+ hrs Optimized Sleep ☐   Deep _____ REM _____

Weight _____ lbs   Ketones _____ mmol/L   Super Water ☐   Cognitive Coffee ☐☐

Red light* ☐   Ice Bath/Cold Shower ☐   Prayer/Meditation/Gratitude ☐

Optional

DEEP WORK WINDOW 1: Be Brilliant. ☐

Day 1 Workout					
Core: 30 rest between sets (6:20)	15 reps				
Incline Sit-up					
Leg Raises					
Strength Warmup 20-20-10 Compound Movement					
Strength: 5 sets x 5 reps (3-min rest)	5 reps				
Incline Bench Press					
Accessory: 4 sets x 6-8 reps (2-min rest)	6-8 reps				
Overhead Press					x
Volume: 4 sets x 10 reps of 4 exercises (30-sec rest)	10 reps				
Side Raises					x
Front Raises					x
Dips					x
Deltoid Flys					x
Burnout: 2 exercises x 50 reps each (Side Raises, Triceps Press downs)					☐

DAY 17 Friday   (Continued)

GPP: Farmer's Walk: 3 rounds - 30 secs on, 30 secs off	☐
Cognitive Walk/Sprint: 30 Minutes (HIIT Sprint) 2:30 walk, 30 Second Sprint 10 Rounds	☐

Complete First 85oz Water (Morning)	☐

Post-Workout Recovery	
20 Minutes Sauna*	☐
20 Minutes of Morning Sun	☐
Cold Shower	☐

DEEP WORK WINDOW 2: Six to Eight 20-minute deep work window sprints, 10-min break, 10 Kettle bell swings and look outside in the distance 1 minute to adjust eyes.	☐

Jump Start Nutrition Plan: Do the .8 calculation to understand exactly the amount of grass fed beef you must consume today.	
Organic Bone Broth (2 cups)	☐
Grass-Fed Beef	g
2oz Liver or Organ Meat	☐
4 Eggs Men, 2 Eggs Women	☐
1 large Avocado	☐
40 Raspberries	☐
20 Pecans or 23 Almonds	☐
50g of Raw Cheese	☐

Afternoon Recharge: HBOT*, Compression* or Cognitive Reset Rest: No more than 1 hour.	☐
Post Recharge: Cognitive Coffee & Collagen	☐

DAY 17 Friday   (Continued)

DEEP WORK WINDOW 3: Output ☐

Afternoon Nature Ideation Walk: 30 Min. – 1 hour. Think Big, Walk & Work, Dream Big. Call an Employee ☐

DEEP WORK WINDOW 4: Tactical ☐

Begin Optimized Nighttime Routine

Complete Second 85oz Water	☐
Blue Light Blocker Glasses	☐
No Water after 5 PM for uninterrupted sleep	☐
Sunset Ice Bath* or Cold Shower (2-3 hours before sleep)	☐
Red light*	☐
Prayer & Gratitude	☐
Create Optimal Sleep Environment: 65 degrees, No Cell Phone/EMF	☐

Completed Perfect Day ☐

Notes: How I win tomorrow.

DAY 18 — Saturday

> "The greatest leader is not necessarily the one who does the greatest things. He is the one that gets the people to do the greatest things."
>
> - Ronald Reagan

Wake Up_____am Sleep: 7+ hrs Optimized Sleep ☐ Deep_____REM_____

Weight_____lbs Ketones_____mmol/L Super Water ☐ Cognitive Coffee ☐ ☐

Red light* ☐   Ice Bath/Cold Shower ☐   Prayer/Meditation/Gratitude ☐

* Optional

DEEP WORK WINDOW 1: Be Brilliant. ☐

Day 2 Workout					
Core: 30 rest between sets (6:20)	15 reps				
Incline Sit-up					
Leg Raises					
Strength Warmup 20-20-10 Compound Movement					
Strength: 5 sets x 5 reps (3-min rest)	5 reps				
Dead Lift					
Accessory: 4 sets x 6-8 reps (2-min rest)	6-8 reps				
Row					x
Volume: 4 sets x 10 reps of 4 exercises (30-sec rest)	10 reps				
Lat Pulldown/Pullup					x
Hammer Curl					x
Row					x

DAY 18 Saturday   (Continued)

Individual Bicep Curl					x
Burnout: 2 exercises x 50 reps each (50 Rows, 50 Bicep Curls)					☐
GPP: 3 rounds - 30 sec on, 30 sec off: Sled Pulls					☐
Cognitive Walk/Sprint: 30 Minutes (HIIT Sprint) 2:30 walk, 30 Second Sprint 10 Rounds					☐

Complete First 85oz Water (Morning)	☐

Post-Workout Recovery	
20 Minutes Sauna*	☐
20 Minutes of Morning Sun	☐
Cold Shower	☐

DEEP WORK WINDOW 2: Six to Eight 20-minute deep work window sprints, 10-min break, 10 Kettle bell swings and look outside in the distance 1 minute to adjust eyes.	☐

Jump Start Nutrition Plan: Do the .8 calculation to understand exactly the amount of grass fed beef you must consume today.	
Organic Bone Broth (2 cups)	☐
Grass-Fed Beef	g
2oz Liver or Organ Meat	☐
4 Eggs Men, 2 Eggs Women	☐
1 large Avocado	☐
40 Raspberries	☐
20 Pecans or 23 Almonds	☐
50g of Raw Cheese	☐

Afternoon Recharge: HBOT*, Compression* or Cognitive Reset Rest: No more than 1 hour.	☐
Post Recharge: Cognitive Coffee & Collagen	☐

DAY 18 Saturday   (Continued)

DEEP WORK WINDOW 3: Output ☐

Afternoon Nature Ideation Walk: 30 Min. – 1 hour. Think Big, Walk & Work, Dream Big. Call an Employee ☐

DEEP WORK WINDOW 4: Tactical ☐

Begin Optimized Nighttime Routine	
Complete Second 85oz Water	☐
Blue Light Blocker Glasses	☐
No Water after 5 PM for uninterrupted sleep	☐
Sunset Ice Bath* or Cold Shower (2-3 hours before sleep)	☐
Red light*	☐
Prayer & Gratitude	☐
Create Optimal Sleep Environment: 65 degrees, No Cell Phone/EMF	☐

Completed Perfect Day	☐

Notes: How I win tomorrow.

DAY 19 — Sunday

> "The entrepreneur is essentially a visualizer and actualizer... He can visualize something, and when he visualizes it, he sees exactly how to make it happen."
>
> - Robert L. Schwartz

Wake Up _____ am   Sleep: 7+ hrs Optimized Sleep ☐   Deep _____ REM _____

Weight _____ lbs   Ketones _____ mmol/L   Super Water ☐   Cognitive Coffee

Red light* ☐   Ice Bath/Cold Shower ☐   Prayer/Meditation/Gratitude ☐

Optional

DEEP WORK WINDOW 1: Be Brilliant. ☐

Day 3 Workout

Core: 30 rest between sets (6:20)	15 reps			
Incline Sit-up				
Leg Raises				
Strength Warmup 20-20-10 Compound Movement				
Strength: 5 sets x 5 reps (3-min rest)	5 reps			
Squat				
Accessory: 4 sets x 6-8 reps (2-min rest)	6-8 reps			
Bulgarian Split Squats				
Volume: 4 sets x 10 reps of 4 exercises (30-sec rest)	10 reps			
Hip Thrusts				
Squat Jumps				

DAY 19 Sunday (Continued)

Calf Raises						
Bulgarian Split Squats						
Burnout: 2 exercises x 50 reps each (Air Squats, Calf Raises)	☐
GPP: 3 rounds - 30 sec on, 30 sec off: Sled Push	☐
Cognitive Walk/Sprint: 30 Minutes (HIIT Sprint) 2:30 walk, 30 Second Sprint 10 Rounds	☐

Complete First 85oz Water (Morning)	☐

Post-Workout Recovery	
20 Minutes Sauna*	☐
20 Minutes of Morning Sun	☐
Cold Shower	☐

DEEP WORK WINDOW 2: Six to Eight 20-minute deep work window sprints, 10-min break, 10 Kettle bell swings and look outside in the distance 1 minute to adjust eyes.	☐

Jump Start Nutrition Plan: Do the .8 calculation to understand exactly the amount of grass fed beef you must consume today.	
Organic Bone Broth (2 cups)	☐
Grass-Fed Beef	g
2oz Liver or Organ Meat	☐
4 Eggs Men, 2 Eggs Women	☐
1 large Avocado	☐
40 Raspberries	☐
20 Pecans or 23 Almonds	☐
50g of Raw Cheese	☐

Afternoon Recharge: HBOT*, Compression* or Cognitive Reset Rest: No more than 1 hour.	☐

DAY 19 Sunday   (Continued)

| Post Recharge: Cognitive Coffee & Collagen | ☐ |

| **DEEP WORK WINDOW 3:** Output | ☐ |

| Afternoon Nature Ideation Walk: 30 Min. – 1 hour. Think Big, Walk & Work, Dream Big. Call an Employee | ☐ |

| **DEEP WORK WINDOW 4:** Tactical | ☐ |

Begin Optimized Nighttime Routine	
Complete Second 85oz Water	☐
Blue Light Blocker Glasses	☐
No Water after 5 PM for uninterrupted sleep	☐
Sunset Ice Bath* or Cold Shower (2-3 hours before sleep)	☐
Red light*	☐
Prayer & Gratitude	☐
Create Optimal Sleep Environment: 65 degrees, No Cell Phone/EMF	☐

| Completed Perfect Day | ☐ |

Notes: How I win tomorrow.

DAY 20 — Monday

> "The true measure of the value of any business leader is performance."
>
> - Brian Tracy

Wake Up _____ am   Sleep: 7+ hrs Optimized Sleep ☐   Deep _____ REM _____

Weight _____ lbs   Ketones _____ mmol/L   Super Water ☐   Cognitive Coffee ☐ ☐

Red light* ☐   Ice Bath/Cold Shower ☐   Prayer/Meditation/Gratitude ☐

* Optional

DEEP WORK WINDOW 1: Be Brilliant. ☐

Day 1 Workout					
Core: 30 rest between sets (6:20)	15 reps				
Incline Sit-up					
Leg Raises					
Strength Warmup 20-20-10 Compound Movement					
Strength: 5 sets x 5 reps (3-min rest)	5 reps				
Incline Bench Press					
Accessory: 4 sets x 6-8 reps (2-min rest)	6-8 reps				
Overhead Press					x
Volume: 4 sets x 10 reps of 4 exercises (30-sec rest)	10 reps				
Side Raises					x
Front Raises					x
Dips					x
Deltoid Flys					x

DAY 20 Monday   (Continued)

Burnout: 2 exercises x 50 reps each (Side Raises, Triceps Press downs)	☐
GPP: Farmer's Walk: 3 rounds - 30 secs on, 30 secs off	☐
Cognitive Walk/Sprint: 30 Minutes (HIIT Sprint) 2:30 walk, 30 Second Sprint 10 Rounds	☐

Complete First 85oz Water (Morning)	☐

Post-Workout Recovery	
20 Minutes Sauna*	☐
20 Minutes of Morning Sun	☐
Cold Shower	☐

DEEP WORK WINDOW 2: Six to Eight 20-minute deep work window sprints, 10-min break, 10 Kettle bell swings and look outside in the distance 1 minute to adjust eyes.	☐

Jump Start Nutrition Plan: Do the .8 calculation to understand exactly the amount of Wild-caught salmon you must consume today.	
Organic Bone Broth (2 cups)	☐
Wild-caught salmon	g
2oz Liver or Organ Meat	☐
4 Eggs Men, 2 Eggs Women	☐
1 large Avocado	☐
40 Raspberries	☐
20 Pecans or 23 Almonds	☐
50g of Raw Cheese	☐

Afternoon Recharge: HBOT*, Compression* or Cognitive Reset Rest: No more than 1 hour.	☐
Post Recharge: Cognitive Coffee & Collagen	☐

DAY 20 Monday   (Continued)

DEEP WORK WINDOW 3: Output	☐
Afternoon Nature Ideation Walk: 30 Min. – 1 hour. Think Big, Walk & Work, Dream Big. Call an Employee	☐

DEEP WORK WINDOW 4: Tactical	☐

Begin Optimized Nighttime Routine	
Complete Second 85oz Water	☐
Blue Light Blocker Glasses	☐
No Water after 5 PM for uninterrupted sleep	☐
Sunset Ice Bath* or Cold Shower (2-3 hours before sleep)	☐
Red light*	☐
Prayer & Gratitude	☐
Create Optimal Sleep Environment: 65 degrees, No Cell Phone/EMF	☐

Completed Perfect Day	☐

Notes: How I win tomorrow.

DAY 21 — Tuesday

> "The best time to plant a tree was 20 years ago. The second-best time is now."
>
> - Chinese Proverb

Wake Up_____am   Sleep: 7+ hrs Optimized Sleep ☐   Deep_____REM_____

Weight_____lbs   Ketones_____mmol/L   Super Water ☐   Cognitive Coffee ☐ ☐

Red light* ☐   Ice Bath/Cold Shower ☐   Prayer/Meditation/Gratitude ☐

* Optional

DEEP WORK WINDOW 1: Be Brilliant. ☐

Day 2 Workout					
Core: 30 rest between sets (6:20)	15 reps				
Incline Sit-up					
Leg Raises					
Strength Warmup 20-20-10 Compound Movement					
Strength: 5 sets x 5 reps (3-min rest)	5 reps				
Dead Lift					
Accessory: 4 sets x 6-8 reps (2-min rest)	6-8 reps				
Row					x
Volume: 4 sets x 10 reps of 4 exercises (30-sec rest)	10 reps				
Lat Pulldown/Pullup					x
Hammer Curl					x
Row					x
Individual Bicep Curl					x

DAY 21 Tuesday   (Continued)

Burnout: 2 exercises x 50 reps each (50 Rows, 50 Bicep Curls)	☐
GPP: 3 rounds - 30 sec on, 30 sec off: Sled Pulls	☐
Cognitive Walk/Sprint: 30 Minutes (HIIT Sprint) 2:30 walk, 30 Second Sprint 10 Rounds	☐

Week 4:

Complete First 85oz Water (Morning)	☐

Post-Workout Recovery	
20 Minutes Sauna*	☐
20 Minutes of Morning Sun	☐
Cold Shower	☐

DEEP WORK WINDOW 2: Six to Eight 20-minute deep work window sprints, 10-min break, 10 Kettle bell swings and look outside in the distance 1 minute to adjust eyes.	☐

Jump Start Nutrition Plan: Do the .8 calculation to understand exactly the amount of grass fed beef you must consume today.	
Organic Bone Broth (2 cups)	☐
Grass-Fed Beef	g
2oz Liver or Organ Meat	☐
4 Eggs Men, 2 Eggs Women	☐
1 large Avocado	☐
40 Raspberries	☐
20 Pecans or 23 Almonds	☐
50g of Raw Cheese	☐

Afternoon Recharge: HBOT*, Compression* or Cognitive Reset Rest: No more than 1 hour.	☐

DAY 21 Tuesday   (Continued)

| Post Recharge: Cognitive Coffee & Collagen | ☐ |

| **DEEP WORK WINDOW 3:** Output | ☐ |

| Afternoon Nature Ideation Walk: 30 Min. – 1 hour. Think Big, Walk & Work, Dream Big. Call an Employee | ☐ |

| **DEEP WORK WINDOW 4:** Tactical | ☐ |

Begin Optimized Nighttime Routine	
Complete Second 85oz Water	☐
Blue Light Blocker Glasses	☐
No Water after 5 PM for uninterrupted sleep	☐
Sunset Ice Bath* or Cold Shower (2-3 hours before sleep)	☐
Red light*	☐
Prayer & Gratitude	☐
Create Optimal Sleep Environment: 65 degrees, No Cell Phone/EMF	☐

| Completed Perfect Day | ☐ |

Notes: How I win tomorrow.

DAY 22 Wednesday

"Don't be afraid to give up the good to go for the great."
- John D. Rockefeller

Wake Up_____am Sleep: 7+ hrs Optimized Sleep ☐ Deep_____REM_____
Weight_____lbs Ketones_____mmol/L Super Water ☐ Cognitive Coffee ☐ ☐
Red light* ☐   Ice Bath/Cold Shower ☐   Prayer/Meditation/Gratitude ☐

* Optional

DEEP WORK WINDOW 1: Be Brilliant. ☐

Day 3 Workout					
Core: 30 rest between sets (6:20)	15 reps				
Incline Sit-up					
Leg Raises					
Strength Warmup 20-20-10 Compound Movement					
Strength: 5 sets x 5 reps (3-min rest)	5 reps				
Squat					
Accessory: 4 sets x 6-8 reps (2-min rest)	6-8 reps				
Bulgarian Split Squats					
Volume: 4 sets x 10 reps of 4 exercises (30-sec rest)	10 reps				
Hip Thrusts					
Squat Jumps					
Calf Raises					
Bulgarian Split Squats					

DAY 22 Wednesday (Continued)

Burnout: 2 exercises x 50 reps each (Air Squats, Calf Raises)	☐
GPP: 3 rounds - 30 sec on, 30 sec off: Sled Push	☐
Cognitive Walk/Sprint: 30 Minutes (HIIT Sprint) 2:30 walk, 30 Second Sprint 10 Rounds	☐

Complete First 85oz Water (Morning)	☐

Post-Workout Recovery	
20 Minutes Sauna*	☐
20 Minutes of Morning Sun	☐
Cold Shower	☐

DEEP WORK WINDOW 2: Six to Eight 20-minute deep work window sprints, 10-min break, 10 Kettle bell swings and look outside in the distance 1 minute to adjust eyes.	☐

Jump Start Nutrition Plan: Do the .8 calculation to understand exactly the amount of grass fed beef you must consume today.	
Organic Bone Broth (2 cups)	☐
Grass-Fed Beef	g
2oz Liver or Organ Meat	☐
4 Eggs Men, 2 Eggs Women	☐
1 large Avocado	☐
40 Raspberries	☐
20 Pecans or 23 Almonds	☐
50g of Raw Cheese	☐

Afternoon Recharge: HBOT*, Compression* or Cognitive Reset Rest: No more than 1 hour.	☐
Post Recharge: Cognitive Coffee & Collagen	☐

DAY 22 Wednesday   (Continued)

DEEP WORK WINDOW 3: Output ☐

Afternoon Nature Ideation Walk: 30 Min. – 1 hour. Think Big, Walk & Work, Dream Big. Call an Employee	☐

DEEP WORK WINDOW 4: Tactical ☐

Begin Optimized Nighttime Routine	
Complete Second 85oz Water	☐
Blue Light Blocker Glasses	☐
No Water after 5 PM for uninterrupted sleep	☐
Sunset Ice Bath* or Cold Shower (2-3 hours before sleep)	☐
Red light*	☐
Prayer & Gratitude	☐
Create Optimal Sleep Environment: 65 degrees, No Cell Phone/EMF	☐

Completed Perfect Day	☐

Notes: How I win tomorrow.

DAY 23 — Thursday

> "The true entrepreneur is a doer, not a dreamer."
> — Nolan Bushnell

Wake Up _____ am   Sleep: 7+ hrs Optimized Sleep ☐   Deep _____ REM _____

Weight _____ lbs   Ketones _____ mmol/L   Super Water ☐   Cognitive Coffee ☐ ☐

Red light* ☐   Ice Bath/Cold Shower ☐   Prayer/Meditation/Gratitude ☐

* Optional

DEEP WORK WINDOW 1: Be Brilliant. ☐

Day 1 Workout					
Core: 30 rest between sets (6:20)	15 reps				
Incline Sit-up					
Leg Raises					
Strength Warmup 20-20-10 Compound Movement					
Strength: 5 sets x 5 reps (3-min rest)	5 reps				
Incline Bench Press					
Accessory: 4 sets x 6-8 reps (2-min rest)	6-8 reps				
Overhead Press					x
Volume: 4 sets x 10 reps of 4 exercises (30-sec rest)	10 reps				
Side Raises					x
Front Raises					x
Dips					x
Deltoid Flys					x
Burnout: 2 exercises x 50 reps each (Side Raises, Triceps Press downs)					☐

DAY 23 Thursday (Continued)

GPP: Farmer's Walk: 3 rounds - 30 secs on, 30 secs off	☐
Cognitive Walk/Sprint: 30 Minutes (HIIT Sprint) 2:30 walk, 30 Second Sprint 10 Rounds	☐

Complete First 85oz Water (Morning)	☐

Post-Workout Recovery	
20 Minutes Sauna*	☐
20 Minutes of Morning Sun	☐
Cold Shower	☐

DEEP WORK WINDOW 2: Six to Eight 20-minute deep work window sprints, 10-min break, 10 Kettle bell swings and look outside in the distance 1 minute to adjust eyes.	☐

Jump Start Nutrition Plan: Today you will be doing your 48hr Fast.

48

Afternoon Recharge: HBOT*, Compression* or Cognitive Reset Rest: No more than 1 hour.	☐
Post Recharge: Cognitive Coffee & Collagen	☐

DEEP WORK WINDOW 3: Output	☐

Afternoon Nature Ideation Walk: 30 Min. – 1 hour. Think Big, Walk & Work, Dream Big. Call an Employee	☐

DAY 23 Thursday   (Continued)

DEEP WORK WINDOW 4: Tactical ☐

Begin Optimized Nighttime Routine	
Complete Second 85oz Water	☐
Blue Light Blocker Glasses	☐
No Water after 5 PM for uninterrupted sleep	☐
Sunset Ice Bath* or Cold Shower (2-3 hours before sleep)	☐
Red light*	☐
Prayer & Gratitude	☐
Create Optimal Sleep Environment: 65 degrees, No Cell Phone/EMF	☐

Completed Perfect Day	☐

Notes: How I win tomorrow.

DAY 24 — Friday

> "Success usually comes to those who are too busy to be looking for it."
>
> - Henry David Thoreau

Wake Up_____am   Sleep: 7+ hrs Optimized Sleep ☐   Deep_____REM_____

Weight_____lbs   Ketones_____mmol/L   Super Water ☐   Cognitive Coffee ☐ ☐

Red light* ☐   Ice Bath/Cold Shower ☐   Prayer/Meditation/Gratitude ☐

* Optional

DEEP WORK WINDOW 1: Be Brilliant. ☐

Day 2 Workout

Core: 30 rest between sets (6:20)	15 reps				
Incline Sit-up					
Leg Raises					
Strength Warmup 20-20-10 Compound Movement					
Strength: 5 sets x 5 reps (3-min rest)	5 reps				
Dead Lift					
Accessory: 4 sets x 6-8 reps (2-min rest)	6-8 reps				
Row					x
Volume: 4 sets x 10 reps of 4 exercises (30-sec rest)	10 reps				
Lat Pulldown/Pullup					x
Hammer Curl					x
Row					x
Individual Bicep Curl					x

DAY 24 Friday   (Continued)

Burnout: 2 exercises x 50 reps each (50 Rows, 50 Bicep Curls)	☐
GPP: 3 rounds - 30 sec on, 30 sec off: Sled Pulls	☐
Cognitive Walk/Sprint: 30 Minutes (HIIT Sprint) 2:30 walk, 30 Second Sprint 10 Rounds	☐

Complete First 85oz Water (Morning)	☐

Post-Workout Recovery	
20 Minutes Sauna*	☐
20 Minutes of Morning Sun	☐
Cold Shower	☐

DEEP WORK WINDOW 2: Six to Eight 20-minute deep work window sprints, 10-min break, 10 Kettle bell swings and look outside in the distance 1 minute to adjust eyes.	☐

Jump Start Nutrition Plan: Do the .8 calculation to understand exactly the amount of grass fed beef you must consume today.	
Organic Bone Broth (2 cups)	☐
Grass-Fed Beef	g
2oz Liver or Organ Meat	☐
4 Eggs Men, 2 Eggs Women	☐
1 large Avocado	☐
40 Raspberries	☐
20 Pecans or 23 Almonds	☐
50g of Raw Cheese	☐

Afternoon Recharge: HBOT*, Compression* or Cognitive Reset Rest: No more than 1 hour.	☐
Post Recharge: Cognitive Coffee & Collagen	☐

DAY 24 Friday (Continued)

DEEP WORK WINDOW 3: Output ☐

Afternoon Nature Ideation Walk: 30 Min. – 1 hour. Think Big, Walk & Work, Dream Big. Call an Employee ☐

DEEP WORK WINDOW 4: Tactical ☐

Begin Optimized Nighttime Routine	
Complete Second 85oz Water	☐
Blue Light Blocker Glasses	☐
No Water after 5 PM for uninterrupted sleep	☐
Sunset Ice Bath* or Cold Shower (2-3 hours before sleep)	☐
Red light*	☐
Prayer & Gratitude	☐
Create Optimal Sleep Environment: 65 degrees, No Cell Phone/EMF	☐

Completed Perfect Day	☐

Notes: How I win tomorrow.

DAY 25 — Saturday

"Every strike brings me closer to the next home run."
— Babe Ruth

Wake Up _____ am   Sleep: 7+ hrs Optimized Sleep ☐   Deep _____ REM _____

Weight _____ lbs   Ketones _____ mmol/L   Super Water ☐   Cognitive Coffee ☐ ☐

Red light* ☐   Ice Bath/Cold Shower ☐   Prayer/Meditation/Gratitude ☐

* Optional

DEEP WORK WINDOW 1: Be Brilliant.   ☐

Day 3 Workout

Core: 30 rest between sets (6:20)			15 reps		
Incline Sit-up					
Leg Raises					
Strength Warmup 20-20-10 Compound Movement					
Strength: 5 sets x 5 reps (3-min rest)			5 reps		
Squat					
Accessory: 4 sets x 6-8 reps (2-min rest)			6-8 reps		
Bulgarian Split Squats					
Volume: 4 sets x 10 reps of 4 exercises (30-sec rest)			10 reps		
Hip Thrusts					
Squat Jumps					
Calf Raises					
Bulgarian Split Squats					
Burnout: 2 exercises x 50 reps each (Air Squats, Calf Raises)					☐

DAY 25 Saturday   (Continued)

GPP: 3 rounds - 30 sec on, 30 sec off: Sled Push	☐
Cognitive Walk/Sprint: 30 Minutes (HIIT Sprint) 2:30 walk, 30 Second Sprint 10 Rounds	☐

Complete First 85oz Water (Morning)	☐

Post-Workout Recovery	
20 Minutes Sauna*	☐
20 Minutes of Morning Sun	☐
Cold Shower	☐

DEEP WORK WINDOW 2: Six to Eight 20-minute deep work window sprints, 10-min break, 10 Kettle bell swings and look outside in the distance 1 minute to adjust eyes.	☐

Jump Start Nutrition Plan: Do the .8 calculation to understand exactly the amount of grass fed beef you must consume today.	
Organic Bone Broth (2 cups)	☐
Grass-Fed Beef	g
2oz Liver or Organ Meat	☐
4 Eggs Men, 2 Eggs Women	☐
1 large Avocado	☐
40 Raspberries	☐
20 Pecans or 23 Almonds	☐
50g of Raw Cheese	☐

Afternoon Recharge: HBOT*, Compression* or Cognitive Reset Rest: No more than 1 hour.	☐
Post Recharge: Cognitive Coffee & Collagen	☐

DAY 25 Saturday   (Continued)

DEEP WORK WINDOW 3: Output ☐

Afternoon Nature Ideation Walk: 30 Min. – 1 hour. Think Big, Walk & Work, Dream Big. Call an Employee ☐

DEEP WORK WINDOW 4: Tactical ☐

Begin Optimized Nighttime Routine	
Complete Second 85oz Water	☐
Blue Light Blocker Glasses	☐
No Water after 5 PM for uninterrupted sleep	☐
Sunset Ice Bath* or Cold Shower (2-3 hours before sleep)	☐
Red light*	☐
Prayer & Gratitude	☐
Create Optimal Sleep Environment: 65 degrees, No Cell Phone/EMF	☐

Completed Perfect Day ☐

Notes: How I win tomorrow.

DAY 26 — Sunday

> "The successful warrior is the average man, with laser-like focus."
> — Bruce Lee

Wake Up _____ am   Sleep: 7+ hrs Optimized Sleep ☐   Deep _____ REM _____
Weight _____ lbs   Ketones _____ mmol/L   Super Water ☐   Cognitive Coffee ☐ ☐
Red light* ☐   Ice Bath/Cold Shower ☐   Prayer/Meditation/Gratitude ☐

Optional

DEEP WORK WINDOW 1: Be Brilliant. ☐

Day 1 Workout					
Core: 30 rest between sets (6:20)	15 reps				
Incline Sit-up					
Leg Raises					
Strength Warmup 20-20-10 Compound Movement					
Strength: 5 sets x 5 reps (3-min rest)	5 reps				
Incline Bench Press					
Accessory: 4 sets x 6-8 reps (2-min rest)	6-8 reps				
Overhead Press					x
Volume: 4 sets x 10 reps of 4 exercises (30-sec rest)	10 reps				
Side Raises					x
Front Raises					x
Dips					x
Deltoid Flys					x

DAY 26 Sunday (Continued)

Burnout: 2 exercises x 50 reps each (Side Raises, Triceps Press downs)	☐
GPP: Farmer's Walk: 3 rounds - 30 secs on, 30 secs off	☐
Cognitive Walk/Sprint: 30 Minutes (HIIT Sprint) 2:30 walk, 30 Second Sprint 10 Rounds	☐

Complete First 85oz Water (Morning)	☐

Post-Workout Recovery	
20 Minutes Sauna*	☐
20 Minutes of Morning Sun	☐
Cold Shower	☐

DEEP WORK WINDOW 2: Six to Eight 20-minute deep work window sprints, 10-min break, 10 Kettle bell swings and look outside in the distance 1 minute to adjust eyes.	☐

Jump Start Nutrition Plan: Do the .8 calculation to understand exactly the amount of grass fed beef you must consume today.	
Organic Bone Broth (2 cups)	☐
Grass-Fed Beef	g
2oz Liver or Organ Meat	☐
4 Eggs Men, 2 Eggs Women	☐
1 large Avocado	☐
40 Raspberries	☐
20 Pecans or 23 Almonds	☐
50g of Raw Cheese	☐

Afternoon Recharge: HBOT*, Compression* or Cognitive Reset Rest: No more than 1 hour.	☐
Post Recharge: Cognitive Coffee & Collagen	☐

DAY 26 Sunday   (Continued)

DEEP WORK WINDOW 3: Output ☐

Afternoon Nature Ideation Walk: 30 Min. – 1 hour. Think Big, Walk & Work, Dream Big. Call an Employee ☐

DEEP WORK WINDOW 4: Tactical ☐

Begin Optimized Nighttime Routine

Complete Second 85oz Water	☐
Blue Light Blocker Glasses	☐
No Water after 5 PM for uninterrupted sleep	☐
Sunset Ice Bath* or Cold Shower (2-3 hours before sleep)	☐
Red light*	☐
Prayer & Gratitude	☐
Create Optimal Sleep Environment: 65 degrees, No Cell Phone/EMF	☐

Completed Perfect Day	☐

Notes: How I win tomorrow.

DAY 27 — Monday

> "The price of victory is high, but so are the rewards."
> - Paul Bryant

Wake Up _____ am   Sleep: 7+ hrs Optimized Sleep ☐   Deep _____ REM _____

Weight _____ lbs   Ketones _____ mmol/L   Super Water ☐   Cognitive Coffee

Red light* ☐   Ice Bath/Cold Shower ☐   Prayer/Meditation/Gratitude ☐

Optional

DEEP WORK WINDOW 1: Be Brilliant. ☐

Day 2 Workout

Core: 30 rest between sets (6:20)	15 reps				
Incline Sit-up					
Leg Raises					
Strength Warmup 20-20-10 Compound Movement					
Strength: 5 sets x 5 reps (3-min rest)	5 reps				
Dead Lift					
Accessory: 4 sets x 6-8 reps (2-min rest)	6-8 reps				
Row					x
Volume: 4 sets x 10 reps of 4 exercises (30-sec rest)	10 reps				
Lat Pulldown/Pullup					x
Hammer Curl					x
Row					x
Individual Bicep Curl					x
Burnout: 2 exercises x 50 reps each (50 Rows, 50 Bicep Curls)					☐

DAY 27 Monday (Continued)

GPP: 3 rounds - 30 sec on, 30 sec off: Sled Pulls	☐
Cognitive Walk/Sprint: 30 Minutes (HIIT Sprint) 2:30 walk, 30 Second Sprint 10 Rounds	☐

Complete First 85oz Water (Morning)	☐

Post-Workout Recovery	
20 Minutes Sauna*	☐
20 Minutes of Morning Sun	☐
Cold Shower	☐

DEEP WORK WINDOW 2: Six to Eight 20-minute deep work window sprints, 10-min break, 10 Kettle bell swings and look outside in the distance 1 minute to adjust eyes.	☐

Jump Start Nutrition Plan: Do the .8 calculation to understand exactly the amount of Wild-caught salmon you must consume today.	
Organic Bone Broth (2 cups)	☐
Wild-caught salmon	g
2oz Liver or Organ Meat	☐
4 Eggs Men, 2 Eggs Women	☐
1 large Avocado	☐
40 Raspberries	☐
20 Pecans or 23 Almonds	☐
50g of Raw Cheese	☐

Afternoon Recharge: HBOT*, Compression* or Cognitive Reset Rest: No more than 1 hour.	☐
Post Recharge: Cognitive Coffee & Collagen	☐

DAY 27 Monday   (Continued)

| **DEEP WORK WINDOW 3:** Output | ☐ |

| Afternoon Nature Ideation Walk: 30 Min. – 1 hour. Think Big, Walk & Work, Dream Big. Call an Employee | ☐ |

| **DEEP WORK WINDOW 4:** Tactical | ☐ |

Begin Optimized Nighttime Routine	
Complete Second 85oz Water	☐
Blue Light Blocker Glasses	☐
No Water after 5 PM for uninterrupted sleep	☐
Sunset Ice Bath* or Cold Shower (2-3 hours before sleep)	☐
Red light*	☐
Prayer & Gratitude	☐
Create Optimal Sleep Environment: 65 degrees, No Cell Phone/EMF	☐

| Completed Perfect Day | ☐ |

Notes: How I win tomorrow.

DAY 28

Tuesday

> "The world is changed by your example, not by your opinion."
> - Paulo Coelho

Wake Up _____ am   Sleep: 7+ hrs Optimized Sleep ☐   Deep _____ REM _____

Weight _____ lbs   Ketones _____ mmol/L   Super Water ☐   Cognitive Coffee ☐ ☐

Red light* ☐   Ice Bath/Cold Shower ☐   Prayer/Meditation/Gratitude ☐

* Optional

DEEP WORK WINDOW 1: Be Brilliant. ☐

Day 3 Workout					
Core: 30 rest between sets (6:20)	15 reps				
Incline Sit-up					
Leg Raises					
Strength Warmup 20-20-10 Compound Movement					
Strength: 5 sets x 5 reps (3-min rest)	5 reps				
Squat					
Accessory: 4 sets x 6-8 reps (2-min rest)	6-8 reps				
Bulgarian Split Squats					
Volume: 4 sets x 10 reps of 4 exercises (30-sec rest)	10 reps				
Hip Thrusts					
Squat Jumps					
Calf Raises					
Bulgarian Split Squats					

DAY 28 Tuesday   (Continued)

Burnout: 2 exercises x 50 reps each (Air Squats, Calf Raises)	☐
GPP: 3 rounds - 30 sec on, 30 sec off: Sled Push	☐
Cognitive Walk/Sprint: 30 Minutes (HIIT Sprint) 2:30 walk, 30 Second Sprint 10 Rounds	☐

Week 5:

Complete First 85oz Water (Morning)	☐

Post-Workout Recovery	
20 Minutes Sauna*	☐
20 Minutes of Morning Sun	☐
Cold Shower	☐

DEEP WORK WINDOW 2: Six to Eight 20-minute deep work window sprints, 10-min break, 10 Kettle bell swings and look outside in the distance 1 minute to adjust eyes.	☐

Jump Start Nutrition Plan: Do the .8 calculation to understand exactly the amount of grass fed beef you must consume today.	
Organic Bone Broth (2 cups)	☐
Grass-Fed Beef	g
2oz Liver or Organ Meat	☐
4 Eggs Men, 2 Eggs Women	☐
1 large Avocado	☐
40 Raspberries	☐
20 Pecans or 23 Almonds	☐
50g of Raw Cheese	☐

Afternoon Recharge: HBOT*, Compression* or Cognitive Reset Rest: No more than 1 hour.	☐

DAY 28 Tuesday   (Continued)

| Post Recharge: Cognitive Coffee & Collagen | ☐ |

| **DEEP WORK WINDOW 3:** Output | ☐ |

| Afternoon Nature Ideation Walk: 30 Min. – 1 hour. Think Big, Walk & Work, Dream Big. Call an Employee | ☐ |

| **DEEP WORK WINDOW 4:** Tactical | ☐ |

Begin Optimized Nighttime Routine	
Complete Second 85oz Water	☐
Blue Light Blocker Glasses	☐
No Water after 5 PM for uninterrupted sleep	☐
Sunset Ice Bath* or Cold Shower (2-3 hours before sleep)	☐
Red light*	☐
Prayer & Gratitude	☐
Create Optimal Sleep Environment: 65 degrees, No Cell Phone/EMF	☐

| Completed Perfect Day | ☐ |

Notes: How I win tomorrow.

DAY 29 — Wednesday

> "I never dreamed about success. I worked for it."
> - Estée Lauder

Wake Up _____ am   Sleep: 7+ hrs Optimized Sleep ☐   Deep _____ REM _____

Weight _____ lbs   Ketones _____ mmol/L   Super Water ☐   Cognitive Coffee ☐ ☐

Red light* ☐   Ice Bath/Cold Shower ☐   Prayer/Meditation/Gratitude ☐

Optional

DEEP WORK WINDOW 1: Be Brilliant. ☐

Day 1 Workout				
Core: 30 rest between sets (6:20)	15 reps			
Incline Sit-up				
Leg Raises				
Strength Warmup 20-20-10 Compound Movement				
Strength: 5 sets x 5 reps (3-min rest)	5 reps			
Incline Bench Press				
Accessory: 4 sets x 6-8 reps (2-min rest)	6-8 reps			
Overhead Press				x
Volume: 4 sets x 10 reps of 4 exercises (30-sec rest)	10 reps			
Side Raises				x
Front Raises				x
Dips				x
Deltoid Flys				x
Burnout: 2 exercises x 50 reps each (Side Raises, Triceps Press downs)				☐

DAY 29 Wednesday   (Continued)

GPP: Farmer's Walk: 3 rounds - 30 secs on, 30 secs off	☐
Cognitive Walk/Sprint: 30 Minutes (HIIT Sprint) 2:30 walk, 30 Second Sprint 10 Rounds	☐

Complete First 85oz Water (Morning)	☐

Post-Workout Recovery	
20 Minutes Sauna*	☐
20 Minutes of Morning Sun	☐
Cold Shower	☐

DEEP WORK WINDOW 2: Six to Eight 20-minute deep work window sprints, 10-min break, 10 Kettle bell swings and look outside in the distance 1 minute to adjust eyes.	☐

Jump Start Nutrition Plan: Do the .8 calculation to understand exactly the amount of grass fed beef you must consume today.	
Organic Bone Broth (2 cups)	☐
Grass-Fed Beef	g
2oz Liver or Organ Meat	☐
4 Eggs Men, 2 Eggs Women	☐
1 large Avocado	☐
40 Raspberries	☐
20 Pecans or 23 Almonds	☐
50g of Raw Cheese	☐

Afternoon Recharge: HBOT*, Compression* or Cognitive Reset Rest: No more than 1 hour.	☐
Post Recharge: Cognitive Coffee & Collagen	☐

DAY 29 Wednesday   (Continued)

DEEP WORK WINDOW 3: Output ☐

Afternoon Nature Ideation Walk: 30 Min. – 1 hour. Think Big, Walk & Work, Dream Big. Call an Employee	☐

DEEP WORK WINDOW 4: Tactical ☐

Begin Optimized Nighttime Routine	
Complete Second 85oz Water	☐
Blue Light Blocker Glasses	☐
No Water after 5 PM for uninterrupted sleep	☐
Sunset Ice Bath* or Cold Shower (2-3 hours before sleep)	☐
Red light*	☐
Prayer & Gratitude	☐
Create Optimal Sleep Environment: 65 degrees, No Cell Phone/EMF	☐

Completed Perfect Day	☐

Notes: How I win tomorrow.

DAY 30 Thursday

> "Passion is energy. Feel the power that comes from focusing on what excites you."
>
> — Oprah Winfrey

Wake Up _____ am Sleep: 7+ hrs Optimized Sleep ☐ Deep _____ REM _____

Weight _____ lbs Ketones _____ mmol/L Super Water ☐ Cognitive Coffee ☐ ☐

Red light* ☐   Ice Bath/Cold Shower ☐   Prayer/Meditation/Gratitude ☐

Optional

DEEP WORK WINDOW 1: Be Brilliant. ☐

Day 2 Workout					
Core: 30 rest between sets (6:20)	15 reps				
Incline Sit-up					
Leg Raises					
Strength Warmup 20-20-10 Compound Movement					
Strength: 5 sets x 5 reps (3-min rest)	5 reps				
Dead Lift					
Accessory: 4 sets x 6-8 reps (2-min rest)	6-8 reps				
Row					x
Volume: 4 sets x 10 reps of 4 exercises (30-sec rest)	10 reps				
Lat Pulldown/Pullup					x
Hammer Curl					x
Row					x
Individual Bicep Curl					x

DAY 30 Thursday (Continued)

Burnout: 2 exercises x 50 reps each (50 Rows, 50 Bicep Curls)	☐
GPP: 3 rounds - 30 sec on, 30 sec off: Sled Pulls	☐
Cognitive Walk/Sprint: 30 Minutes (HIIT Sprint) 2:30 walk, 30 Second Sprint 10 Rounds	☐

Complete First 85oz Water (Morning)	☐

Post-Workout Recovery	
20 Minutes Sauna*	☐
20 Minutes of Morning Sun	☐
Cold Shower	☐

DEEP WORK WINDOW 2: Six to Eight 20-minute deep work window sprints, 10-min break, 10 Kettle bell swings and look outside in the distance 1 minute to adjust eyes.	☐

Jump Start Nutrition Plan: Today you will be doing your 48hr Fast.

48

Afternoon Recharge: HBOT*, Compression* or Cognitive Reset Rest: No more than 1 hour.	☐
Post Recharge: Cognitive Coffee & Collagen	☐

DEEP WORK WINDOW 3: Output	☐

Afternoon Nature Ideation Walk: 30 Min. – 1 hour. Think Big, Walk & Work, Dream Big. Call an Employee	☐

DAY 30 Thursday   (Continued)

DEEP WORK WINDOW 4: Tactical	☐

Begin Optimized Nighttime Routine	
Complete Second 85oz Water	☐
Blue Light Blocker Glasses	☐
No Water after 5 PM for uninterrupted sleep	☐
Sunset Ice Bath* or Cold Shower (2-3 hours before sleep)	☐
Red light*	☐
Prayer & Gratitude	☐
Create Optimal Sleep Environment: 65 degrees, No Cell Phone/EMF	☐

Completed Perfect Day	☐

Notes: How I win tomorrow.

DAY 31 — Friday

> "It's not about ideas.
> It's about making ideas happen."
> – Scott Belsky

Wake Up _____ am   Sleep: 7+ hrs Optimized Sleep ☐   Deep _____ REM _____
Weight _____ lbs   Ketones _____ mmol/L   Super Water ☐   Cognitive Coffee ☐☐
Red light* ☐   Ice Bath/Cold Shower ☐   Prayer/Meditation/Gratitude ☐

Optional

DEEP WORK WINDOW 1: Be Brilliant. ☐

Day 3 Workout					
Core: 30 rest between sets (6:20)	15 reps				
Incline Sit-up					
Leg Raises					
Strength Warmup 20-20-10 Compound Movement					
Strength: 5 sets x 5 reps (3-min rest)	5 reps				
Squat					
Accessory: 4 sets x 6-8 reps (2-min rest)	6-8 reps				
Bulgarian Split Squats					
Volume: 4 sets x 10 reps of 4 exercises (30-sec rest)	10 reps				
Hip Thrusts					
Squat Jumps					
Calf Raises					
Bulgarian Split Squats					

DAY 31 Friday   (Continued)

Burnout: 2 exercises x 50 reps each (Air Squats, Calf Raises)	☐
GPP: 3 rounds - 30 sec on, 30 sec off: Sled Push	☐
Cognitive Walk/Sprint: 30 Minutes (HIIT Sprint) 2:30 walk, 30 Second Sprint 10 Rounds	☐

Complete First 85oz Water (Morning)	☐

Post-Workout Recovery	
20 Minutes Sauna*	☐
20 Minutes of Morning Sun	☐
Cold Shower	☐

DEEP WORK WINDOW 2: Six to Eight 20-minute deep work window sprints, 10-min break, 10 Kettle bell swings and look outside in the distance 1 minute to adjust eyes.	☐

Jump Start Nutrition Plan: Do the .8 calculation to understand exactly the amount of grass fed beef you must consume today.	
Organic Bone Broth (2 cups)	☐
Grass-Fed Beef	g
2oz Liver or Organ Meat	☐
4 Eggs Men, 2 Eggs Women	☐
1 large Avocado	☐
40 Raspberries	☐
20 Pecans or 23 Almonds	☐
50g of Raw Cheese	☐

Afternoon Recharge: HBOT*, Compression* or Cognitive Reset Rest: No more than 1 hour.	☐
Post Recharge: Cognitive Coffee & Collagen	☐

DAY 31 Friday   (Continued)

DEEP WORK WINDOW 3: Output ☐

Afternoon Nature Ideation Walk: 30 Min. – 1 hour. Think Big, Walk & Work, Dream Big. Call an Employee ☐

DEEP WORK WINDOW 4: Tactical ☐

Begin Optimized Nighttime Routine

Complete Second 85oz Water	☐
Blue Light Blocker Glasses	☐
No Water after 5 PM for uninterrupted sleep	☐
Sunset Ice Bath* or Cold Shower (2-3 hours before sleep)	☐
Red light*	☐
Prayer & Gratitude	☐
Create Optimal Sleep Environment: 65 degrees, No Cell Phone/EMF	☐

Completed Perfect Day	☐

Notes: How I win tomorrow.

DAY 32 — Saturday

> "If you can't stop thinking about it, don't stop working for it."
> - Michael Jordan

Wake Up _____ am   Sleep: 7+ hrs Optimized Sleep ☐   Deep _____ REM _____
Weight _____ lbs   Ketones _____ mmol/L   Super Water ☐   Cognitive Coffee ☐ ☐
Red light* ☐   Ice Bath/Cold Shower ☐   Prayer/Meditation/Gratitude ☐

Optional

DEEP WORK WINDOW 1: Be Brilliant. ☐

Day 1 Workout

Core: 30 rest between sets (6:20)	15 reps				
Incline Sit-up					
Leg Raises					
Strength Warmup 20-20-10 Compound Movement					
Strength: 5 sets x 5 reps (3-min rest)	5 reps				
Incline Bench Press					
Accessory: 4 sets x 6-8 reps (2-min rest)	6-8 reps				
Overhead Press					x
Volume: 4 sets x 10 reps of 4 exercises (30-sec rest)	10 reps				
Side Raises					x
Front Raises					x
Dips					x
Deltoid Flys					x

DAY 32 Saturday   (Continued)

Burnout: 2 exercises x 50 reps each (Side Raises, Triceps Press downs)	☐
GPP: Farmer's Walk: 3 rounds - 30 secs on, 30 secs off	☐
Cognitive Walk/Sprint: 30 Minutes (HIIT Sprint) 2:30 walk, 30 Second Sprint 10 Rounds	☐

Complete First 85oz Water (Morning)	☐

Post-Workout Recovery	
20 Minutes Sauna*	☐
20 Minutes of Morning Sun	☐
Cold Shower	☐

DEEP WORK WINDOW 2: Six to Eight 20-minute deep work window sprints, 10-min break, 10 Kettle bell swings and look outside in the distance 1 minute to adjust eyes.	☐

Jump Start Nutrition Plan: Do the .8 calculation to understand exactly the amount of grass fed beef you must consume today.	
Organic Bone Broth (2 cups)	☐
Grass-Fed Beef	g
2oz Liver or Organ Meat	☐
4 Eggs Men, 2 Eggs Women	☐
1 large Avocado	☐
40 Raspberries	☐
20 Pecans or 23 Almonds	☐
50g of Raw Cheese	☐

Afternoon Recharge: HBOT*, Compression* or Cognitive Reset Rest: No more than 1 hour.	☐
Post Recharge: Cognitive Coffee & Collagen	☐

DAY 32 Saturday   (Continued)

DEEP WORK WINDOW 3: Output ☐

Afternoon Nature Ideation Walk: 30 Min. – 1 hour. Think Big, Walk & Work, Dream Big. Call an Employee	☐

DEEP WORK WINDOW 4: Tactical ☐

Begin Optimized Nighttime Routine	
Complete Second 85oz Water	☐
Blue Light Blocker Glasses	☐
No Water after 5 PM for uninterrupted sleep	☐
Sunset Ice Bath* or Cold Shower (2-3 hours before sleep)	☐
Red light*	☐
Prayer & Gratitude	☐
Create Optimal Sleep Environment: 65 degrees, No Cell Phone/EMF	☐

Completed Perfect Day	☐

Notes: How I win tomorrow.

DAY 33

Sunday

> "The secret of change is to focus all of your energy, not on fighting the old, but on building the new."
>
> - Socrates

Wake Up_____am   Sleep: 7+ hrs Optimized Sleep ☐   Deep_____REM_____
Weight_____lbs   Ketones_____mmol/L   Super Water ☐   Cognitive Coffee ☐ ☐
Red light* ☐   Ice Bath/Cold Shower ☐   Prayer/Meditation/Gratitude ☐

Optional

DEEP WORK WINDOW 1: Be Brilliant. ☐

Day 2 Workout					
Core: 30 rest between sets (6:20)	15 reps				
Incline Sit-up					
Leg Raises					
Strength Warmup 20-20-10 Compound Movement					
Strength: 5 sets x 5 reps (3-min rest)	5 reps				
Dead Lift					
Accessory: 4 sets x 6-8 reps (2-min rest)	6-8 reps				
Row					x
Volume: 4 sets x 10 reps of 4 exercises (30-sec rest)	10 reps				
Lat Pulldown/Pullup					x
Hammer Curl					x
Row					x
Individual Bicep Curl					x

DAY 33 Sunday   (Continued)

Burnout: 2 exercises x 50 reps each (50 Rows, 50 Bicep Curls)	☐
GPP: 3 rounds - 30 sec on, 30 sec off: Sled Pulls	☐
Cognitive Walk/Sprint: 30 Minutes (HIIT Sprint) 2:30 walk, 30 Second Sprint 10 Rounds	☐

Complete First 85oz Water (Morning)	☐

Post-Workout Recovery	
20 Minutes Sauna*	☐
20 Minutes of Morning Sun	☐
Cold Shower	☐

DEEP WORK WINDOW 2: Six to Eight 20-minute deep work window sprints, 10-min break, 10 Kettle bell swings and look outside in the distance 1 minute to adjust eyes.	☐

Jump Start Nutrition Plan: Do the .8 calculation to understand exactly the amount of grass fed beef you must consume today.	
Organic Bone Broth (2 cups)	☐
Grass-Fed Beef	g
2oz Liver or Organ Meat	☐
4 Eggs Men, 2 Eggs Women	☐
1 large Avocado	☐
40 Raspberries	☐
20 Pecans or 23 Almonds	☐
50g of Raw Cheese	☐

Afternoon Recharge: HBOT*, Compression* or Cognitive Reset Rest: No more than 1 hour.	☐
Post Recharge: Cognitive Coffee & Collagen	☐

DAY 33 Sunday   (Continued)

DEEP WORK WINDOW 3: Output ☐

Afternoon Nature Ideation Walk: 30 Min. – 1 hour. Think Big, Walk & Work, Dream Big. Call an Employee	☐

DEEP WORK WINDOW 4: Tactical ☐

Begin Optimized Nighttime Routine

Complete Second 85oz Water	☐
Blue Light Blocker Glasses	☐
No Water after 5 PM for uninterrupted sleep	☐
Sunset Ice Bath* or Cold Shower (2-3 hours before sleep)	☐
Red light*	☐
Prayer & Gratitude	☐
Create Optimal Sleep Environment: 65 degrees, No Cell Phone/EMF	☐

Completed Perfect Day	☐

Notes: How I win tomorrow.

DAY 34 — Monday

> "I attribute my success to this:
> I never gave or took an excuse."
> — Florence Nightingale

Wake Up _____ am   Sleep: 7+ hrs Optimized Sleep ☐   Deep _____ REM _____

Weight _____ lbs   Ketones _____ mmol/L   Super Water ☐   Cognitive Coffee ☐ ☐

Red light* ☐   Ice Bath/Cold Shower ☐   Prayer/Meditation/Gratitude ☐

Optional

DEEP WORK WINDOW 1: Be Brilliant. ☐

Day 3 Workout

Core: 30 rest between sets (6:20)	15 reps				
Incline Sit-up					
Leg Raises					
Strength Warmup 20-20-10 Compound Movement					
Strength: 5 sets x 5 reps (3-min rest)	5 reps				
Squat					
Accessory: 4 sets x 6-8 reps (2-min rest)	6-8 reps				
Bulgarian Split Squats					
Volume: 4 sets x 10 reps of 4 exercises (30-sec rest)	10 reps				
Hip Thrusts					
Squat Jumps					
Calf Raises					
Bulgarian Split Squats					

DAY 34 Monday   (Continued)

Burnout: 2 exercises x 50 reps each (Air Squats, Calf Raises)	☐
GPP: 3 rounds - 30 sec on, 30 sec off: Sled Push	☐
Cognitive Walk/Sprint: 30 Minutes (HIIT Sprint) 2:30 walk, 30 Second Sprint 10 Rounds	☐

Complete First 85oz Water (Morning)	☐

Post-Workout Recovery	
20 Minutes Sauna*	☐
20 Minutes of Morning Sun	☐
Cold Shower	☐

DEEP WORK WINDOW 2: Six to Eight 20-minute deep work window sprints, 10-min break, 10 Kettle bell swings and look outside in the distance 1 minute to adjust eyes.	☐

Jump Start Nutrition Plan: Do the .8 calculation to understand exactly the amount of Wild-caught salmon you must consume today.	
Organic Bone Broth (2 cups)	☐
Wild-caught salmon	g
2oz Liver or Organ Meat	☐
4 Eggs Men, 2 Eggs Women	☐
1 large Avocado	☐
40 Raspberries	☐
20 Pecans or 23 Almonds	☐
50g of Raw Cheese	☐

Afternoon Recharge: HBOT*, Compression* or Cognitive Reset Rest: No more than 1 hour.	☐
Post Recharge: Cognitive Coffee & Collagen	☐

DAY 34 Monday   (Continued)

DEEP WORK WINDOW 3: Output ☐

Afternoon Nature Ideation Walk: 30 Min. – 1 hour. Think Big, Walk & Work, Dream Big. Call an Employee ☐

DEEP WORK WINDOW 4: Tactical ☐

Begin Optimized Nighttime Routine

Complete Second 85oz Water	☐
Blue Light Blocker Glasses	☐
No Water after 5 PM for uninterrupted sleep	☐
Sunset Ice Bath* or Cold Shower (2-3 hours before sleep)	☐
Red light*	☐
Prayer & Gratitude	☐
Create Optimal Sleep Environment: 65 degrees, No Cell Phone/EMF	☐

Completed Perfect Day ☐

Notes: How I win tomorrow.

DAY 35 — Tuesday

> "Obsessed is a word the lazy use to describe the dedicated."
> — Unknown

Wake Up _____ am   Sleep: 7+ hrs Optimized Sleep ☐   Deep _____ REM _____

Weight _____ lbs   Ketones _____ mmol/L   Super Water ☐   Cognitive Coffee ☐☐

Red light* ☐   Ice Bath/Cold Shower ☐   Prayer/Meditation/Gratitude ☐

* Optional

DEEP WORK WINDOW 1: Be Brilliant. ☐

Day 1 Workout

Core: 30 rest between sets (6:20)	15 reps				
Incline Sit-up					
Leg Raises					
Strength Warmup 20-20-10 Compound Movement					
Strength: 5 sets x 5 reps (3-min rest)	5 reps				
Incline Bench Press					
Accessory: 4 sets x 6-8 reps (2-min rest)	6-8 reps				
Overhead Press					x
Volume: 4 sets x 10 reps of 4 exercises (30-sec rest)	10 reps				
Side Raises					x
Front Raises					x
Dips					x
Deltoid Flys					x

DAY 35 Tuesday   (Continued)

Burnout: 2 exercises x 50 reps each (Side Raises, Triceps Press downs)	☐
GPP: Farmer's Walk: 3 rounds - 30 secs on, 30 secs off	☐
Cognitive Walk/Sprint: 30 Minutes (HIIT Sprint) 2:30 walk, 30 Second Sprint 10 Rounds	☐

Week 6:

Complete First 85oz Water (Morning)	☐

Post-Workout Recovery	
20 Minutes Sauna*	☐
20 Minutes of Morning Sun	☐
Cold Shower	☐

DEEP WORK WINDOW 2: Six to Eight 20-minute deep work window sprints, 10-min break, 10 Kettle bell swings and look outside in the distance 1 minute to adjust eyes.	☐

Jump Start Nutrition Plan: Do the .8 calculation to understand exactly the amount of grass fed beef you must consume today.	
Organic Bone Broth (2 cups)	☐
Grass-Fed Beef	g
2oz Liver or Organ Meat	☐
4 Eggs Men, 2 Eggs Women	☐
1 large Avocado	☐
40 Raspberries	☐
20 Pecans or 23 Almonds	☐
50g of Raw Cheese	☐

DAY 35 Tuesday (Continued)

Afternoon Recharge: HBOT*, Compression* or Cognitive Reset Rest: No more than 1 hour.	☐
Post Recharge: Cognitive Coffee & Collagen	☐

DEEP WORK WINDOW 3: Output	☐

Afternoon Nature Ideation Walk: 30 Min. – 1 hour. Think Big, Walk & Work, Dream Big. Call an Employee	☐

DEEP WORK WINDOW 4: Tactical	☐

Begin Optimized Nighttime Routine	
Complete Second 85oz Water	☐
Blue Light Blocker Glasses	☐
No Water after 5 PM for uninterrupted sleep	☐
Sunset Ice Bath* or Cold Shower (2-3 hours before sleep)	☐
Red light*	☐
Prayer & Gratitude	☐
Create Optimal Sleep Environment: 65 degrees, No Cell Phone/EMF	☐

Completed Perfect Day	☐

Notes: How I win tomorrow.

DAY 36

Wednesday

"Strength grows in the moments when you think you can't go on but you keep going anyway."

— Unknown

Wake Up _____ am   Sleep: 7+ hrs Optimized Sleep ☐   Deep _____ REM _____

Weight _____ lbs   Ketones _____ mmol/L   Super Water ☐   Cognitive Coffee ☐ ☐

Red light* ☐   Ice Bath/Cold Shower ☐   Prayer/Meditation/Gratitude ☐

* Optional

DEEP WORK WINDOW 1: Be Brilliant. ☐

Day 2 Workout					
Core: 30 rest between sets (6:20)	15 reps				
Incline Sit-up					
Leg Raises					
Strength Warmup 20-20-10 Compound Movement					
Strength: 5 sets x 5 reps (3-min rest)	5 reps				
Dead Lift					
Accessory: 4 sets x 6-8 reps (2-min rest)	6-8 reps				
Row					x
Volume: 4 sets x 10 reps of 4 exercises (30-sec rest)	10 reps				
Lat Pulldown/Pullup					x
Hammer Curl					x
Row					x
Individual Bicep Curl					x

DAY 36 Wednesday   (Continued)

Burnout: 2 exercises x 50 reps each (50 Rows, 50 Bicep Curls)	☐
GPP: 3 rounds - 30 sec on, 30 sec off: Sled Pulls	☐
Cognitive Walk/Sprint: 30 Minutes (HIIT Sprint) 2:30 walk, 30 Second Sprint 10 Rounds	☐

Complete First 85oz Water (Morning)	☐

Post-Workout Recovery	
20 Minutes Sauna*	☐
20 Minutes of Morning Sun	☐
Cold Shower	☐

DEEP WORK WINDOW 2: Six to Eight 20-minute deep work window sprints, 10-min break, 10 Kettle bell swings and look outside in the distance 1 minute to adjust eyes.	☐

Jump Start Nutrition Plan: Do the .8 calculation to understand exactly the amount of grass fed beef you must consume today.	
Organic Bone Broth (2 cups)	☐
Grass-Fed Beef	g
2oz Liver or Organ Meat	☐
4 Eggs Men, 2 Eggs Women	☐
1 large Avocado	☐
40 Raspberries	☐
20 Pecans or 23 Almonds	☐
50g of Raw Cheese	☐

Afternoon Recharge: HBOT*, Compression* or Cognitive Reset Rest: No more than 1 hour.	☐
Post Recharge: Cognitive Coffee & Collagen	☐

DAY 36 Wednesday   (Continued)

DEEP WORK WINDOW 3: Output ☐

Afternoon Nature Ideation Walk: 30 Min. – 1 hour. Think Big, Walk & Work, Dream Big. Call an Employee	☐

DEEP WORK WINDOW 4: Tactical ☐

Begin Optimized Nighttime Routine	
Complete Second 85oz Water	☐
Blue Light Blocker Glasses	☐
No Water after 5 PM for uninterrupted sleep	☐
Sunset Ice Bath* or Cold Shower (2-3 hours before sleep)	☐
Red light*	☐
Prayer & Gratitude	☐
Create Optimal Sleep Environment: 65 degrees, No Cell Phone/EMF	☐

Completed Perfect Day	☐

Notes: How I win tomorrow.

DAY 37 — Thursday

> "Chase the vision, not the money;
> the money will end up following you."
> - Tony Hsieh

Wake Up_____am   Sleep: 7+ hrs Optimized Sleep ☐   Deep_____REM_____

Weight_____lbs   Ketones_____mmol/L   Super Water ☐   Cognitive Coffee ☐ ☐

Red light* ☐   Ice Bath/Cold Shower ☐   Prayer/Meditation/Gratitude ☐

* Optional

DEEP WORK WINDOW 1: Be Brilliant. ☐

Day 3 Workout				
Core: 30 rest between sets (6:20)	15 reps			
Incline Sit-up				
Leg Raises				
Strength Warmup 20-20-10 Compound Movement				
Strength: 5 sets x 5 reps (3-min rest)	5 reps			
Squat				
Accessory: 4 sets x 6-8 reps (2-min rest)	6-8 reps			
Bulgarian Split Squats				
Volume: 4 sets x 10 reps of 4 exercises (30-sec rest)	10 reps			
Hip Thrusts				
Squat Jumps				
Calf Raises				
Bulgarian Split Squats				

DAY 37 Thursday (Continued)

Burnout: 2 exercises x 50 reps each (Air Squats, Calf Raises)	☐
GPP: 3 rounds - 30 sec on, 30 sec off: Sled Push	☐
Cognitive Walk/Sprint: 30 Minutes (HIIT Sprint) 2:30 walk, 30 Second Sprint 10 Rounds	☐

Complete First 85oz Water (Morning)	☐

Post-Workout Recovery	
20 Minutes Sauna*	☐
20 Minutes of Morning Sun	☐
Cold Shower	☐

DEEP WORK WINDOW 2: Six to Eight 20-minute deep work window sprints, 10-min break, 10 Kettle bell swings and look outside in the distance 1 minute to adjust eyes.	☐

Jump Start Nutrition Plan: Today you will be doing your 48hr Fast.

48

Afternoon Recharge: HBOT*, Compression* or Cognitive Reset Rest: No more than 1 hour.	☐
Post Recharge: Cognitive Coffee & Collagen	☐

DEEP WORK WINDOW 3: Output	☐

Afternoon Nature Ideation Walk: 30 Min. – 1 hour. Think Big, Walk & Work, Dream Big. Call an Employee	☐

DAY 37 Thursday   (Continued)

DEEP WORK WINDOW 4: Tactical ☐

Begin Optimized Nighttime Routine	
Complete Second 85oz Water	☐
Blue Light Blocker Glasses	☐
No Water after 5 PM for uninterrupted sleep	☐
Sunset Ice Bath* or Cold Shower (2-3 hours before sleep)	☐
Red light*	☐
Prayer & Gratitude	☐
Create Optimal Sleep Environment: 65 degrees, No Cell Phone/EMF	☐

Completed Perfect Day	☐

Notes: How I win tomorrow.

DAY 38 — Friday

> "Passion is the genesis of genius."
> - Galileo Galilei

Wake Up _____ am   Sleep: 7+ hrs Optimized Sleep ☐ Deep _____ REM _____

Weight _____ lbs   Ketones _____ mmol/L   Super Water ☐   Cognitive Coffee ☐ ☐

Red light* ☐   Ice Bath/Cold Shower ☐   Prayer/Meditation/Gratitude ☐

* Optional

DEEP WORK WINDOW 1: Be Brilliant. ☐

Day 1 Workout

Day 1 Workout					
Core: 30 rest between sets (6:20)	15 reps				
Incline Sit-up					
Leg Raises					
Strength Warmup 20-20-10 Compound Movement					
Strength: 5 sets x 5 reps (3-min rest)	5 reps				
Incline Bench Press					
Accessory: 4 sets x 6-8 reps (2-min rest)	6-8 reps				
Overhead Press					x
Volume: 4 sets x 10 reps of 4 exercises (30-sec rest)	10 reps				
Side Raises					x
Front Raises					x
Dips					x
Deltoid Flys					x
Burnout: 2 exercises x 50 reps each (Side Raises, Triceps Press downs) ☐					

DAY 38 Friday (Continued)

GPP: Farmer's Walk: 3 rounds - 30 secs on, 30 secs off	☐
Cognitive Walk/Sprint: 30 Minutes (HIIT Sprint) 2:30 walk, 30 Second Sprint 10 Rounds	☐

Complete First 85oz Water (Morning)	☐

Post-Workout Recovery	
20 Minutes Sauna*	☐
20 Minutes of Morning Sun	☐
Cold Shower	☐

DEEP WORK WINDOW 2: Six to Eight 20-minute deep work window sprints, 10-min break, 10 Kettle bell swings and look outside in the distance 1 minute to adjust eyes.	☐

Jump Start Nutrition Plan: Do the .8 calculation to understand exactly the amount of grass fed beef you must consume today.	
Organic Bone Broth (2 cups)	☐
Grass-Fed Beef	g
2oz Liver or Organ Meat	☐
4 Eggs Men, 2 Eggs Women	☐
1 large Avocado	☐
40 Raspberries	☐
20 Pecans or 23 Almonds	☐
50g of Raw Cheese	☐

Afternoon Recharge: HBOT*, Compression* or Cognitive Reset Rest: No more than 1 hour.	☐
Post Recharge: Cognitive Coffee & Collagen	☐

DAY 38 Friday   (Continued)

DEEP WORK WINDOW 3: Output	☐

Afternoon Nature Ideation Walk: 30 Min. – 1 hour. Think Big, Walk & Work, Dream Big. Call an Employee	☐

DEEP WORK WINDOW 4: Tactical	☐

Begin Optimized Nighttime Routine	
Complete Second 85oz Water	☐
Blue Light Blocker Glasses	☐
No Water after 5 PM for uninterrupted sleep	☐
Sunset Ice Bath* or Cold Shower (2-3 hours before sleep)	☐
Red light*	☐
Prayer & Gratitude	☐
Create Optimal Sleep Environment: 65 degrees, No Cell Phone/EMF	☐

Completed Perfect Day	☐

Notes: How I win tomorrow.

DAY 39 — Saturday

> "The greater the obstacle, the more glory in overcoming it."
>
> - Molière

Wake Up_____am   Sleep: 7+ hrs Optimized Sleep ☐ Deep_____REM_____

Weight_____lbs   Ketones_____mmol/L   Super Water ☐   Cognitive Coffee ☐ ☐

Red light* ☐   Ice Bath/Cold Shower ☐   Prayer/Meditation/Gratitude ☐

* Optional

DEEP WORK WINDOW 1: Be Brilliant. ☐

Day 2 Workout

Core: 30 rest between sets (6:20)	15 reps			
Incline Sit-up				
Leg Raises				
Strength Warmup 20-20-10 Compound Movement				
Strength: 5 sets x 5 reps (3-min rest)	5 reps			
Dead Lift				
Accessory: 4 sets x 6-8 reps (2-min rest)	6-8 reps			
Row				x
Volume: 4 sets x 10 reps of 4 exercises (30-sec rest)	10 reps			
Lat Pulldown/Pullup				x
Hammer Curl				x
Row				x
Individual Bicep Curl				x

DAY 39 Saturday (Continued)

Burnout: 2 exercises x 50 reps each (50 Rows, 50 Bicep Curls)	☐
GPP: 3 rounds - 30 sec on, 30 sec off: Sled Pulls	☐
Cognitive Walk/Sprint: 30 Minutes (HIIT Sprint) 2:30 walk, 30 Second Sprint 10 Rounds	☐

Complete First 85oz Water (Morning)	☐

Post-Workout Recovery	
20 Minutes Sauna*	☐
20 Minutes of Morning Sun	☐
Cold Shower	☐

DEEP WORK WINDOW 2: Six to Eight 20-minute deep work window sprints, 10-min break, 10 Kettle bell swings and look outside in the distance 1 minute to adjust eyes.	☐

Jump Start Nutrition Plan: Do the .8 calculation to understand exactly the amount of grass fed beef you must consume today.	
Organic Bone Broth (2 cups)	☐
Grass-Fed Beef	g
2oz Liver or Organ Meat	☐
4 Eggs Men, 2 Eggs Women	☐
1 large Avocado	☐
40 Raspberries	☐
20 Pecans or 23 Almonds	☐
50g of Raw Cheese	☐

Afternoon Recharge: HBOT*, Compression* or Cognitive Reset Rest: No more than 1 hour.	☐
Post Recharge: Cognitive Coffee & Collagen	☐

DAY 39 Saturday   (Continued)

DEEP WORK WINDOW 3: Output	☐

Afternoon Nature Ideation Walk: 30 Min. – 1 hour. Think Big, Walk & Work, Dream Big. Call an Employee	☐

DEEP WORK WINDOW 4: Tactical	☐

Begin Optimized Nighttime Routine	
Complete Second 85oz Water	☐
Blue Light Blocker Glasses	☐
No Water after 5 PM for uninterrupted sleep	☐
Sunset Ice Bath* or Cold Shower (2-3 hours before sleep)	☐
Red light*	☐
Prayer & Gratitude	☐
Create Optimal Sleep Environment: 65 degrees, No Cell Phone/EMF	☐

Completed Perfect Day	☐

Notes: How I win tomorrow.

DAY 40

Sunday

> "Success is not the result of spontaneous combustion. You must set yourself on fire."
>
> - Arnold H. Glasow

Wake Up _____ am   Sleep: 7+ hrs Optimized Sleep ☐   Deep _____ REM _____

Weight _____ lbs   Ketones _____ mmol/L   Super Water ☐   Cognitive Coffee ☐ ☐

Red light* ☐   Ice Bath/Cold Shower ☐   Prayer/Meditation/Gratitude ☐

* Optional

DEEP WORK WINDOW 1: Be Brilliant. ☐

Day 3 Workout					
Core: 30 rest between sets (6:20)	15 reps				
Incline Sit-up					
Leg Raises					
Strength Warmup 20-20-10 Compound Movement					
Strength: 5 sets x 5 reps (3-min rest)	5 reps				
Squat					
Accessory: 4 sets x 6-8 reps (2-min rest)	6-8 reps				
Bulgarian Split Squats					
Volume: 4 sets x 10 reps of 4 exercises (30-sec rest)	10 reps				
Hip Thrusts					
Squat Jumps					
Calf Raises					
Bulgarian Split Squats					

DAY 40 Sunday   (Continued)

Burnout: 2 exercises x 50 reps each (Air Squats, Calf Raises)	☐
GPP: 3 rounds - 30 sec on, 30 sec off: Sled Push	☐
Cognitive Walk/Sprint: 30 Minutes (HIIT Sprint) 2:30 walk, 30 Second Sprint 10 Rounds	☐

Complete First 85oz Water (Morning)	☐

Post-Workout Recovery	
20 Minutes Sauna*	☐
20 Minutes of Morning Sun	☐
Cold Shower	☐

DEEP WORK WINDOW 2: Six to Eight 20-minute deep work window sprints, 10-min break, 10 Kettle bell swings and look outside in the distance 1 minute to adjust eyes.	☐

Jump Start Nutrition Plan: Do the .8 calculation to understand exactly the amount of grass fed beef you must consume today.	
Organic Bone Broth (2 cups)	☐
Grass-Fed Beef	g
2oz Liver or Organ Meat	☐
4 Eggs Men, 2 Eggs Women	☐
1 large Avocado	☐
40 Raspberries	☐
20 Pecans or 23 Almonds	☐
50g of Raw Cheese	☐

Afternoon Recharge: HBOT*, Compression* or Cognitive Reset Rest: No more than 1 hour.	☐
Post Recharge: Cognitive Coffee & Collagen	☐

DAY 40 Sunday   (Continued)

DEEP WORK WINDOW 3: Output ☐

Afternoon Nature Ideation Walk: 30 Min. – 1 hour. Think Big, Walk & Work, Dream Big. Call an Employee ☐

DEEP WORK WINDOW 4: Tactical ☐

Begin Optimized Nighttime Routine	
Complete Second 85oz Water	☐
Blue Light Blocker Glasses	☐
No Water after 5 PM for uninterrupted sleep	☐
Sunset Ice Bath* or Cold Shower (2-3 hours before sleep)	☐
Red light*	☐
Prayer & Gratitude	☐
Create Optimal Sleep Environment: 65 degrees, No Cell Phone/EMF	☐

Completed Perfect Day	☐

Notes: How I win tomorrow.

DAY 41 — Monday

> "Strength does not come from physical capacity. It comes from an indomitable will."
> - Mahatma Gandhi

Wake Up_____am   Sleep: 7+ hrs Optimized Sleep ☐ Deep_____REM_____

Weight_____lbs   Ketones_____mmol/L   Super Water ☐   Cognitive Coffee ☐☐

Red light* ☐   Ice Bath/Cold Shower ☐   Prayer/Meditation/Gratitude ☐

* Optional

DEEP WORK WINDOW 1: Be Brilliant. ☐

Day 1 Workout					
Core: 30 rest between sets (6:20)	15 reps				
Incline Sit-up					
Leg Raises					
Strength Warmup 20-20-10 Compound Movement					
Strength: 5 sets x 5 reps (3-min rest)	5 reps				
Incline Bench Press					
Accessory: 4 sets x 6-8 reps (2-min rest)	6-8 reps				
Overhead Press					x
Volume: 4 sets x 10 reps of 4 exercises (30-sec rest)	10 reps				
Side Raises					x
Front Raises					x
Dips					x
Deltoid Flys					x

DAY 41 Monday   (Continued)

Burnout: 2 exercises x 50 reps each (Side Raises, Triceps Press downs)	☐
GPP: Farmer's Walk: 3 rounds - 30 secs on, 30 secs off	☐
Cognitive Walk/Sprint: 30 Minutes (HIIT Sprint) 2:30 walk, 30 Second Sprint 10 Rounds	☐

Complete First 85oz Water (Morning)	☐

Post-Workout Recovery	
20 Minutes Sauna*	☐
20 Minutes of Morning Sun	☐
Cold Shower	☐

DEEP WORK WINDOW 2: Six to Eight 20-minute deep work window sprints, 10-min break, 10 Kettle bell swings and look outside in the distance 1 minute to adjust eyes.	☐

Jump Start Nutrition Plan: Do the .8 calculation to understand exactly the amount of Wild-caught salmon you must consume today.	
Organic Bone Broth (2 cups)	☐
Wild-caught salmon	g
2oz Liver or Organ Meat	☐
4 Eggs Men, 2 Eggs Women	☐
1 large Avocado	☐
40 Raspberries	☐
20 Pecans or 23 Almonds	☐
50g of Raw Cheese	☐

Afternoon Recharge: HBOT*, Compression* or Cognitive Reset Rest: No more than 1 hour.	☐
Post Recharge: Cognitive Coffee & Collagen	☐

DAY 41 Monday   (Continued)

DEEP WORK WINDOW 3: Output ☐

Afternoon Nature Ideation Walk: 30 Min. – 1 hour. Think Big, Walk & Work, Dream Big. Call an Employee	☐

DEEP WORK WINDOW 4: Tactical ☐

Begin Optimized Nighttime Routine	
Complete Second 85oz Water	☐
Blue Light Blocker Glasses	☐
No Water after 5 PM for uninterrupted sleep	☐
Sunset Ice Bath* or Cold Shower (2-3 hours before sleep)	☐
Red light*	☐
Prayer & Gratitude	☐
Create Optimal Sleep Environment: 65 degrees, No Cell Phone/EMF	☐

Completed Perfect Day	☐

Notes: How I win tomorrow.

DAY 42 — Tuesday

> "Winning takes talent, to repeat takes character."
> - John Wooden

Wake Up _____ am   Sleep: 7+ hrs Optimized Sleep ☐   Deep _____ REM _____

Weight _____ lbs   Ketones _____ mmol/L   Super Water ☐   Cognitive Coffee ☐ ☐

Red light* ☐   Ice Bath/Cold Shower ☐   Prayer/Meditation/Gratitude ☐

* Optional

DEEP WORK WINDOW 1: Be Brilliant. ☐

Day 2 Workout

Core: 30 rest between sets (6:20)	15 reps				
Incline Sit-up					
Leg Raises					
Strength Warmup 20-20-10 Compound Movement					
Strength: 5 sets x 5 reps (3-min rest)	5 reps				
Dead Lift					
Accessory: 4 sets x 6-8 reps (2-min rest)	6-8 reps				
Row					x
Volume: 4 sets x 10 reps of 4 exercises (30-sec rest)	10 reps				
Lat Pulldown/Pullup					x
Hammer Curl					x
Row					x
Individual Bicep Curl					x
Burnout: 2 exercises x 50 reps each (50 Rows, 50 Bicep Curls)	☐				

DAY 42 Tuesday (Continued)

GPP: 3 rounds - 30 sec on, 30 sec off: Sled Pulls	☐
Cognitive Walk/Sprint: 30 Minutes (HIIT Sprint) 2:30 walk, 30 Second Sprint 10 Rounds	☐

Complete First 85oz Water (Morning)	☐

Post-Workout Recovery	
20 Minutes Sauna*	☐
20 Minutes of Morning Sun	☐
Cold Shower	☐

DEEP WORK WINDOW 2: Six to Eight 20-minute deep work window sprints, 10-min break, 10 Kettle bell swings and look outside in the distance 1 minute to adjust eyes.	☐

Jump Start Nutrition Plan: Do the .8 calculation to understand exactly the amount of grass fed beef you must consume today.	
Organic Bone Broth (2 cups)	☐
Grass-Fed Beef	g
2oz Liver or Organ Meat	☐
4 Eggs Men, 2 Eggs Women	☐
1 large Avocado	☐
40 Raspberries	☐
20 Pecans or 23 Almonds	☐
50g of Raw Cheese	☐

Afternoon Recharge: HBOT*, Compression* or Cognitive Reset Rest: No more than 1 hour.	☐
Post Recharge: Cognitive Coffee & Collagen	☐

DAY 42   Tuesday   (Continued)

DEEP WORK WINDOW 3: Output ☐

Afternoon Nature Ideation Walk: 30 Min. – 1 hour. Think Big, Walk & Work, Dream Big. Call an Employee ☐

DEEP WORK WINDOW 4: Tactical ☐

Begin Optimized Nighttime Routine	
Complete Second 85oz Water	☐
Blue Light Blocker Glasses	☐
No Water after 5 PM for uninterrupted sleep	☐
Sunset Ice Bath* or Cold Shower (2-3 hours before sleep)	☐
Red light*	☐
Prayer & Gratitude	☐
Create Optimal Sleep Environment: 65 degrees, No Cell Phone/EMF	☐

Completed Perfect Day	☐

Notes: How I win tomorrow.

DAY 43 — Wednesday

> "The difference between try and triumph is just a little 'umph'."
> – Marvin Phillips

Wake Up _____ am   Sleep: 7+ hrs Optimized Sleep ☐   Deep _____ REM _____

Weight _____ lbs   Ketones _____ mmol/L   Super Water ☐   Cognitive Coffee ☐☐

Red light* ☐   Ice Bath/Cold Shower ☐   Prayer/Meditation/Gratitude ☐

Optional

DEEP WORK WINDOW 1: Be Brilliant. ☐

Day 3 Workout				
Core: 30 rest between sets (6:20)	15 reps			
Incline Sit-up				
Leg Raises				
Strength Warmup 20-20-10 Compound Movement				
Strength: 5 sets x 5 reps (3-min rest)	5 reps			
Squat				
Accessory: 4 sets x 6-8 reps (2-min rest)	6-8 reps			
Bulgarian Split Squats				
Volume: 4 sets x 10 reps of 4 exercises (30-sec rest)	10 reps			
Hip Thrusts				
Squat Jumps				
Calf Raises				
Bulgarian Split Squats				

DAY 43 Wednesday   (Continued)

Burnout: 2 exercises x 50 reps each (Air Squats, Calf Raises)	☐
GPP: 3 rounds - 30 sec on, 30 sec off: Sled Push	☐
Cognitive Walk/Sprint: 30 Minutes (HIIT Sprint) 2:30 walk, 30 Second Sprint 10 Rounds	☐

Complete First 85oz Water (Morning)	☐

Post-Workout Recovery	
20 Minutes Sauna*	☐
20 Minutes of Morning Sun	☐
Cold Shower	☐

DEEP WORK WINDOW 2: Six to Eight 20-minute deep work window sprints, 10-min break, 10 Kettle bell swings and look outside in the distance 1 minute to adjust eyes.	☐

Jump Start Nutrition Plan: Do the .8 calculation to understand exactly the amount of grass fed beef you must consume today.	
Organic Bone Broth (2 cups)	☐
Grass-Fed Beef	g
2oz Liver or Organ Meat	☐
4 Eggs Men, 2 Eggs Women	☐
1 large Avocado	☐
40 Raspberries	☐
20 Pecans or 23 Almonds	☐
50g of Raw Cheese	☐

Afternoon Recharge: HBOT*, Compression* or Cognitive Reset Rest: No more than 1 hour.	☐
Post Recharge: Cognitive Coffee & Collagen	☐

DAY 43 Wednesday   (Continued)

DEEP WORK WINDOW 3: Output ☐

Afternoon Nature Ideation Walk: 30 Min. – 1 hour. Think Big, Walk & Work, Dream Big. Call an Employee	☐

DEEP WORK WINDOW 4: Tactical ☐

Begin Optimized Nighttime Routine	
Complete Second 85oz Water	☐
Blue Light Blocker Glasses	☐
No Water after 5 PM for uninterrupted sleep	☐
Sunset Ice Bath* or Cold Shower (2-3 hours before sleep)	☐
Red light*	☐
Prayer & Gratitude	☐
Create Optimal Sleep Environment: 65 degrees, No Cell Phone/EMF	☐

Completed Perfect Day	☐

Notes: How I win tomorrow.

DAY 44 — Thursday

> "Physical fitness is the basis for all other forms of excellence."
>
> - John F. Kennedy

Wake Up_____am   Sleep: 7+ hrs Optimized Sleep ☐   Deep_____REM_____

Weight_____lbs   Ketones_____mmol/L   Super Water ☐   Cognitive Coffee ☐ ☐

Red light* ☐   Ice Bath/Cold Shower ☐   Prayer/Meditation/Gratitude ☐

* Optional

DEEP WORK WINDOW 1: Be Brilliant. ☐

Day 1 Workout					
Core: 30 rest between sets (6:20)	15 reps				
Incline Sit-up					
Leg Raises					
Strength Warmup 20-20-10 Compound Movement					
Strength: 5 sets x 5 reps (3-min rest)	5 reps				
Incline Bench Press					
Accessory: 4 sets x 6-8 reps (2-min rest)	6-8 reps				
Overhead Press					x
Volume: 4 sets x 10 reps of 4 exercises (30-sec rest)	10 reps				
Side Raises					x
Front Raises					x
Dips					x
Deltoid Flys					x

DAY 44 Thursday (Continued)

Burnout: 2 exercises x 50 reps each (Side Raises, Triceps Press downs)	☐
GPP: Farmer's Walk: 3 rounds - 30 secs on, 30 secs off	☐
Cognitive Walk/Sprint: 30 Minutes (HIIT Sprint) 2:30 walk, 30 Second Sprint 10 Rounds	☐

Complete First 85oz Water (Morning)	☐

Post-Workout Recovery	
20 Minutes Sauna*	☐
20 Minutes of Morning Sun	☐
Cold Shower	☐

DEEP WORK WINDOW 2: Six to Eight 20-minute deep work window sprints, 10-min break, 10 Kettle bell swings and look outside in the distance 1 minute to adjust eyes.	☐

Jump Start Nutrition Plan: Today you will be doing your first 72hr fast.

72

Afternoon Recharge: HBOT*, Compression* or Cognitive Reset Rest: No more than 1 hour.	☐
Post Recharge: Cognitive Coffee & Collagen	☐

DEEP WORK WINDOW 3: Output	☐

Afternoon Nature Ideation Walk: 30 Min. – 1 hour. Think Big, Walk & Work, Dream Big. Call an Employee	☐

DAY 44 Thursday   (Continued)

DEEP WORK WINDOW 4: Tactical ☐

Begin Optimized Nighttime Routine	
Complete Second 85oz Water	☐
Blue Light Blocker Glasses	☐
No Water after 5 PM for uninterrupted sleep	☐
Sunset Ice Bath* or Cold Shower (2-3 hours before sleep)	☐
Red light*	☐
Prayer & Gratitude	☐
Create Optimal Sleep Environment: 65 degrees, No Cell Phone/EMF	☐

Completed Perfect Day	☐

Notes: How I win tomorrow.

DAY 45 Friday

> "The finish line is just the beginning of a whole new race."
> - Unknown

Wake Up _____ am   Sleep: 7+ hrs Optimized Sleep ☐   Deep _____ REM _____
Weight _____ lbs   Ketones _____ mmol/L   Super Water ☐   Cognitive Coffee ☐ ☐
Red light* ☐   Ice Bath/Cold Shower ☐   Prayer/Meditation/Gratitude ☐

* Optional

DEEP WORK WINDOW 1: Be Brilliant. ☐

Day 2 Workout					
Core: 30 rest between sets (6:20)	15 reps				
Incline Sit-up					
Leg Raises					
Strength Warmup 20-20-10 Compound Movement					
Strength: 5 sets x 5 reps (3-min rest)	5 reps				
Dead Lift					
Accessory: 4 sets x 6-8 reps (2-min rest)	6-8 reps				
Row					x
Volume: 4 sets x 10 reps of 4 exercises (30-sec rest)	10 reps				
Lat Pulldown/Pullup					x
Hammer Curl					x
Row					x
Individual Bicep Curl					x

DAY 45 Friday   (Continued)

Burnout: 2 exercises x 50 reps each (50 Rows, 50 Bicep Curls)	☐
GPP: 3 rounds - 30 sec on, 30 sec off: Sled Pulls	☐
Cognitive Walk/Sprint: 30 Minutes (HIIT Sprint) 2:30 walk, 30 Second Sprint 10 Rounds	☐

Complete First 85oz Water (Morning)	☐

Post-Workout Recovery	
20 Minutes Sauna*	☐
20 Minutes of Morning Sun	☐
Cold Shower	☐

DEEP WORK WINDOW 2: Six to Eight 20-minute deep work window sprints, 10-min break, 10 Kettle bell swings and look outside in the distance 1 minute to adjust eyes.	☐

Jump Start Nutrition Plan: Today you will be doing your first 72hr fast.

72

Afternoon Recharge: HBOT*, Compression* or Cognitive Reset Rest: No more than 1 hour.	☐
Post Recharge: Cognitive Coffee & Collagen	☐

DEEP WORK WINDOW 3: Output	☐

Afternoon Nature Ideation Walk: 30 Min. – 1 hour. Think Big, Walk & Work, Dream Big. Call an Employee	☐

DAY 45 Friday   (Continued)

| **DEEP WORK WINDOW 4:** Tactical | ☐ |

Begin Optimized Nighttime Routine	
Complete Second 85oz Water	☐
Blue Light Blocker Glasses	☐
No Water after 5 PM for uninterrupted sleep	☐
Sunset Ice Bath* or Cold Shower (2-3 hours before sleep)	☐
Red light*	☐
Prayer & Gratitude	☐
Create Optimal Sleep Environment: 65 degrees, No Cell Phone/EMF	☐

| Completed Perfect Day | ☐ |

Notes: How I win tomorrow.

Final Thoughts

The Speed of the Leader Determines the Rate of the Pack

You've done it! You have become part of the new breed of optimized executives collectively raising the bar with the future of entrepreneurial leadership. You've learned how to optimize your cognitive performance for business and entrepreneurial success while learning the tools to become the strongest human you have ever been. By following the 45-Day Action Plan, you've incorporated all of the best techniques to maximize both your physical and cognitive functions. In short, you are badass.

You now stand as a testament to the limitless power of the Performance CEO mindset. Armed with fasting, OMAD, strength training, and strategic recovery, you have harnessed your brain's full potential, transforming it into your ultimate competitive advantage in the dynamic realm of entrepreneurship.

Through this rigorous Protocol, you have discovered the true essence of resilience and the profound impact of nurturing your mind and body in harmony. The amalgamation of intermittent fasting and one meal a day has not only sharpened your cognitive acuity but has also instilled discipline, offering you a newfound clarity of purpose and focus. Harnessing the strength within, both mental and physical, you have transcended boundaries and limitations, demonstrating unwavering determination in the pursuit of excellence.

In making your brain the fulcrum of entrepreneurial success, you have unlocked a universe of creativity and innovation. The strategic implementation of strength training and recovery has not only honed your physical prowess but has also amplified your mental adaptability, enabling you to embrace challenges with poise and confidence. The interplay of these elements has cemented your role as the Performance CEO, a leader who not only drives business growth but also empowers a culture of resilience and passion among your team.

Beyond the walls of the Extreme Cognitive Protocol, your journey as the Performance CEO has just begun. Armed with newfound clarity, resilience, and an unyielding pursuit of excellence, you are now equipped to navigate the turbulent tides of entrepreneurship with a steadfast commitment to both business success and personal well-being. Your journey is an inspiration to me and those who dare to embrace the unconventional, to those who believe that the mind is not just a tool but a force that can shape destinies.

As you embark on the next chapter of your entrepreneurial voyage, may the Performance CEO mindset continue to be your guiding light, propelling you to new heights of accomplishment and fulfillment. Remember that your brain remains your greatest asset, and through relentless dedication and strategic optimization, there are no bounds to the extraordinary impact you can create in the world. The path of the Performance CEO beckons, and you stand poised to seize the future with the unwavering conviction that you are the author of your success. Congratulations, Performance CEO, for embracing the Extreme Cognitive Protocol and paving the way for a future of limitless possibilities.

This Protocol doesn't make you automatically successful. But it puts you in a situation where you're cognitively and biologically at your best. The result will be the result, but you will never wonder "what if?"

Welcome to the Rest of your Entrepreneurial Life

In **The Performance CEO**, we embarked on a transformative journey, empowering ambitious entrepreneurs like yourself to embrace a Protocol for cognitive optimization. We shatter the conventional norms that have confined business leaders to traditional paradigms, and we usher in an era of unapologetic ambition, strategic optimization, and holistic well-being. Through cutting-edge research, expert insights, and real-life success stories, this book delves into the foundational principles of the Extreme Cognitive Protocol. With a focus on fasting, OMAD, strength training, and recovery, we equip you with the tools to revolutionize your approach to business and unleash the full potential of your brain, making it the driving force behind your entrepreneurial success.

As you venture out now at your cognitive best, you will witness a complete shift in your leadership style. Your journey from an entrepreneur to the Performance CEO involves an empowering transformation that extends beyond how you previously led. Fasting and OMAD cultivate mental clarity and focus, leading to decisive, visionary leadership that inspires and motivates. Strength training instills confidence, poise, and physical presence, elevating your influence as a leader. Your commitment to strategic recovery will resonate throughout your organization, fostering a culture that embraces well-being, productivity, and collective growth. Empowered with this newfound perspective, you will redefine leadership and chart a course for unprecedented success.

The Performance CEO is not merely a 45-day program but a lifelong commitment to sustained cognitive excellence, focus, passing on your new knowledge to create, and a legacy of impact. As you conclude the Extreme Cognitive Protocol, you will discover that it is simply the beginning of a journey fueled by continual growth and unwavering tenacity. Armed with the Performance CEO philosophy, knowledge, and tools, you will propel your business to unprecedented heights, fostering a thriving ecosystem of innovation, adaptability, and well-being. Your pursuit of excellence will inspire others to follow in your footsteps, creating a ripple effect that transforms not just individual lives but your entire industry.

Welcome to a new world where your brain becomes your ultimate competitive advantage, and your journey becomes an indelible mark on the landscape of entrepreneurship. You are now fully prepared to have an optimized brain. Treat this book, *The Performance CEO*, as an evolving practice to continue upgrading your body and mind from the inside out and strive each and every day to maximize your output. You have learned proven biohacking techniques to help you reach new levels and thrive in any high-paced environment. This cutting-edge Protocol isn't for everyone; it's for the physically and mentally strong; it's for those who have proven they are the elite of the elite; it's for those wanting to push themselves further than they ever have before. It's for you. You are now the Performance CEO.

Final Thoughts

We stand at the threshold of a new era in optimized entrepreneurship—one defined by cognitive performance, strategic optimization, and the unwavering pursuit of excellence. The journey you have undertaken through this Extreme Cognitive Protocol has revealed the immense power of your brain—your power of will and this fusion will be the driving force behind your success as the Performance CEO. You now hold the keys to unlocking your full potential as a visionary leader and a catalyst for real change. You are the future.

Embrace the Performance CEO within you—the audacious dreamer who defies limitations, the agile strategist who navigates uncharted waters, and the compassionate leader who empowers others to rise. By aligning your entrepreneurial endeavors with the principles of this transformative journey, you embody the essence of resilience, adaptability, and holistic well-being.

As the pages of this book close, remember that the journey to becoming the Performance CEO is never-ending. Continually seek growth, embrace challenges, and evolve as a leader. Empower your brain, the heart of your competitive advantage, and foster a legacy that impacts not just your business but the world around you.

In the relentless pursuit of excellence, remember that greatness lies not solely in the achievements of your organization, but in the lives you touch and the inspiration you ignite. Now, go forth, Performance CEO, and lead with passion, purpose, and unyielding determination. Your story is one of triumph and transformation, and the world eagerly awaits the legacy you will create. This is not just the end of a book; it is the beginning of a newly-emerging optimized entrepreneurial journey.

Let's crush our goals together as Performance CEO, builders, and the new breed of optimized leaders.

Please keep me updated during your journey. I am honored and humbled to be a part of it. LFG. Nothing is impossible.

@michaelkochceo
Twitter @michaelkochceo
IG @michaelkochceo
FB
LinkedIn
LinkTree
Amazon Review

Bibliography and References

1. Mattson, M. P. (2014). Fasting: Molecular Mechanisms and Clinical Applications. Cell Metabolism, 19(2), 181-192.

2. Longo, V. D., & Mattson, M. P. (2014). Fasting: Molecular Mechanisms and Clinical Applications. Cell Metabolism, 19(2), 181-192.

3. Chaix, A., Zarrinpar, A., Miu, P., & Panda, S. (2014). Time-Restricted Feeding Is a Preventative and Therapeutic Intervention against Diverse Nutritional Challenges. Cell Metabolism, 20(6), 991-1005.

4. Lee, J., Duan, W., & Mattson, M. P. (2002). Evidence that brain-derived neurotrophic factor is required for basal neurogenesis and mediates, in part, the enhancement of neurogenesis by dietary restriction in the hippocampus. Journal of Neurochemistry, 82(6), 1367-1375.

5. Molteni, R., Wu, A., Vaynman, S., Ying, Z., Barnard, R. J., & Gomez-Pinilla, F. (2004). Exercise reverses the harmful effects of consumption of a high-fat diet on synaptic and behavioral plasticity associated to the action of brain-derived neurotrophic factor. Neuroscience, 123(2), 429-440.

6. Yau, S. Y., Li, A., Hoo, R. L., Ching, Y. P., Christie, B. R., & Lee, T. M. (2014). Physical exercise-induced hippocampal neurogenesis and antidepressant effects are mediated by the adipocyte hormone

adiponectin. Proceedings of the National Academy of Sciences, 111(44), 15810-15815.

7. Brandt, R., Franke, S., & Giavalisco, P. (2019). Molecular mechanisms of plant resilience to deregulated redox balance and their manipulation for biohacking crops. Plant, Cell & Environment, 42(3), 765-772.

8. Ives, S. J., Bloom, O. J., & Matias, A. (2017). Neurobiology of exercise and cognitive processes. In Routledge Handbook of Sport and Exercise Systems Genetics (pp. 288-305). Routledge.

9. Cotman, C. W., & Berchtold, N. C. (2002). Exercise: a behavioral intervention to enhance brain health and plasticity. Trends in Neurosciences, 25(6), 295-301.

10. Erickson, K. I., Voss, M. W., & Prakash, R. S. (2011). Exercise training increases size of hippocampus and improves memory. Proceedings of the National Academy of Sciences, 108(7), 3017-3022.

11. Mattson, M. P., & Wan, R. (2005). Beneficial effects of intermittent fasting and caloric restriction on the cardiovascular and cerebrovascular systems. The Journal of Nutritional Biochemistry, 16(3), 129-137.

12. Martin, B., Ji, S., & Maudsley, S. (2010). "Control" laboratory rodents are metabolically morbid: why it matters. Proceedings of the National Academy of Sciences, 107(14), 6127-6133.

13. van Praag, H., Kempermann, G., & Gage, F. H. (1999). Running increases cell proliferation and neurogenesis in the adult mouse dentate gyrus. Nature Neuroscience, 2(3), 266-270.

14. Vaynman, S., & Gomez-Pinilla, F. (2005). License to run: exercise impacts functional plasticity in the intact and injured central nervous system by using neurotrophins. Neurorehabilitation and Neural Repair, 19(4), 283-295.

15. Woo, J., Shin, K. O., & Park, S. Y. (2013). The effects of detraining and retraining on muscle strength and brain-derived neurotrophic

factor (BDNF) levels in elderly females. Archives of Gerontology and Geriatrics, 56(2), 413-419.

16. Voss, M. W., Erickson, K. I., & Prakash, R. S. (2010). Functional connectivity: a source of variance in the association between cardiorespiratory fitness and cognition?. Neuropsychologia, 48(5), 1394-1406.

17. Raichlen, D. A., & Alexander, G. E. (2017). Exercise, APOE genotype, and the evolution of the human lifespan. Trends in Neurosciences, 40(7), 447-449.

18. Dinoff, A., Herrmann, N., & Swardfager, W. (2017). The effect of exercise training on resting concentrations of peripheral brain-derived neurotrophic factor (BDNF): a meta-analysis. PloS One, 12(9), e0183666.

19. Suwabe, K., Byun, K., Hyodo, K., & Fukuie, T. (2018). Rapid stimulation of human dentate gyrus function with acute mild exercise. Proceedings of the National Academy of Sciences, 115(41), 10487-10492.

20. Zoladz, J. A., Pilc, A., & Majerczak, J. (2018). Endurance training increases plasma brain-derived neurotrophic factor concentration in young healthy men. Journal of Physiology and Pharmacology, 69(3).

21. Marosi, K., Bori, Z., & Hart, N. (2016). Long-term exercise treatment reduces oxidative stress in the hippocampus of aging rats. Neuroscience, 320, 157-163.

22. Gómez-Pinilla, F., Hillman, C., & Castellanos, V. H. (2013). The influence of dietary factors in central nervous system plasticity and injury recovery. PM&R, 5(6), S44-S51.

23. Rasmussen, P., Brassard, P., & Adser, H. (2009). Evidence for a release of brain-derived neurotrophic factor from the brain during exercise. Experimental Physiology, 94(10), 1062-1069.

24. McMorris, T., Mielcarz, G., & Suchomel, A. (2011). Effect of 7 days of creatine supplementation on memory and cognition in a

older population. Journal of Aging and Physical Activity, 19(1), 251-257.

25. Hillman, C. H., Erickson, K. I., & Kramer, A. F. (2008). Be smart, exercise your heart: exercise effects on brain and cognition. Nature Reviews Neuroscience, 9(1), 58-65.

26. Dallman, M. F., & Pecoraro, N. C. (2005). Chronic stress and comfort foods: Self-medication and abdominal obesity. Brain, Behavior, and Immunity, 19(4), 275-280.

27. Griesbach, G. S., Hovda, D. A., & Gomez-Pinilla, F. (2009). Exercise-induced improvement in cognitive performance after traumatic brain injury in rats is dependent on BDNF activation. Brain Research, 1288, 105-115.

28. Li, J., Tang, Y., & Cai, D. (2018). Effects of strength training on cognitive function of elderly individuals with mild cognitive impairment. BioMed Research International, 2018.

29. Voss, M. W., Weng, T. B., & Nagamatsu, L. S. (2016). The impact of physical activity on structure and function of the aging brain. In Neuropsychology of Aging (pp. 227-245). Springer, Cham.

30. Kandola, A., Ashdown-Franks, G., & Stubbs, B. (2019). Physical activity and depression: Towards understanding the antidepressant mechanisms of physical activity. Neuroscience & Biobehavioral Reviews, 107, 525-539.

31. Cotman, C. W., Berchtold, N. C., & Christie, L. A. (2007). Exercise builds brain health: key roles of growth factor cascades and inflammation. Trends in Neurosciences, 30(9), 464-472.

32. Yang, J. L., Lin, Y. T., & Chuang, P. C. (2012). Role of physical activity in reducing cognitive decline in older adults: a systematic review. Journal of Nursing Research, 20(4), 268-281.

33. Phillips, C., & Baktir, M. A. (2010). Neuroprotective effects of physical activity on the brain: a closer look at trophic factor signaling. Frontiers in Cellular Neuroscience, 8(6), 170.

34. Manini, T. M., & Patel, K. V. (2010). Lifestyles for successful cognitive aging. American Journal of Lifestyle Medicine, 4(1), 17-21.
35. Macpherson, H., Teo, W. P., & Schneider, L. A. (2013). Weight training improves cognitive functions in older adults: A review. Journal of Aging and Physical Activity, 21(4), 496-509.
36. Kraemer, W. J., & Ratamess, N. A. (2005). Hormonal responses and adaptations to resistance exercise and training. Sports Medicine, 35(4), 339-361.
37. Nyberg, J., Aberg, M. A. I., & Schiöth, H. B. (2014). Cardiovascular and cognitive fitness at age 18 and risk of early-onset dementia. Brain, 137(5), 1514-1523.
38. Erickson, K. I., Gildengers, A. G., & Butters, M. A. (2010). Exercise-induced brain plasticity in older adults. Archives of Internal Medicine, 170(2), 171-178.
39. Leckie, R. L., Oberlin, L. E., & Voss, M. W. (2014). BDNF mediates improvements in executive function following a 1-year exercise intervention. Frontiers in Human Neuroscience, 8, 985.
40. Hopkins, M. E., Nitecki, R., & Bucci, D. J. (2011). Physical exercise during adolescence versus adulthood: differential effects on object recognition memory and brain-derived neurotrophic factor levels. Neuroscience, 194, 84-94.
41. Gomes da Silva, S., & Arida, R. M. (2015). Physical activity and brain development. Expert Review of Neurotherapeutics, 15(10), 1121-1130.
42. Steiner, J. L., & Murphy, E. A. (2016). Importance of physical activity and cardiorespiratory fitness in the prevention of chronic diseases. Journal of Healthcare Engineering, 2016.
43. Lozano, L. D., & Mourot, L. (2016). How can aerobic exercise influence brain morphology? International Journal of Environmental Research and Public Health, 13(11), 1102.
44. Coelho, F. G., Vital, T. M., Stein, A. M., & Teodorov, E. (2014). Acute aerobic exercise increases brain-derived neurotrophic factor

levels in elderly with Alzheimer's disease. Journal of Alzheimer's Disease, 39(2), 401-408.

45. Rasmussen, P., Brassard, P., & Adser, H. (2009). Evidence for a release of brain-derived neurotrophic factor from the brain during exercise. Experimental Physiology, 94(10), 1062-1069.

46. Lee, J., Duan, W., & Mattson, M. P. (2002). Evidence that brain-derived neurotrophic factor is required for basal neurogenesis and mediates, in part, the enhancement of neurogenesis by dietary restriction in the hippocampus. Journal of Neurochemistry, 82(6), 1367-1375.

47. Lopez-Lopez, C., LeRoith, D., & Torres-Aleman, I. (2004). Insulin-like growth factor I is required for vessel remodeling in the adult brain. Proceedings of the National Academy of Sciences, 101(26), 9833-9838.

48. Håkansson, K., Ledreux, A., Daffner, K., & Terjestam, Y. (2017). BDNF responses in healthy older persons to 35 minutes of physical exercise, cognitive training, and mindfulness: associations with working memory function. Journal of Alzheimer's Disease, 55(2), 645-657.

49. Valenzuela, P. L., Castillo-García, A., & Morales, J. S. (2018). Physical exercise in the oldest old. Journal of Aging and Physical Activity, 26(3), 365-371.

50. Maass, A., Düzel, S., Brigadski, T., & Goerke, M. (2015). Relationships of peripheral IGF-1, VEGF and BDNF levels to exercise-related changes in memory, hippocampal perfusion and volumes in older adults. NeuroImage, 131, 142-154.

Endnotes

1. A scientific study of brain circuits confirmed that our creative activity is highest during and immediately after sleep (Morning Ideation), while the analytical parts of the brain (the editing, researching, and proofreading parts) become more active as the day progresses.

   Title: "Sleep Inspires Insight and Enhances Creativity"

   Authors: Sara C. Mednick, Denise Cai, Tristan A. Kanady, Sarnoff A. Mednick

   Published in the Journal of Sleep Research, Volume 18, Issue 2, June 2009, Pages 115-123.

   Link: https://doi.org/10.1111/j.1365-2869.2008.00756.x

2. Research indicates that an hour of natural light in the morning will help you sleep better.

   Title: "Exposure to Room Light before Bedtime Suppresses Melatonin Onset and Shortens Melatonin Duration in Humans"

   Authors: Joshua J. Gooley, Rajaratnam S. M. W., Shantha M. W. Rajaratnam, Eliza Van Reen, Jamie M. Czeisler, Steven W. Lockley

   Published in The Journal of Clinical Endocrinology & Metabolism, Volume 96, Issue 3, 1 March 2011, Pages E463–E472.

   Link: https://doi.org/10.1210/jc.2010-2098

3. Research shows that a walk can increase cerebral blood flow, creativity, and overall executive function.

    Title: "The Cognitive Benefits of Interacting With Nature"

    Authors: Marc G. Berman, John Jonides, and Stephen Kaplan

    Published in Psychological Science, Volume 19, Issue 12, December 2008, Pages 1207–1212.

    Link: https://journals.sagepub.com/doi/10.1111/j.1467-9280.2008.02225.x

4. Science tells us that the heart and brain love ketones. They are an essential part of your cognitive health journey. Utilizing ketones as fuel is the leading way to boost cognitive performance. This is proven. Even the military and government agencies are now using it to heighten brain performance. Higher ketone levels lead to better cognitive function and provide neuroprotective effects.

    Title: "The Ketogenic Diet: Metabolic Influences on Brain Epilepsy and Beyond"

    Authors: Jong M. Rho, Mark P. S. M. P. M. P. Dingledine

    Published in the Epilepsia journal, Volume 47, Issue 4, April 2006, Pages 82-83.

    Link: https://doi.org/10.1111/j.1528-1167.2006.00478_1.x

5. Fasting can increase your brain's BDNF by 100 to 400 percent.

    Title: "Fasting induces a neuron-autonomous circadian clock in the hippocampus via BDNF and metabotropic glutamate receptor signaling."

    Authors: Rachel S. Edgar, Marco J. D. Riera, Adilson L. Guilherme, et al.

    Published in eLife, Volume 7, 2018, e33053.

    Link: https://doi.org/10.7554/eLife.33053

6. Fasting for more than 23 hours has been proven to reduce inflammation by decreasing oxidative stress in cells. We do it every day. Recent updated research and clinical trials suggest that sustained fasting regimens maintained over months or even years may also improve memory, along with executive function and overall cognition.

   Title: "Fasting-mimicking diet and markers/risk factors for aging, diabetes, cancer, and cardiovascular disease."
   Authors: Min Wei, Sebastian Brandhorst, Mahshid Shelehchi, et al.
   Published in Science Translational Medicine, Volume 9, Issue 377, March 2017.
   Link: https://doi.org/10.1126/scitranslmed.aai8700

7. Fasting can improve cardiovascular health. In addition, it can help fight certain kinds of cancer, and even help preserve memory, as well as improve metabolic health.

   Title: "Fasting: Molecular Mechanisms and Clinical Applications"
   Authors: Mark P. Mattson, Valter D. Longo, and Michelle Harvie
   Published in Cell Metabolism, Volume 27, Issue 4, April 2018, Pages 738-752.
   Link: https://doi.org/10.1016/j.cmet.2018.03.021

8. One study found that fasting for more than 23 hours lowered inflammation by reducing oxidative stress in cells. Another study showed that both intermittent fasting and alternate-day fasting were effective at reducing insulin resistance, which is the precursor to type 2 diabetes (an inflammatory condition).

Title: "Intermittent Fasting and Human Metabolic Health"

Authors: Mark P. Mattson, R. J. et al.

Published in Journal of the Academy of Nutrition and Dietetics, Volume 115, Issue 8, August 2015, Pages 1203-1212.

Link: https://doi.org/10.1016/j.jand.2015.02.018

9. Research shows that people who practice regular intermittent fasting have lower body fat, lower resting heart rates, lower blood sugar and insulin levels, and lower unhealthy cholesterol and bad blood fats.

Title: "Effects of Intermittent Fasting on Health, Aging, and Disease"

Authors: Mark P. Mattson, Valter D. Longo, and Michelle Harvie

Published in The New England Journal of Medicine, Volume 381, Issue 26, December 2019, Pages 2541-2551.

Link: https://doi.org/10.1056/NEJMra1905136

10. Studies have shown that induced autophagy through fasting in hippocampal neurons is necessary to boost activity in memory and promote the stimuli needed to improve cognitive fitness.

Title: "Fasting enhances the response of autophagy to hormonal signaling in skeletal muscle of 8-month-old rats."

Authors: Ferreira A, et al.

Published in J Gerontol A Biol Sci Med Sci. 2021;76(6):974-980.

Link: https://doi.org/10.1093/gerona/glaa256

11. According to a study, intermittent fasting switches on DNA-repairing genes that help reduce inflammation in the body. This helps the skin to heal and repair, as cells are renewed more rapidly. Plus, production of a hormone called somatropin increases, helping to minimize wrinkles and fine lines, to slow the aging process and increase longevity by cleaning our cells. And so, fasting not only evokes that optimal fuel-burning, which means you think and perform at your mental peak, but you will also look amazing while doing it.

Title: "Cellular and molecular mechanisms of autophagy in metabolic disorders"

Authors: Congcong Zhang, Xiaokun Gang, Feng Zhang, et al.

Published in Biological Chemistry, Volume 399, Issue 8, August 2018, Pages 821–830.

Link: https://www.degruyter.com/document/doi/10.1515/hsz-2018-0108/html

www.ingramcontent.com/pod-product-compliance
Lightning Source LLC
LaVergne TN
LVHW042251070526
838201LV00105B/301/J